CURIOUS
AVATAR

EXPLORING REALITY,
SPIRITUAL ENERGY,
PERSONAL TRANSFORMATION,
AND THE MEANING OF LIFE

MARC MAX POLLOCK

ISBN Paperback: 979-8-9876731-1-9
ISBN Electronic: 979-8-9876731-0-2

Library of Congress Control Number: 2023902829

Portions of this book are works of nonfiction. Certain names and identifying characteristics have been changed.

Published in the United States of America by Max Media Publishing.

FIRST PRINT EDITION

Marc Max Pollock
Max Media Publishing
www.maxmediapublishing.net

Dear Reader,

Please be advised that the author is not a trained counselor, psychotherapist, or physician. Any advice or teaching in this book is not intended to replace the services of a physician or mental health professional, nor to provide an alternative to professional medical treatment. The reader is advised to proceed at their own risk.

This book is dedicated to the many Souls who
graciously agreed to help me evolve through this lifetime.
I am especially grateful to my wife and children
for their limitless supply of love and joy.
I am truly blessed beyond measure.

HOW TO USE THIS BOOK

THIS BOOK HIGHLIGHTS DISCOVERIES AT the foundation of my personal evolution. Each chapter focuses on a particular *insight* that provides form and context to the inner workings of reality and details how these forces affect change in this material realm. These *insights* not only highlight the relationship between God and humanity but provide a roadmap for harnessing the power of Source-Energy so we can create a better life.

The chapters begin with *backdrop* information that provides real-world context (based on my personal experience) around the subject of each *insight*. The purpose of the *backdrop* is to help orient the reader around the origins of the *insight* that follows.

After each *insight*, I offer an *activation* instruction as a practical guide you can use to apply the *insight* principles to your life. The *activation* highlights the same successful process of discovery and experimentation I use in my life. It also serves as a platform for reorienting YOUR mind to accept a new, dynamic view of reality. In addition, certain *activations* contain specific *exercises* designed to help you integrate the power of the *insight* information.

The chapters in this book are organized into Sections I through V. Each section is themed around a specific characteristic of reality and is designed to help the reader progress through concepts and theories that contribute to the book's overarching narrative. Each section builds upon the information from the previous one. To avoid confusion over terminology and the meaning behind certain concepts, the book is meant to be read sequentially at first, and then the reader may pick the book up and reread any topic of interest. Also, the core ideas have been repeated across chapters to ensure that each chapter can stand alone. Additional clarification can be found in the Glossary of Terms, as well as in the illustrations scattered throughout the book.

I hope you enjoy reading *Curious Avatar*, and I hope your curiosity will guide you along your path to enlightenment.

—Marc

PREFACE

LIFE IS MAGICAL. NOT THE deceptive, sleight-of-hand kind of magic. Not the mythological magic conjured up from imagination. Not even the magic we assign to things we can't explain or don't understand. I am talking about the wide-eyed, rational, intentional ability to create something real and tangible out of "thin air." There is "real" magic available to every one of us. How do I know? Because there is no other way to explain my own improbable arc through this lifetime.

Picture, if you will, a thirteen-year-old boy and his mother sitting nervously in front of a school counselor as he shuffles through the results of the boy's seventh-grade standardized testing. The administrator glances at the hapless pair over black-rimmed glasses, then pulls out the final page of the report. Shaking his head, as if in disbelief, he barks at the boy's mother, "Marc has tested in the *bottom* five percent of all seventh graders in the country. The boy appears to have serious learning problems. It is my recommendation that he undergo a professional evaluation to determine *what* he can do with his life. Maybe he can be directed toward a trade of some sort."

"HEY BUDDY," I thought, "I'm sitting right in front of you!" To say I felt distraught and defeated would be a gross understatement. I felt damaged beyond repair. What this asshole did not know, or take the time to inquire about, was my backstory.

When I was six, the emotional instability of both my parents, along with my mother's ongoing relationship with her former high school sweetheart (who was not my father), set a torch to an already tumultuous marriage, sending my father running from Texas to work in the Alaska oilfields. Even before his silhouette disappeared over the horizon, Mom shacked up with (and later married), her former high school beau. (We'll call him J.W.). J.W.

was not a sweetheart. He was an alcoholic ex-marine with a volatile, violent personality. For me, this began a four-year cycle of beatings and emotional terror, culminating in a daring escape.

My mother, younger brother, and I went into hiding—we were essentially homeless. We relied on government food stamps to eat and the charity from churches and acquaintances for shelter. Often, we camped out in our rusting, rattletrap Oldsmobile named "Big Blue."

From the time of my parents' divorce until seventh grade, my academic participation was practically nonexistent. Between J.W.'s transient occupation and later, our nomadic life in hiding, we lived in a constant state of floundering chaos. As a result, I skipped large chunks of each school year, only to be dropped into a random class now and then, with no chance of absorbing anything useful. By the time I hit junior high school, I had missed the prerequisites for attending seventh grade. My tumultuous life had left me unstable, uneducated... an emotional basket case. Just to top things off, here I was, sitting across from an insensitive jerk, telling me I was mentally handicapped with no hope of a normal life.

So, how in the world did I emerge from this shit show to create the life of abundance and prosperity I now enjoy? And most extraordinarily, how was I granted a view of the inner workings of reality that I used to make this possible? Well, it all began many years ago, when, out of sheer desperation, I did something drastic—I committed to annihilating all my ideologies.

It is an unnatural thing to turn your life upside down—to abandon your carefully constructed notions of God, Reality, and Life—and to ride, scorched earth, across the landscape, burning every vestige of belief to the ground. Madness! This is not the behavior of a healthy, rational human being. This can only manifest from a tortured soul who is beyond desperate. I had nothing to lose, so I rolled the dice and sacrificed all my beliefs upon the grievous altar of fear and insecurity, with the faint, anguished hope that a new truth would emerge... my truth.

Why is life so hard? Can we make sense of existence? What is the purpose of all this? Are we stuck here, hoarding chits that will grant us passage to a grand afterlife? I know; these are the same hackneyed questions we have all been positing from the beginning. After all, we human beings invented religion and philosophy to construct guardrails around these mysteries.

All the ideologies in my world had fallen flat. For me, religion was worse than useless—it had revealed itself as nothing more than a relic of deception and control. In fact, I came to identify all the "thought merchants" in my life as either hacks or frauds. I was in deep pain and could delude myself no longer. I had to find the answers or end up in a pit of nihilism. Not to be melodramatic, but like many who head down this path, my continued existence hung in the balance.

As I marched (or rather crawled) into my uncertain future, I resolved to hold fast to one, and only one, precept: I would no longer accept at face value anyone else's vision of reality! Instead, every concept, belief, doctrine, creed, tenet, and conviction had to first pass through my scientific process of examination and experimentation. In this way, I resolved to build a reality based on objective experience. Either I applied a concept to affect "real-world" change in my daily existence, or it was discarded. I think of this experimental process as a form of science—spiritual science.

With the winds of desperation filling my sails, and the polestar of spiritual science navigating the way, I began my journey into the void. I became a consumer of innovative scientific discoveries and far-flung philosophical and mystical thought. Throughout my explorations, I considered all new discoveries without preconceived bias or judgment. No idea was out of bounds, no matter how crazy it seemed. Living within this framework allowed me to mix scientific data and hypotheses with spiritual concepts and philosophies. The validity of each new insight was weighed against my emerging view of reality and then filtered through the trial and error of my experience.

Once I was committed to this process, mind-blowing events manifested around me. I experienced a level of synchronicity and serendipity I can only describe as miraculous. A steady stream of resources materialized at the right moment, each leading me step by painful step toward the holistic, unified concept of life I was seeking. A view of reality that resonates with both mind and spirit emerged—a simple, elegant theory of everything that permits science and mysticism to coexist within creation's harmonious framework.

To my amazement, I discovered that each of us is a direct extension, an *avatar*, if you will, of the same universal intelligence that creates everything in our material realm. In addition, our avatar bodies are imbued with the creative power to perfect our individual and collective realities. (The term "avatar" in this book describes the embodiment or physical manifestation of an individual's Spiritual identity.)

As I plumb the mysteries of my avatar powers, the world transforms before me in miraculous ways. To my constant amazement, I have the power to affect real, dramatic change in my life. Serious physical illness has given way to health and vitality; torturous mental illness has been replaced by a clear, healthy mind; anxiety and depression have transitioned to peace and happiness; and abject poverty has been displaced by a level of material prosperity and abundance beyond my wildest imagination.

Just as important as learning to wield creative power is the knowledge I have gained about the inner workings of reality. I have a logical framework that answers most of the "Big Questions" I was asking myself: "What is the purpose of life? What are the origins of existence? What awaits us after death? What are the controlling forces of reality?"

What follows are concepts I have used to transform my life. It is my great hope this book will assist you (the reader) in your own journey of discovery and evolution. As you move through, keep in mind that these are my ideas about how reality works. They are important to me—they work for me—but they may or may not apply to any other person on the planet. The point is you should focus on discovering reality from your unique perspective. Take any ideas of interest to you and use your own life as a testing ground. Develop your own unique view of reality—the one that works for you.

I wish blessings upon you, my fellow Curious Avatar... my friend!
—Marc Max Pollock

TABLE OF CONTENTS

SECTION I: THE REALM OF ENERGY

SECTION I:
THE REALM OF ENERGY

Framework for Section I: The Realm of Energy

Lᴇᴛ ᴜs ʙᴇɢɪɴ ᴏᴜʀ ᴇxᴘʟᴏʀᴀᴛɪᴏɴ of reality at the broadest point—beyond time, space, and matter; beyond existence as we know it—in the traditional God-realm, the invisible field from which our universe emerged some 13.8 billion years ago.

Of course, human beings have explored this realm from the very beginning. Not only do our sentient brains want a logical explanation for the force that created the universe, but we also crave connection with this force. We are searching for answers to two very Big Questions:

1. Who/What created the universe?
2. What is our relationship with this creative force?

While traditional religions refer to this creator as "God," a term that now makes some people uneasy, "God" as revealed in this book is a *Creative Energetic Force*. This Creative-Force has three distinct characteristics. This Force is:

1. Infinite,
2. Creative, and
3. Evolutionary.

My various labels (synonyms) for this Force correspond to each of these three characteristics:

1. God as Infinite: Core, Core-Energy, Source, Source-Energy, God of Being, God, God-Force.

2. God as Creative: Creative-Energy, Creative-Field, Creative-Impulse, Creative-Force, Field of Energy, Field.[1]
3. God as Evolutionary: Spirit, Spirit-Self, Spiritual-Personality, Spiritual-Center, Spiritual-Voice, Soul, Real-Self, Mind of God.

We can also visualize the attributes of this Creative Energetic Source in relation to humankind. We will explore each of these dynamics in greater detail, but here is a broad description:

1. Source as *infinite*: In this definition, God is conceived of as existing beyond this material realm. It is the source of energy that exists outside of space and time as we know it—the original Core-Energy responsible for this universe, the concept of infinity. It exists before the beginning and after the end of this universe—the Alpha and the Omega.[2]
2. Source as *creative*: This is the concept of a Creative-Energy responsible for making everything in our material existence. It is the Energy that flows from God to create reality. This ever-present Field of Energy is channeled into our material realm to transform the world.
3. Source as *evolutionary*: The concept that this material realm is in a constant state of growth and expansion. We are individual expressions of God, tasked with developing and improving our connection to Core-Energy. This is the personalized Soul, existing in energetic form, that connects us with both Core-Energy and Creative-Energy. It is the author of who we are outside of the confines of this material realm, the Spirit propelling our impulse to grow and progress. This is God's link to matter.

In this section, we will examine the attributes of the Creative Energetic Force, which brings our material universe into existence and continues its evolutionary transformation. We will lay the foundation for understanding how this Force interacts with each

---

[1] Lynne McTaggart, *The Field: The Quest for the Secret Force of The Field*, 1st ed. (United States: Harper Collins, 2002).
[2] Rev. 1:8 (NIV).

of us and introduce the ways in which the Creative Energetic Force interacts with humanity. To comprehend this relationship, it is important to understand the differences between our biologically based and Energy-based cognitive processes. We are two separate beings wrapped up in one material package. We are at once an infinite expression of Energy and a temporal manifestation of life. Our thoughts, feelings, and actions either originate from Divinity (our Spiritual-Mind), or they are tied to our biological brain.

Throughout this book, we will explore this dichotomy. However, for clarity, please be aware that I use "brain," "mind," and "ego" to describe thoughts and behaviors that originate from our biological form (as opposed to our link to Source-Energy). "Mind" and "brain" are used interchangeably to represent our complex, grey-matter organ with all its "hardwired" proclivities originating from millions of years of human evolution. The term "ego" represents the impact a person's history (socialization, childhood, experiences, beliefs, etc.) has on the mind/brain.

Now, let's take a journey into the Realm of Energy.

THE CREATIVE ENERGETIC FORCE

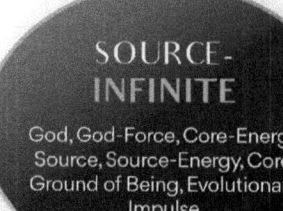

SOURCE-INFINITE

God, God-Force, Core-Energy, Source, Source-Energy, Core, Ground of Being, Evolutionary Impulse

SPIRIT-CREATIVE

Spiritual-Self, Soul, True-Self, Spiritual-Personality, Spiritual-Mind, Spirit

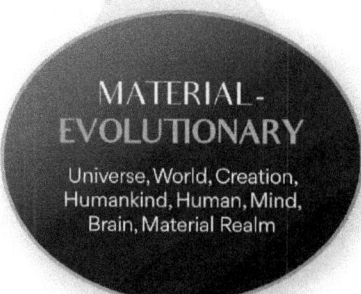

MATERIAL-EVOLUTIONARY

Universe, World, Creation, Humankind, Human, Mind, Brain, Material Realm

This diagram highlights the descriptive synonyms used in this book for each of the Three Realms that contribute to our reality.

CHAPTER 1:

EVERYTHING IS CONNECTED

During my formative years, I was immersed in fundamentalist Christianity. Like many religions, the focus was on the intrinsic separation between God and humanity. Sure, God created reality, but as soon as human beings entered the picture, a schism erupted between God and creation.

Although I tried to grasp this concept, I could never reconcile the paradox of a benevolent Creative-Force designing something, all the while intending to sever its relationship with the very thing it created. As I watched those around me beg "God" to reconnect with their life—to intervene in their existence—I became ever more disillusioned by the notion of an autocratic, authoritarian God. It made no sense, and it did not correspond to the world I saw around me.

I asked myself, "What if the notion of God advanced by Christianity and many other religions is wrong? If I wipe the slate clean and conceptualize a unifying Creative-Force that jives with both my observations and with science, what would it look like?" These questions drove me to investigate the existence of an interconnected Field of Energy that binds all of reality.

Everything Is Connected

That life emerged on this planet from the same materials that make up the most distant star is only the first chapter in the astounding story of our interconnected universe. We now understand that our material universe originated from a cosmic singularity that emerged from an unseen dimension... From that moment on, the creative force behind this event continued to evolve in complexity. From a sea of subatomic particles... to star systems... to simple life forms... to human beings, this originating force is the common denominator that binds all of creation.

In literature, this sea of Intelligent Energy is referred to by many names: the Etheric Field, Source-Energy, Core-Energy, Spiritual-Energy, the Astral Field, the Akashic Field, the Universal Energy Field, and even God—to name a few. The label for this force does not matter. It is only important to recognize there is an energetic presence that binds all of reality and to learn how to interact with this force.

Science Supports the Existence of the Field

The latest science points to the location of this Field of Energy as being in a dimension other than the one that occupies our five senses. Using our most sensitive technology, physicists can detect matter forming, out of "nowhere," and then just as mysteriously dematerializing back into a realm for which they cannot provide a rational explanation. Albert Einstein postulated that matter originates from a conversion of energy,[3] and that energy can neither be

---

[3] Don Lincoln, "Quantum Foam," *Fermilab Today* (Feb. 1, 2013). https://news.fnal.gov/2013/02/quantum-foam/; Sidney Perkowitz, "E = mc²," Encyclopedia Britannica (16 Aug. 2022), https://www.britannica.com/science/E-mc2-equation, Accessed 18 November 2022.

created nor destroyed.[4] Therefore, the manifestation of matter from nothing, or out of nowhere, presents a major ongoing problem for modern science.

We can observe the manifestation of energy coming from this enigmatic Field, but we have no scientific explanation for its occurrence. To complicate things, this Field possesses all the hallmark characteristics of an intelligent "God-Force." From observing the growth of distant star systems to pondering the improbable miracle of life here on Earth, it is obvious there is a force driving matter toward ever-increasing levels of intricacy. From a scientific perspective, matter continuing to gain in complexity violates the basic scientific concept of entropy,[5] which states that, over time, energy disburses and dissolves into chaos. The only way to avoid entropy in a closed system is to feed energy from an outside source into the system. If you consider that our universe is a giant closed system, then some kind of outside force is necessary to create what we see around us. In fact, from the very beginning, our universe has defied the notion of entropy. It has emerged from a dark soup of subatomic particles to evolving intelligent life!

There is no getting around the evidence that we are immersed in a field of directed energy that is omnipresent, omniscient, and creative. The more technologically sophisticated our experimental techniques become, the more we face the unflinching reality that everything in our material universe (ourselves included) is crafted from an immersive, interactive matrix of intelligent design.[6]

---

[4] Britannica, The Editors of Encyclopaedia, "energy," Encyclopedia Britannica (18 Oct. 2022), https://www.britannica.com/science/energy, Accessed 18 November 2022.
[5] Stephon Alexander and Salvador Almagro-Moreno, "Is Life The Result Of The Laws of Entropy?" New Scientist (June 11, 2022), https://www.newscientist.com/article/2323820-is-life-the-result-of-the-laws-of-entropy/; Boston University, "Entropy and the second law" (December 12, 1999), http://physics.bu.edu/~duffy/py105/Secondlaw.html.
[6] Casey Luskin, "An Introduction to Intelligent Design," *Intelligent Design and Evolution Awareness Center*, https://www.discovery.org/m/2015/08/Introduction_to_ID_Luskin_2015.pdf.

Ancient Wisdom Foretold the Existence of Creative-Energy

This notion of a multidimensional, creative Field is far from novel. From the beginning of recorded history, ancient wisdom has espoused that with which modern science now grapples. Everything we experience with our five senses spawned from somewhere other than this material realm.

Religions often address this notion by envisioning realms of heaven and hell that serve as a repository for the pervasive Creative-Force. Irrespective of what deity or deities occupy these hidden dimensions, the message that matter originates from a vehicle of intelligent design, beyond our three-dimensional existence, remains the same.

Also pervasive within many shamanic and mystical traditions is the idea of interconnectedness. From this perspective, each of us is a material projection of an interconnected blanket of Intelligent Energy that some refer to as "God." Everything is related to everything else.

We are entering a truly exciting time that sees both science and ancient wisdom coming to an agreement that there is, indeed, a Field of Energy beyond our material realm that is responsible for existence. This Field is the true birthplace of our material universe, and the force that drives the existence of every particle in every moment. It is the source of energy that connects all reality.

Tuning into the Creative-Field

Tuning into the Creative-Field involves expanding one's attention beyond the brain's customary machinations and toward the Spiritual-Mind. There are many paths to accomplishing this capacity, but a great place to start is to use your five senses to tune into your innate link to the Field.

EXERCISE
CONNECTING WITH THE SPIRITUAL MIND

Step One:
Let's take a moment to connect with the amazing material realm around you. Reach out with each of your five senses, one by one. Open your eyes and ears and draw in the entire panorama of sights and sounds around you. Breathing deeply through your nose, absorb the smells dancing on air particles rushing through your nostrils. Expand your lungs. Pick up your beverage, feel the heat or cold of the container. Take a sip. Concentrate on the taste. Stroke your garment. Feel the subtle variations in the weave and texture. In this way, you bring attention to the present moment.

Step Two:
Now continue this thought experiment by expanding your sensory attention outward. Imagine using your five senses to absorb everything in your room. Now expand to absorb everything in your house... your neighborhood... your city... the world... the universe! All material existence is now flooding into your awareness... into your consciousness. Feel the connection you have with all of creation!

Step Three:
Next, bring this thought experience inward. Draw that connection to every cell in your body. Imagine each cell pulling energy from the sun, the air, the minerals, and your food and converting this energy for the greater good of your material self. Sit with this connection to the universe. Let it radiate through your being.

Step Four:
Breathe deeply. Visualize your inseparable link to the whole of creation. All the particles in our universe—whether those that make up the cells in your body, or those that make up the farthest corner of the universe—originated from the same source of energy. You are linked to everything in existence. We are all inexorably connected to *The Field of Creation*!

THE CREATIVE FIELD

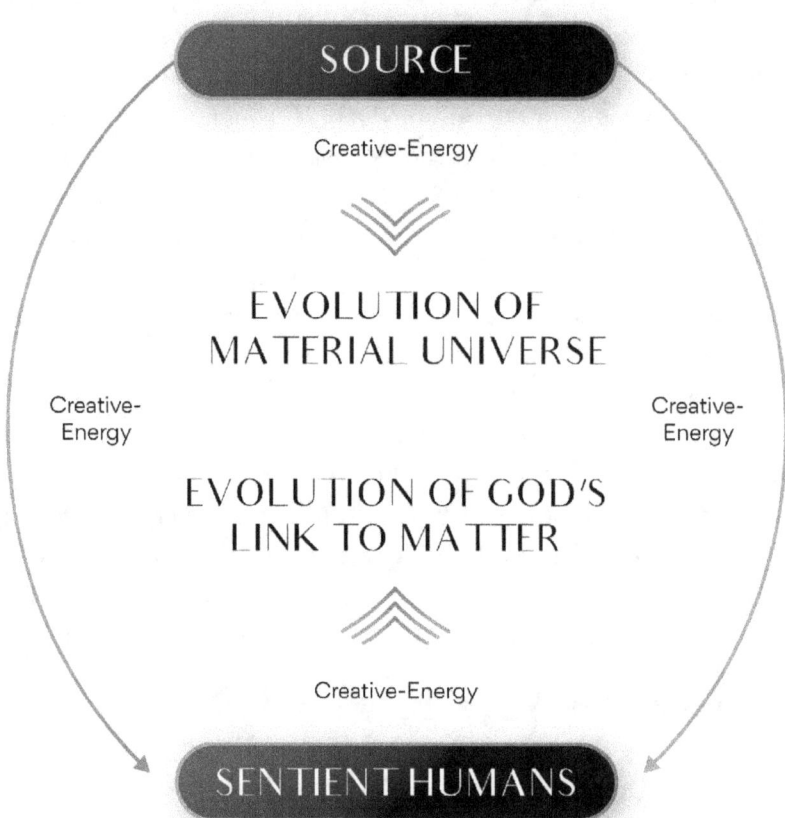

Creative-Energy exists within a Field that encompasses all of reality. This Creative Field is the foundation for all the energy channeled through Source to create the Universe, as well as all the energy channeled through humanity to create our reality and evolve our link back to Source.

CHAPTER 2:

THE MEANING OF EXISTENCE IS THE ONLY IMPORTANT QUESTION

Aʜ, "Wʜᴀᴛ ɪꜱ ᴛʜᴇ Mᴇᴀɴɪɴɢ of Life?" There is a reason we human beings are obsessed with this question. We are programmed to believe that unless we can arrive at a satisfactory explanation for why we are here, there is no possibility of peace or happiness. We seek the shelter of religion, or (like me) we engage in self-exploration. We have an evolutionary urge to know what is unknown—to assign meaning to our existence. This same hunger drives the creation of technology, personal development, and advancements of every kind.

I discovered that this impulse originates not in our brain but from our direct link to Source-Energy. Our desire for knowledge is inseparable from Source's appetite for evolution.

Why are you here—in this life—at this place and at this time? What are any of us doing here? What is the grand purpose of all of this? Of all the Big Questions of life, pondering the meaning of your existence is one of the most important.

The Evolution of Intelligent Energy

For the broad answer to these pertinent questions, one must examine the evolution of intelligent energy. Imagine you are a pure, intelligent energy, existing in ethereal realms comprising energy with no expression in material reality. In this scenario, there are no visceral experiences tied to matter and our material world—no way to feel the warmth of the sun on your face, or a sensual touch of your skin. There are no colors, no smells, no music. There is no way to experience the incredible profusion of sensory stimulation we enjoy in our material existence.

Now imagine you had the power to convert your energy into matter; to create a dimension that would provide you with the varied, wonderful, tactile experiences of the material world. Well, this is the origin story of our universe. To continue with this thought experiment, if you could create a material realm, you would want to merge your creative intelligence with your material creation—so your mind too could be expressed in material form. Human beings represent the highest (known) expression of this intent.

The Meaning of Life

One drawback of transforming energy into matter (then into biological matter, and further into the sentient biology represented by creative-thinking, self-reflective humans) is what I call *the challenge of emerging complexity*. As things grow in complexity, they carry with them remnants of their lesser-evolved past. Like pulling a wagon while steadily piling on the weight of our accumulated social and biological history, it takes more and more effort to progress forward. The past places an ever-increasing drag on our future evolution. For example, our brain and central nervous system are legacies of a long, evolutionary process. Since our emergence as primitive life forms, we have accumulated genetic material and programming which influences our current status as advanced sentient beings. As we embark on our next evolutionary step (of merging holistically with Creative-Energy), we must adapt the primitive aspects of our brain to align with Source-Energy. And this, my friend, is why we are here! This existence—in this lifetime—represents the next step in merging our material form with our Creative Source Energy. This is the meaning of LIFE!

Connecting to Source-Energy

Perfecting our connection to Source-Energy involves learning to use the full power of Creation itself. You already have the potential to manifest what you desire; you need to learn to use the tools at your disposal. You came into this life with certain creative strengths and weaknesses. It is your job to leverage your strengths and work on your areas of weakness. You have your Spiritual-Self and the whole of Source-Energy to support you in this endeavor.

EXERCISE
IDENTIFYING YOUR CREATIVE STRENGTHS AND WEAKNESSES

Take a hard look at your life. Ask yourself two questions:

1. What strengths and gifts do I possess? These can be identified by contemplating the following questions:
    a. What actions seem to come naturally (or easily) to me?
    b. What actions bring joy and fulfillment to my life?
    c. When considering my dreams and aspirations, what thoughts elevate my energy and bring a sense of excitement?
2. What weaknesses, challenges, and obstacles are prevalent in my life? These can be identified by contemplating the following questions:
    a. What areas of life are causing me anxiety, fear, anger, depression, or frustration?
    b. What actions are creating negative or undesirable consequences?
    c. What about my life is dreadful or unfulfilling?

Identifying and leveraging both your *strengths* and *weaknesses* should be viewed as valuable for developing your connection to Source-Energy. It is important to resist the impulse to bury the painful parts of life while only concentrating on what makes you feel good.

You occupy this lifetime for a purpose—not only to elevate humanity through the expression of your gifts but also to do the hard work necessary to root out your pathologies and underlying obstacles to growth. Resolving your individual weaknesses, challenges, and obstacles will expand and strengthen your evolution and that of humanity as a whole.

EVOLUTION OF MATTER

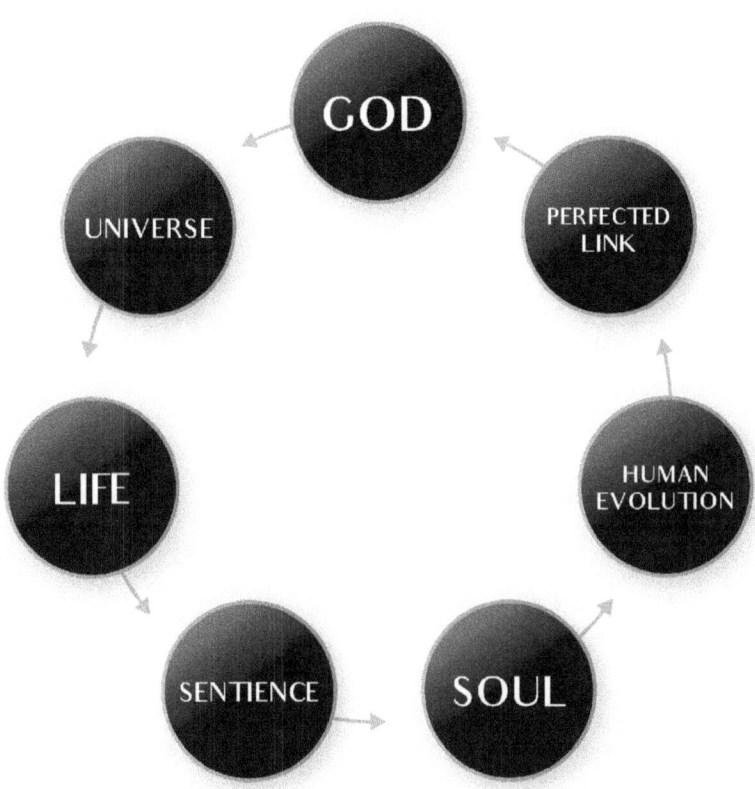

God is evolving matter so that "energy" can fully and completely enjoy the sensorial experience of the material realm. The diagram shows the process of this development. First there was the Big Bang and the creation of the Universe. Life evolved to become sentient. Humankind came to be. Since then, humankind has been the driving force for perfecting the link between energy and matter, and between God and our material existence.

CHAPTER 3 :

YOUR MIND CHANNELS EXISTENCE

Endeavoring to synthesize a belief system based on truth, I have turned to science to lead the way. To my continuing amazement, the emergent study of quantum physics is destroying the barriers between "rational" science and esoteric mysticism. There is much that science does not understand about the subatomic world that underpins reality, but what we can observe supports the existence of an intelligent, other-dimensional Creative-Force.

A Revolution in Science

The beginning of the twentieth century jumpstarted an upheaval within the scientific community as it became apparent that the underpinnings of the universe were far beyond our understanding.

Up to that point, physicists had relied on a classical Newtonian, cause-and-effect model to explain everything from the orbits of planets to the fundamental building blocks of matter.[7] However, as the sophistication of experimental technology developed, scientists discovered there are forces at work that cannot be explained by this traditional view of physics.

Everything in our material realm emerges from a mysterious *quantum-Field* of Energy[8] that possesses the characteristics of an intelligent Creative-Force. These characteristics have been espoused by mystics for thousands of years:

1. Creative-Energy emerges from a dimension outside of our four-dimensional (length, width, depth, and time) universe.[9]
2. This energy possesses creative intelligence.[10]
3. This energy interacts with the human mind and can be shared, directed, and manipulated.[11]
4. This energy transfers (between objects in a quantum state)[12] at a rate of speed greater than the speed of light (instantaneously).
5. This energy is not bound by time, place, or distance.[13]

[7] Ilyak Shapiro and Guilherme de Berredo-Peixoto, *Lecture Notes on Newtonian Mechanics: Lessons from Modern Concepts* (New York: Springer, 2013).

[8] Ethan Siegel, "Starts with a Bang: 70-year-old quantum prediction comes true, as something is created from nothing," *Big Think* (Sept. 13, 2022), https://bigthink.com/starts-with-a-bang/something-from-nothing/.

[9] Lisa Zyga, "Physicists investigate lower dimensions of the universe," *Physics.org* (March 18, 2011), https://phys.org/news/2011-03-physicists-dimensions-universe.html.

10 Raymond Bergner, "Intelligent Design: Maybe True, Maybe False, But Not Absurd" (2017), 10.13140/RG.2.2.15653.91367.

[11] Dean Radin, Leena Michel, Karla Galdamez, et al. (2012), "Consciousness and the double-slit interference pattern: Six experiments," *Physics Essays*, 25: 157-171. 10.4006/0836-1398-25.2.157, https://hal.archives-ouvertes.fr/hal-00719707; Andy Ridgway, "Your quantum brain: A new theory suggests that the bizarre world of quantum physics could be at play between our ears," Magzter.com, *BBC Focus* (March 2017), https://www.magzter.com/stories/Science/BBC-Focus-Science-Technology/Your-QuantumBrain.

[12] Clara Moskowitz, "Tangled Up in Spacetime," *Scientific American* (January 2017): 33-37.

[13] Jennifer Chu, MIT News Office, "Light from ancient quasars helps confirm quantum entanglement." Results are among the strongest evidence yet for 'spooky action at a distance,'" (August 19, 2018), https://news.mit.edu/2018/light-ancient-quasars-helps-confirm-quantum-entanglement-0820; George Musser, "Quantum Weirdness Now a Matter of Time," *Quanta Magazine* (January 19, 2016), https://www.quantamagazine.org/time-entanglement-raises-quantum-mysteries-20160119/; Stephanie Pappas, "Faster-Than-Light Discovery Raises Prospect of Time Travel, *"Live Science* (January 31, 2022), https://www.livescience.com/16207-faster-light-discovery-time-travel.html.

As confounding as quantum energy is to modern science, ancient wisdom has a long tradition of harnessing the power of this energy to assist us in our human journey. The most important tool at our disposal is our ability to use our mind to channel and manipulate Creative-Energy. Simply put, our mind uses thought patterns to convert raw energy into reality—we literally "think" things into existence. Our physical connection to foundational energy has developed to where we are directing quantum forces and creating our reality.

Therefore, in accordance with many ancient teachings, if we want to take control of reality, we must first learn to take control of our minds.

Controlling Reality by Controlling the Mind

Thoughts zip in and out of your mind every moment of every day. As you move through time, these thoughts serve as the building blocks for the reality unfolding before you. Therefore, if you want to control the reality you create, you must learn to control your thoughts. Most of us exercise very little control over what we think about. We allow our minds to dominate our thought agenda, which results in a reactive, chaotic existence that mirrors the primitive inclinations of the biological brain. Breaking this cycle requires intervention from your Core-Self. You must learn the skill of witnessing your thoughts and changing them to suit your needs. This is the practice of *awareness*.

The practice of awareness involves acknowledging thoughts as they enter your mind. Once you are conscious of a thought, you can either amplify it and use it to create your desired reality or filter it out by releasing its energy from your mind. This might sound easy, but few of us are aware of the constant flood of negative, counterproductive thoughts flooding into our brains. So, a tip to help identify damaging thoughts is to use your body and feelings as an early warning system. If your body feels tight, uncomfortable, or sick; or if emotionally you feel sad, stressed, or irritable, take a moment to notice your thoughts. Reset your mind.

EXERCISE
BREATHING TECHNIQUE TO BRING AWARENESS

Breathing techniques are the easiest, most effective way to establish awareness. Take a few deep breaths through your nose. Recognize the negative thoughts contributing to your discomfort. As you observe these thoughts, as though at a distance, identify their source. Your thoughts will represent unconscious, habitual patterns rooted somewhere in your past, or unresolved feelings buried in your subconscious mind. For clarification, the energy from past experiences can be stored within both the mind and body, outside our field of conscious awareness. This "hidden" energy is represented by the terms "unconscious" and "subconscious."

Now recognize that these thoughts and feelings are symbolic projections from the past and that you have the power to change how these projections affect your life. You can eliminate their influence on the present moment! Once you realize this, you are ready to release negative energy from the past and forge a new reality.

As silly as it might seem, for the next step, forgive yourself for your thoughts and emotions. While recognizing that these thoughts and feelings originated from fear or anxiety, extend understanding to your mind. Cleanse these thoughts and feelings with positive energy and release them back to the universe. Now you are prepared to receive new thoughts that support your goals and objectives. You are ready to take the next step toward forging your desired reality.

CHAPTER 4:

EXISTENCE IS TIED TO VIBRATIONAL FREQUENCY

As I EXPERIMENTED WITH VARIOUS techniques for transforming my life, it became apparent that my obstacles to growth were rooted in a wide assortment of negative attitudes and beliefs I had accumulated throughout my lifetime. Discovering the concept of "energy vibration" provided the link I needed to understand the physical relationship between energy and creation. This knowledge gave me a simple set of tools that I use to construct my desired reality.

Everything Vibrates

There is nothing in this universe that is not vibrational. Let's flip this statement: everything in our known reality is vibrating—

everything! Vibration is fundamental to our material realm.[14] From the subatomic particles that make up matter, to the electricity that runs your home, to the hardest minerals and compounds, to the thoughts and emotions in your mind—everything is vibrating. The only differentiating factor between all the objects and forces that make up our existence is the *frequency* at which they vibrate.

Detecting Frequency

We are all familiar with the concept of vibration, but frequency rates on the nanoscale of energy or matter are far beyond our senses' abilities to discern. However, all life on Earth has developed the ability to sense these extreme frequencies on a *subconscious (or unconscious)* level.[15] Somehow, we know if we are engaged with higher or lower frequencies. We can *feel* the difference! These differing frequencies have an immediate effect on the body, the mind, and the emotions—all without us knowing it.

This frequency of communication extends to all of life. Animals can sense these variations in frequency. For example, your pet senses your mood without you saying a word. It has even been proven that plants can respond to and communicate frequency information from the environment (such as the presence of threats).[16]

We live within a web of interconnected energy. No living thing exists in isolation. Energetic communication is happening all around us—whether or not we are consciously aware of it.

---

[14] Tam Hunt, "The Hippies Were Right: It's All About Vibrations, Man!: A New Theory of Consciousness," *Scientific American* (Dec. 5, 2018), https://blogs.scientificamerican.com/observations/the-hippies-were-right-its-all-about-vibrations-man/.

[15] Robert H. Austin, "Detecting nanoscale vibrations as signature of life," *Proceedings of the National Academy of Sciences of the United States of America* (Dec. 29, 2014), https://www.pnas.org/doi/abs/10.1073/pnas.1415348112.

[16] Cornell University, "Plants alert neighbors to threats using common 'language,'" ScienceDaily, (October 3, 2019), www.sciencedaily.com/releases/2019/10/191003135713.htm, and Carnegie Science, "Plants' Threat-Detection Mechanisms Raise the Alarm" (June 13, 2022), https://carnegiescience.edu/plants-threat-detection-mechanisms-raise-alarm-0.

Vibrational Form and Function

The vibrational frequency of energy determines its form and function. Lower energetic frequencies break down to form matter, while higher energetic frequencies are associated with formless manifestations, such as thoughts, feelings, and communication between energy states (including intention, healing, and cross-dimensional interactions).

Within each of these subgroups are frequency bands that impact the nature of what we manifest. For example, our feelings are associated with a specific frequency range that determines how we feel. Higher frequencies within this spectrum are associated with feeling good; lower frequencies lead to negative feelings. As another example, say you intend to create something in our material realm, such as wealth. If you are awash with negative (low-frequency) energy (like feelings of unworthiness or a lack of confidence that you can achieve your goal), your efforts will be stymied. If, on the other hand, you project confidence and visualize your success (high-frequency energy), then this energy will go to work helping you achieve your aim. It is of vital importance to align your energy with what you are trying to achieve.

We human beings are blessed with the capacity to access and use energy in all its forms, regardless of how low or high its frequency is. This ability does not require any conscious decision-making. It is natural within us. In fact, our realities are a product of the energy frequencies we are channeling into life in each moment. Therefore, the key to manifesting a better, more fulfilling life is to learn the art of controlling the frequencies of energy we bring to any situation.

All energy, regardless of the form it takes in our material realm, comes from the same Source. This Source is the common link that connects all of creation. Understanding this creates an intimate bond between you and your environment.

It might be helpful to visualize reality in the same way we view our physical bodies. Every part of you, from your toenails to your heart, originated from the coding of your DNA. Likewise, every part of the universe, from life on planet Earth to the most far-flung galaxies, originated from Source-Energy. Everything is a part of the same superorganism called our material existence. Therefore, every bit of energy channeled into our reality influences life as a whole. This is why it is of vital importance to learn how to control and manage the type of energy you channel into the world.

Learning to Use Energy

If you learn to pay attention, you can not only perceive the frequency of the energy surrounding any situation, but you can manipulate this energy to your advantage. Chances are you have been conditioned from childhood to disregard your intuitive ability to pick up the energy frequencies in your environment. This ability is a bit like a muscle that must be used, or it atrophies. Over time, you lose the faculty to recognize the level of energy coming from people, places, and things around you.

The good news is you can regain this gift by developing a habit of tuning into your feelings and then scanning your environment to identify the energy source behind these feelings. This brings your unconscious emotional reactions into the light of consciousness, giving you power over how best to deal with energy, whether positive or negative.

Use Your Feelings

This same technique of awareness can transform any frequency of energy to your advantage. Say you are trying to create prosperity in your life, but you find yourself mired in doubt and deep-seated feelings of unworthiness. You can transform these low-frequency thoughts by bringing them into consciousness, and then bathing them in higher-frequency emotions of love, forgiveness, and understanding. In this way, you transmute negative energy into beneficial energy.

As your practice of awareness expands, so will your abilities to transform the surrounding energy. Learning the alchemy of raising energy frequencies gives you the power to direct Creative-Energy wherever and however your heart desires.

CHAPTER 5:

ENERGY ATTRACTS
AND COMPOUNDS

For many years, I struggled with prolonged episodes of debilitating depression. I noticed that many of these bouts started with some insignificant bit of negative stimuli—maybe a bad day at work, a fight with my partner, even a rude encounter with a stranger. It could have been anything. From this innocuous crumb, negative thoughts would begin churning in my mind until I was enveloped by a dark cloud of despair. The cloud would lift, but only when something positive caught my mind's attention. From this morsel of positivity, supporting thoughts would emerge, and my mind crawled out of the pit it had dug for itself.

I recognized that the energies associated with my thoughts have an attribute of attraction. If I want to change my mental or emotional state from negative to positive, all I need to do is take control of my mind and bring forward a positive thought and feeling. The simple act of introducing a higher energy thought is often all it takes to reverse a downward spiral of negativity and create a positive outlook. Through practice, I not only cured myself of chronic depression but proved we can leverage the attractive quality of Creative-Energy to enhance every area of life.

Two of the most amazing characteristics of Creative-Energy are that it is attractive and compounding. Similar to the gravitational pull of mass, Creative-Energy projects a force that interacts with the energetic Field surrounding everything. It draws in more energy. If two energy streams are complementary (possessing the same or similar frequency and amplitude), for example, they combine to increase the overall frequency signature of the energetic flow. If two energy streams are dissonant (possessing different frequencies and amplitudes), the combination cancels out all, or a portion, of the energetic flow.

Spiral Flow of Energy

For this process, it is helpful to imagine a spiral shape. To illustrate, let's look at an example using the lower frequency energy associated with negative emotional states and belief systems. As you project low-vibrational energy through your thoughts, emotions, or actions, you invite the energy to validate your expectations. This additional energy is added to the existing negative energy, which further validates your belief system, which attracts more negative energy, and the spiral continues its compounding downward trajectory.[17]

Of course, we can also move this spiral in the opposite direction. Using the same example, what if this individual wanted to put the brakes on a negative energy spiral and enjoy the benefits of attracting positive, higher frequency energy? It is a simple matter of projecting higher-vibrational energy through thoughts, emotions, or actions. Taking a page from physics, once this high energy meets low energy, the effect is to cancel out the conflicting amplitudes of both streams, thus slowing the downward spiral. As more high-frequency energy

---

[17] Ester and Jerry Hicks, *Ask and It Is Given: Learning to Manifest Your Desires* (Carlsbad, California: Hay House Inc., 2004); Don Edward Beck, *Spiral Dynamics in Action: Humanity's Master Code* (United Kingdom: John Wiley & Sons Ltd., 2018).

is pumped into the system, the spiral passes through a neutral point before beginning its turnaround in the positive direction.[18] Once this happens, you will continue to enjoy the compounding effect of the positive energy until you project something that interferes with the upward cycle, thus breaking the spiral's inertia.

Using the example of an energy spiral, the point where the spiral is poised to change direction can be described as the inertia point in the spiral's cycle. Like getting a locomotive to change directions, to elicit positive change, the inertia must be broken. This requires pumping a lot of energy into the system. Enough energy must be applied to put the brakes on the downward spiral, and then, additional energy is required to begin the positive upward momentum. The good news is that once the high-energy spiral begins, the attractive and compounding forces proceed in your favor!

Why do some people seem to have all the luck, while others seem to wallow in one misadventure after another? When things don't turn out the way we would like, the tendency is to point to a host of uncontrollable external forces, but actually, we are in control over the outcome of our reality. It all comes down to the type of energy we project. It is that simple.

Controlling the Mind

So, the key to creating your optimal life—to managing the spiral flow of energy surrounding your existence—is to take control of your thoughts, emotions, and actions. You must take control of your mind. As you go about your day, your thought "habits" are the predominate driver of what you experience. Are you subconsciously expecting conflict or peace, success or failure, or positive or negative experiences?

---

[18] A. Konyukhov, "Wave cancellation conditions for the double impact of finite duration in an arbitrary structure," *Acta Mech* 231, 2773–2798 (2020), https://link.springer.com/article/10.1007/s00707-020-02672-0.

EXERCISE
CONTROLLING YOUR MINDSTATE

If you are not getting what you want, it is time to change your default Mind-State. Like breaking any habit, the first step is *awareness*. It helps to set an intention to catch negative, counterproductive thoughts as they bubble to the surface of your consciousness. Once you identify an obstacle, release it. Replace it with the vision of reality you want to actualize (want to bring into existence). At first, this may seem awkward and will require a great deal of concentration. However, as you continue to go through this process, the mind will habituate to this new vision of reality, and it will take less and less energy to maintain a positive outlook. As your mind becomes focused on creating positive outcomes, the attractive forces of Creative-Energy will manifest an amazing and miraculous transformation of your experiential reality.

You can apply this process to any area of life, from mental health, to relationships, to financial abundance—the basic principles of energy attraction are consistent no matter what you are creating.

CHAPTER 6:

CREATIVE-ENERGY IS NEUTRAL

M ANY OF US DELUDE OURSELVES into thinking there is a fundamental morality behind creation. However, this has no basis. Anywhere you look, you will see destruction and violence manifested on the same scale as creation and peace. The only thing that tips the scale is the intention behind our individual actions.

As human beings, we can create either heaven or hell, not only for ourselves, but for everyone and everything within our sphere of influence. There is no such thing as an external benevolent intercessor—we are solely responsible for the condition of our reality. Early in my spiritual journey, I recognized that there was no "savior" that could swoop in and drag my ass out of the ditch. Instead, I am a direct beneficiary (for good or bad) of the type of Creative-Energy I channel into the world. We each "reap what we sow,"[19] and there is no getting around it.

---

[19] Galatians 6:7 (NIV).

Creative-Energy does not care what it creates. It does not prefer creating one thing over another. It possesses neither value judgments nor a moral or ethical agenda. It does not care if it is channeled by a saint or a sinner. It does not care about the vibrational frequency in which it operates. It is *agnostic and neutral.* It makes things, builds things, expresses things, evolves things. It simply creates! You can view Creative-Energy as the bricks and mortar of consciousness. The brick is part of the construction—it does not decide the design or functionality of the building. Likewise, Creative-Energy is the raw material each of us uses to create our designed reality.

As you move through each moment, you are consciously or unconsciously (through your thoughts and actions) harnessing and directing Creative-Energy. You are molding your reality. If reality sucks, guess what? You are creating a low-frequency life for yourself. You can just as easily use the same energy to create the magnificent life of your dreams.

Using Your Mind to Control Creation

To reiterate, Creative-Energy does not label things as good, bad, positive, or negative. It takes your view of life and creates a reality that matches your expectations and intentions. If you want to change your situation, change the way you think. This means taking control of the way your mind processes information.

Because the workings of the biological brain are a product of experiences, there are often deep-rooted negative pathologies impeding your creative objectives. Are you having trouble manifesting money? You might be conditioned to believe you live in a world of scarcity rather than abundance. Are you unable to manifest success? You might have deep-seated feelings of inadequacy. Are you having trouble manifesting positive relationships? Maybe you have unrecognized feelings that you are unworthy of healthy relationships.

EXERCISE
RESOLVING OBSTACLES

Whatever the underlying issues, moving your creative process forward requires that you bring these issues to light and resolve them in a healthy way.

Step One:
The first step in gaining control over your mind is identifying the underlying obstacle. To determine where you need to make changes, look no further than the problems you are having. The negative aspects of your reality will always point to changes you need to make in your mind.

Step Two:
Next, you need to bring each negative thought pattern forward to the full light of consciousness. As painful as it might be, you must realize the origins of each barrier and the negative impacts they are having on your life and the lives of those around you.

Step Three:
The final step involves releasing the hold that this negative energy has on your present life and replacing it with a positive affirmation that supports your expectations and intentions. Once you bring the monster out of the closet and into the light, you can begin transforming the same energy into a positive reality. An obstacle you identify is an obstacle you can overcome.

CHAPTER 7:

SOURCE-ENERGY IS EVOLUTIONARY

I HAVE ALWAYS BEEN PUZZLED BY the broad display of variety and diversity in humanity. Unlike any other species, we somehow evolved a complex sentient brain that has spawned billions upon billions of individual personalities, each possessing a host of diverse physical and psychological characteristics. The question is, why did life evolve in this way? How and why did sentience (which refers to the mind's capacity for rational thought, self-reflection, and depth of awareness) emerge?

These questions led me to conceptualize and examine three possible explanations:

1. The crazy mishmash of humanity exists for the amusement of some sort of divine entity (i.e., God).
   - Nope. Long ago, I abandoned this religion-based concept of God.

2. The diversity displayed within humanity is the byproduct of natural selection and random adaptation.[20]
    - Doubtful. While natural selection and random adaptation undoubtedly account for some aspects of biological evolution, emerging scientific enquiry makes it clear that both the timing and complexity of human development cannot be explained by these factors alone.[21]
3. The multifarious mélange of humanity affords some sort of advantage to connect energy with matter....
    - Yes. As I reflect on my journey of personal and spiritual development, I realize that my evolution has been enhanced by the variety of challenges I have faced and the experiences I have had. Source-Energy is using this same principle on a massive scale to perfect its link to matter. In short, Source-Energy is using a variation of the strategy "economies of scale" by leveraging the variety and massive numbers of human beings to help it evolve energy's connection to matter.

Source-Energy Uses Distributed Evolution

Consider the possibility that the leap from pure energy into matter is a novel occurrence that requires intelligent energy to figure out the best way to solve this enormously complicated puzzle. Or perhaps our material universe is one of many such structures and is using a tried-and-true technique of linking Source-Energy to matter—one that uses trial and error to develop the connection.

In either case, the enormous complexity of turning matter into a pure conductor of Spiritual-Energy is challenging. Unlike the myth

---

[20] Henry M. Morris, "The Scientific Case Against Evolution," Institute for Creation Research, https://www.icr.org/home/resources/resources_tracts_scientificcaseagainstevolution/.
[21] University of Haifa, "Groundbreaking study uncovers first evidence of long-term directionality in the origination of human mutation, fundamentally challenging Neo-Darwinism," *American Association for the Advancement of Science* (Jan. 31, 2022), https://www.eurekalert.org/news-releases/941828.

of "God the Creator," who can snap His fingers to create what He wants, our energetic Source is evolutionary. It is evolving its connection to matter, step by step. The fastest, most efficient way for Source-Energy to evolve this connection is to distribute the evolutionary load over as many unique entities as possible. This increases the odds for evolution to take place either from a chance occurrence or from learned behavior.

This strategy for distributed evolution began at the moment the universe exploded into existence and will continue (at least) until matter becomes a pure conduit for Creative-Energy. At this stage, the human capacity for abstract reasoning represents a major step toward the seamless integration of Energy and matter. However, there is still a long way to go before our mind and body provide an unobstructed link to Source-Energy.

Creating Individual Expressions of Spirit

This *model* for achieving evolutionary change (distributed evolution), necessitates that we develop individual expressions of Spirit that correspond with our individual material lives. As such, our Spiritual-Self (the energetic expression of our individual consciousness which resides within the Realm of Energy) becomes the energetic repository for our unique gifts, talents, and interests, as well as our distinctive collection of behavioral impulses, pathologies, and the like. Our individualized paths expose us to particular sets of experiences, which facilitate unique expressions of both matter and Spirit.

Therefore, our individual Spiritual-Personality co-evolves along with our material existence. As we shall explore throughout the book, I have reason to believe that this co-evolution occurs over many, many lifetimes.

The big difference between our Spiritual and human forms is that our Spiritual-Personality lives in the Realm of Energy and is informed by the evolutionary desires of Core-Energy, as opposed to our physical existence, which is dominated by the trial-and-error efforts needed to perfect our link to energy.

Each of us is an individual expression of a collective Spirit, (the link between the Creative Energetic Force and human material existence). Some of us are old Souls, and some of us are newer, but each one of us plays an integral part in the evolutionary development of this material realm. One of the beautiful aspects of our individual journey is that Spirit's need to create impels us toward creativity and variety. If Core-Energy is the artist, then your individual expression of Spirit is the paintbrush, and your material form is your colorful pallet of paints. In this way, each of us contributes uniquely to the canvas of life.

Your Unique Expression of Spirit

So, what talents and skills allow you to make your unique contribution to the story of humanity? The good news is you already know! You need to sift through the clutter of your mind and recognize your special gifts. This process begins and ends with a connection to your Spiritual-Self. The more you can condition your brain to respond to your spiritual impulses, the more your creative gifts will flow.

Life wants—no, it *needs* you to create. You have at your disposal an unlimited supply of Creative-Energy. Because energy attracts like energy, creativity begets more creativity. The more you actualize your gifts, the easier it becomes to access your well of Creative-Energy. Your Creative-Energy attracts complementary energy from the world around you. As a result, people and circumstances appear in your environment to assist your creative output.

By expressing your gifts, you contribute to developing humanity's link to Source-Energy. This is why you are here. Each of us is responsible for identifying our unique abilities, and then using them to drive the evolutionary process forward.

Finding Your Gifts

Finding your unique creative gifts is as simple as following your heart. What makes you happy? What gets you excited? What occupies your dreams? What captures your attention and makes time stand still? These are all sparks from your Spiritual-Self that point the way.

Your Brain Is the Obstacle

The programming of your mind often hampers your ability to identify and express your innate gifts. The mind's nature is to conform, to be risk averse, and to shelter within the banal confines of the familiar. In isolation, your mind knows only what has been programmed into it and will resist exploring realms outside of its "known" reality. Therefore, your mind will give you a hundred reasons you should not listen to your Spiritual-Voice (the thoughts emanating from your Spirit). To make matters worse, the clouded minds of the people around you will give you a hundred reasons not to follow your muse.

Training the Mind

Because of its proclivities, you must introduce your brain to a new vision of reality. You must train it to trust and accept the link to your Spiritual-Mind. This reprogramming is accomplished through *experience*, *vigilance*, and *repetition*. As you manifest your gifts, your brain will expand its *experience* and become less critical and more accepting of this strange new path. As always, it takes time and persistence to reprogram the mind. You must be *vigilant* to intercept and bypass negative thoughts. And, *repetition* is required to transform the counterproductive habitual responses of your mind. Over time, your mind will come to view the manifestation of your gifts as blessings and will relinquish its fear.

DISTRIBUTED EVOLUTION

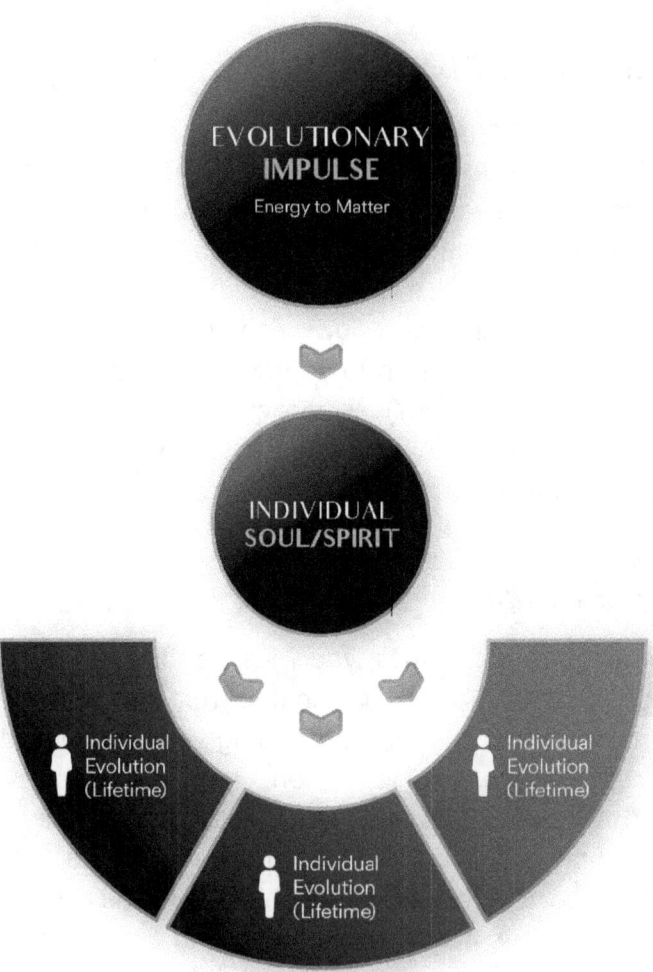

This illustration shows how Source-Energy uses a distributive model to maximize the evolutionary connection between energy and matter. Our individual Spirit sends our material form into each lifetime with a strategy to continue our evolutionary progress. In this way, our Spirit not only co-evolves with our various material expressions through time but also serves as a consistent guide and source of inertia as we perfect the connection between energy and matter.

CHAPTER 8:

YOU ARE INFINITE AND CREATIVE

ONE OF THE PIVOTAL MOMENTS in my spiritual journey came when I was introduced to the work of the famed writer of comparative mythology and religion, Joseph Campbell.[22] His chronicles of the common mythological links between various major theologies provided fertile ground for my budding skepticism of organized religion. Up to that point, I suspected that my fundamentalist Christian indoctrination was rife with lies and half-truths, but in Campbell's work, for the first time, I had evidence that focused a spotlight on the fanciful storytelling that had been sold as cold, hard facts.

This was all I needed! I gave myself permission not only to question my Christian upbringing but to explore the vast landscape of alternative spiritual thought. Thank you, Mr. Campbell.

---

[22] Joseph Campbell, *The Hero with a Thousand Faces*, 3rd ed. (Novato, CA: New World Library, 2012).

Using the world's religions as a basis to explore the nature of God (or Source-Energy) can be confusing. Most Eastern and Western traditions conceptualize God (and the realm of God) as being separate from humanity. This supposition places a clear division between the Divine and its material creation. In other words, God is separate from us lowly humans and dwells in a place removed from our tainted material realm.

Eastern Religion Emphasizes God as Infinite

While they might have similar notions about God's orientation to creation, the religions of East and West differ on how they view the relationship between God and humankind. In the East, the path to God focuses on removing oneself from the tainted framework of creation. The aim is to detach from one's body, mind, and environment and to eliminate all thought, desire, need, and creative ambition. The path to peace and bliss involves disconnecting from this material existence.

Fundamental to this viewpoint is the notion that God is a timeless, formless, omniscient, omnipresent sea of bliss-energy. God is *infinite* in every way. Therefore, to reach God, one must mimic this God-like state of being. To ascend to the status of God requires dropping all attachments to this physical realm. To transcend into Divinity, you must, in effect, rescind your humanity.

Western Religion Emphasizes God as Creative

In contrast, the West emphasizes the opposite path to God. Instead of disconnecting from this material realm, Western traditions place value on both your actions and what you create. For these religions, the stairway to heaven is built upon what is accomplished in this life. The aim is to earn your way to God's favor. It is a philosophy built upon action, upon doing. It emphasizes both the good deeds that one is engaged in and the sin that one commits. From this viewpoint, God's fundamental nature is *creative*, and the path to the Divine relies on how you interact with creation.

God Is Both Infinite and Creative

While deficient on many fronts, the differing philosophies of both Eastern and Western religions provide insight into the two fundamental characteristics of Source-Energy, the Two Faces of God:

- One face is the ecstatic, dynamic, creative compulsion that is most observable when we look at the world. This impulse wants to—in fact, it *must*—make, build, grow, perfect, and evolve. It is the cosmic itch that must be scratched and is the reason anything exists at all.
- The second face is quite different. It is the ground of being that never changes. This is the omnipresent, omnipotent foundation of all that is and all that ever will be. This is the deep, still water of the soul—secure, peaceful, and womb-like. The Bible refers to this quality as the "peace that transcends all understanding."[23]

Though different, these characteristics are two sides of the same coin. Source-Energy is at once creative and beyond creation. God is driven to manifest and is a bottomless well of tranquility.

Each of Us Is, at Once, Infinite and Creative

As products of this God-force, we have the power to tap into both *infinite* and *creative* energies. Not only does our reality represent a synthesis of both Eastern and Western religious viewpoints, but it also adds an important element that contradicts most mainstream religious traditions. Our created realities reflect the truth that *there is no separation between humanity and God*.

As material expressions of the Divine, we are direct projections of God. We can create a more perfect material realm and rest within the peace of our infinite being. In fact, we are charged to do both.

---

[23] Philippians 4:7 (NIV).

Our evolution depends upon our ability to harness both the power to create and the power to dwell beyond this material realm.

As we go about our daily lives, sometimes it is appropriate to access our well of Creative-Energy and to build, create, innovate, and evolve. And other times, we need to align with our infinite, never-changing foundation of bliss and love. Eventually, we will develop to where there is no difference between the two. On that day, there will be no separation between God and this material existence.

Our Brain Is the Barrier

The reason religion has a hard time fusing the two faces of God is because the human brain cannot conceptualize these two singular points of view at the same time. It makes little sense to the logical mind that your nature is action and inaction; creative and passive; that it both drives evolution forward and dwells in infinite stillness. Therefore, the mind focuses on one or the other.

The most difficult aspect of God to comprehend is Its infinite nature. It is hard to conceptualize timelessness, perfect stillness, eternal peace—a realm that contains nothing and everything at once. It is a challenge to find words to describe this facet of God that makes sense to our action-oriented brains. For this reason, groups that focus on this side of God tend to cloister themselves—they remove themselves from society in order to unravel this deep mystery.

You and I, on the other hand, are called to remain in society, and to become complete, whole expressions of God—to merge our creative power with our boundless, formless nature. Therefore, it is important to engage in a spiritual practice that develops the mind's connection to both features of Core-Energy.

That said, it helps if you split your practice by concentrating on one aspect or the other. There will be times when you want to manifest something in your life; to use your mind as a tool to focus Creative-Energy toward a result. There will be other times when you want to align with Divinity. This requires moving beyond thought to a space where your mind disappears and God-nature consumes your awareness. It is important to explore both facets of your divine nature. With practice, your experience in any given moment will reflect the synthesis of both the creative and the infinite aspects of who you are.

CHAPTER 9:

SOURCE-ENERGY IS INTELLIGENT

IT IS NATURAL FOR THE mind to form fixed ideological viewpoints. Eons of evolution have ensured that our brain is hardwired to develop simple, predictable perspectives that require very little processing time before we jump into action. For primitive humans, our very survival depended upon this rigid analysis of the environment around us!

Unfortunately, this evolutionary legacy continues to dominate our brain/mind. For modern humans, the impulse to establish a predictable model of our environment has morphed into a pathological need to hold fixed positions as to what is right and wrong. Our desire to hold these static viewpoints also brings with it a kind of discrimination against perspectives that might challenge our fixed worldview and a rote allegiance to concepts that support our fixed ideologies. We want to be right, so if we reject a concept, our mind will reason that the opposite extreme must be true. And, if we embrace an ideology, our mind rejects anything that challenges its perception of reality. For the mind, the middle ground between two extremes represents uncertainty—and the mind derides uncertainty!

I have struggled with these same issues on my spiritual journey. I bounced from Christian fundamentalism to rabid scientism, and it took years of personal development to understand that my extreme views toward science were just another form of religious absolutism. Under the guise of scientific "objectivism,"[24] I was blinding myself to the most vibrant and amazing aspects of life. It's always the "isms" that get us into trouble!

Creative-Energy is intelligent. However, from a scientific viewpoint, the concept that there is an overarching intelligence guiding our material realm is unpalatable. This is understandable because modern scientific enquiry was birthed, in part, to counteract the creation mythologies of institutionalized religion.

Science Has Become a Religion

However, for modern science, the proverbial pendulum has now swung 180 degrees, which results in science becoming a kind of religion unto itself. In its haste to rid itself of the tyranny of organized religion, it now subscribes to an assortment of biases that create the same barriers to objective thought it is trying to promote. As a result, any notions that contradict these biases are dismissed out of hand, labeled as fantastical, or worse, as lunacy.

One such prejudice involves the prohibition of assigning intelligence to energy. This concept held up pretty well in the age of Newtonian physics, where most things in our observable universe could be explained by cause-and-effects mathematics. Even for those pesky subjects that had no logical explanation (such as gravity and magnetism), we could plug in a placeholder calculation and assure ourselves that it was just a matter of time before we would

---

24 David Kelley, "What is Objectivism?" *The Atlas Society* (June 14, 2010), https://www.atlassociety.org/post/what-is-objectivism.

discover a mechanistic answer to the mystery. We had "faith" in our Newtonian view of the universe.

Superseding Newtonian Physics

This all changed in the early 1900s with quantum physics.[25] It was apparent that the old, reliable scientific view of the world was just scratching the surface. Much to the consternation of the scientific community, quantum theory recognized that the foundations of reality operate in a field of phenomena that supersedes Newtonian physics and for which science has no logical explanation.[26] A mysterious font of pure energy, (a force with the potential to affect material existence), took center stage as the source of everything in our material realm.

From the time of this momentous discovery until the present day, the scientific community has had an enormous problem on its hands. The fact is science has no explanation for the origins or nature of this enigmatic Field of Energy. Where does it come from? How does it know what form to take? How can it communicate with other forms and states of energy? How can quantum communication (through quantum entanglement) happen instantaneously, regardless of distance? How can subatomic particles be in two places at the same time? Why does pre-matter energy respond to its environment?[27] How is it that quantum effects are influenced by our thoughts, feelings, and intentions?[28] How is energy able to predict the future?[29] Science has confirmed all these characteristics,

---

[25] George Gamow, *Thirty Years That Shook Physics: The Story of Quantum Theory* (Dover ed., New York: Dover Publications Inc., 1985).

[26] John Gibbins, "Quantum Physics in 10 Minutes," *BBC Science Focus*, Issue No. 284 (Aug. 2015).

[27] Tim Folger, "The war over reality," *Discover Magazine* (May 2017).

[28] Ethan Siegel, "Observing the Universe Really Does Change the Outcome, and This Experiment Shows How," *Forbes.com* (May 26, 2020), https://www.forbes.com/sites/startswithabang/2020/05/26/observing-the-universe-really-does-change-the-outcome-and-this-experiment-shows-how/?sh=69f5cc4467af.

[29] Henry P. Stapp, "Attention, intention, and will in quantum physics," Ernest Orlando Lawrence Berkley National Laboratory, LBNL-42650 reprint (May 1999), https://escholarship.org/content/qt5xr366vq/qt5xr366vq_noSplash_a451774ff5e46f7a5bdc665ed65c09f8.pdf?t=p21mxm.

but no one has an explanation for the questions of How, What, When, Where, or Why.

Just take a good look at the aforementioned characteristics of energy. Are they not the very definition of an intelligent creative power? Still, mainstream science remains reticent to break free from the ideological prison it has created for itself. Even when faced with irrefutable scientific evidence, it refuses to acknowledge that there is a form of intelligent energy behind the substance of our existence.

Since the Renaissance, science has disavowed any notion of creationism. We are conditioned to view the inner workings of the universe as an insular, mechanistic process—a notion that leaves little room for the existence of an intelligent source of creative power. Of course, this leaves a rather large void within the human psyche for questions pertaining to creation, morality, the afterlife, and such. As usual, organized religions step in to fill these gaps with a host of superstitions, myths, and rules for behavior that are loaded with ulterior motives for expanding their control over their believers instead of offering a viable complement to the shortcomings of modern science.

All Beliefs Must Be Tested

As you expand your view of reality, it is important to consider all the biases, prejudices, and arbitrary notions supplied by both science and religion. Do not be afraid to question anything (and everything). You must bring your beliefs into the light and evaluate them at face value. This includes any notions you might have about reality and your place within it.

Everything must be scrutinized through your own lens, nobody else's. Apply the same evidence-based approach that a scientist might employ—but with no preconceptions. Examine a belief. Test it—and then apply it to your life. Does it hold water? If it does,

Eureka! If it does not, discard it. Move on. Remain open to change and growth. What works today might change tomorrow. Know that only a lazy fool maintains a static view of life. Reality morphs and changes. It evolves, and so must your beliefs.

Personal Discovery

Every person born has the right to undertake a journey of self-discovery. And, as noted, each one of us must do our part to further the evolution of humankind's connection to Source. When this evolution runs counter to the prevailing sentiments of our societal institutions (whether scientific, religious, or governmental), it can create a backlash. When this happens, take heart! Your mission extends far beyond any institutional ideologies. You are a pioneer, blazing a path for future generations.

CHAPTER 10:

CREATIVE-ENERGY WANTS TO EXPAND

COUNTLESS TIMES THROUGHOUT THE YEARS, I have used my life as a proving ground for the expansive quality of Creative-Energy. I started out by observing those around me who were oriented toward "scarcity." It was apparent that their negative belief systems were contributing to the negative reality swirling around them. As I gained exposure to others who were achieving "success" in certain areas of their life, I recognized a stark contrast between them and those who could not achieve their dreams. Not only did those achieving success see what they wanted to create; they believed they could accomplish their goals. They visualized reality as conforming to their dreams, desires, and efforts.

These days, popular culture emphasizes that reality conforms to positive thoughts. While filtering out negative thoughts is important, it is only a piece of a complex process of creation. To get the complete picture, we must understand the foundational nature of Creative-Energy and how this energy manifests in our material realm.

∞

Creation is expansive. It is the nature of Creative-Energy to give, to provide, to fill a void, and to respond to any energetic invitation to bring forth. Whether we are aware of it or not, our individual and collective realities are a direct reflection of this impulse. Just look around—you invited all of this into your life! The amount of abundance (or scarcity) in your life is proportional to the attractive energy you have laid out in front of you. This ability to manipulate reality is an immense amount of power! Learning to harness this power for your own benefit starts with understanding the dynamics behind this expansive force.

The Law of Creative Expansion

Let's begin with an example that should be familiar to everyone. Have you ever moved into a larger dwelling without enough furniture and belongings to fill all the rooms and closets? Before you know it, you have filled all the empty spaces and are left wondering how in the world it happened. Well, you created an environment that allowed for expansion, and the *Law of Creative Expansion* took care of the rest. You set up the energy field to attract more stuff, and the stuff waltzed in the door.

This same principle can apply to any area of life. Take, for example, a business that wants to grow. You can take a conservative approach and maintain just enough office space and staffing to handle the current client load. Or you can expand your facility in anticipation of future growth. In this scenario, Creative-Energy will interpret the conservative approach as a *desire for scarcity* and growth will be difficult to achieve. It will interpret an act of expansion as a *desire for abundance*, and Creative-Energy will go to work to fulfill this aim. This example might seem fanciful, but it is a genuine phenomenon.

Now let's look at a real-life example from the famous comedic actor, Jim Carrey. Several years ago, during an interview, he described his own method of tapping into creative expansion before he was successful and famous.[30] He describes a routine where every night he drove up to a lookout and took in the view of the entire Los Angeles valley. As he looked out over the vast sea of lights, he would visualize himself as a successful entertainer. In fact, he would stay there until he was 100 percent convinced that he was, at that very moment, what he desired to be—the most famous comedic actor in the world! He even wrote himself a $10 million check, dated for the near future, to represent his projected success. Once he "knew" himself as what he desired to become, he drove back down the hill to his tough existence as a struggling artist.

Of course, Jim Carrey ended up becoming the world-famous artist he wanted to be. But what effect did the visualization practice play in all of that? In short, his practice set up a kind of energetic scaffolding for reality to build upon. His thoughts, emotions, and actions aligned to support abundance, and as a result, abundance materialized.

In everyday life, each of us is doing the same thing. Our thoughts, beliefs, emotions, and actions are preparing the foundation for Creative-Energy, and the Law of Creative Expansion takes care of the rest.

The great news is that you can learn to harness power of the Law of Creative Expansion for your benefit.

---

30   Jim Carrey, "What Oprah Learned from Jim Carrey," Oprah's Life Class (1997), Oprah Winfrey Network, 3:50.

EXERCISE
HARNESSING THE POWER OF CREATIVE EXPANSION

Step One:
Awareness: Notice the energy emanating from your thoughts, beliefs, emotions, and actions. Is your attractive energy from these areas supporting or hindering your goals and objectives?

Step Two:
Focus: In order to set the table for actualizing your desires, you must filter the energy emanating from your mind. Disregard any negative thoughts and amplify thoughts and beliefs that will contribute to you realizing your objectives.

Step Three:
Visualize: Consciously dwell in the vision of your desire. See yourself in your new reality. Allow yourself to experience every aspect of this world "as if" it is your reality at this moment.

Step Four:
Activate: Let your actions support your desires and take the steps to pursue your vision. For example: If you want to grow your business, you might move to a larger space that can accommodate the growth.

Remember, you are the source of Creative-Energy and you placed yourself in this material realm to *create*! You have at your disposal the power to channel this energy into the world. *The Law of Creative Expansion* serves as a kind of gravitational force that attaches to your beliefs and expectations, drawing on the persons, circumstances, and resources you need to assist the process. With a focused mind, you can create the reality of your dreams!

LAW OF CREATIVE EXPANSION

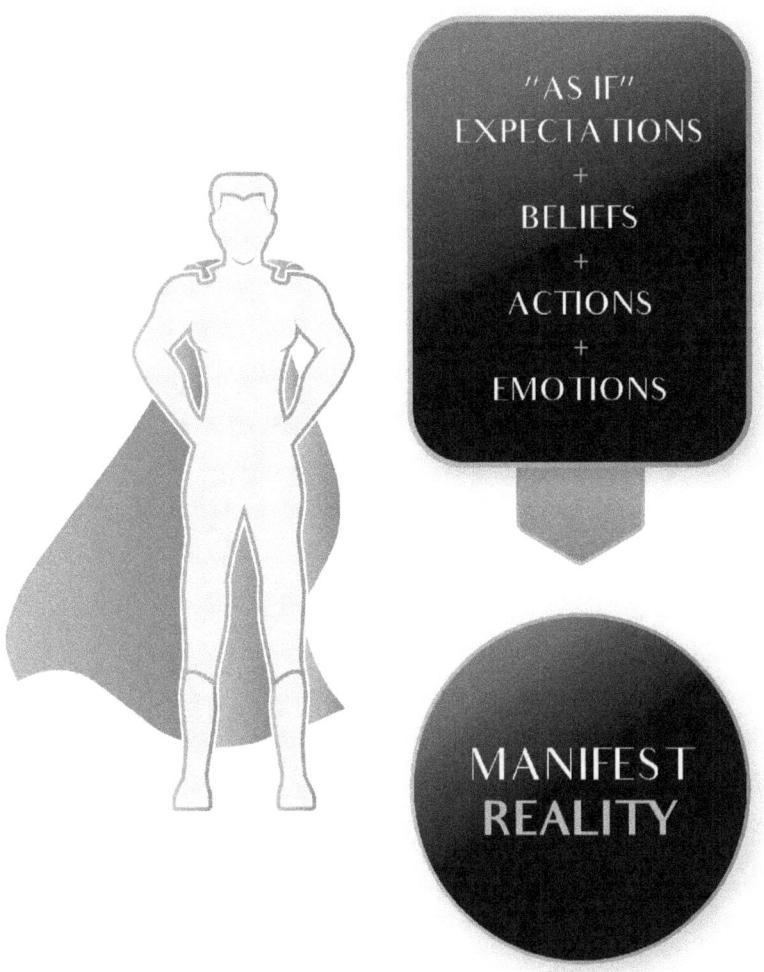

"AS IF"
EXPECTATIONS
+
BELIEFS
+
ACTIONS
+
EMOTIONS

MANIFEST
REALITY

You can use the Law of Creative Expansion to manifest your desired reality in this life. By coordinating your expectations, beliefs, actions, and emotions, you can create the reality of your dreams.

SECTION II: CONVERTING ENERGY TO MATTER

SECTION II:
CONVERTING ENERGY TO MATTER

Framework for Section II: Converting Energy to Matter

IN SECTION I, WE BUILT a case for the existence of an intelligent sea of energy that is the source of everything we know as reality. We examined the characteristics of Source-Energy and discovered that its fundamental nature is to create—it is the "stuff" that transforms energy into matter.

In this section, we begin an exciting journey into the origins of our universe and the purpose behind its existence. We also do a deep-dive into humanity's relationship with Core-Energy and explore the answers to some very Big Questions along the way, including:

- Why are we here? For what purpose do we exist?
- What is our relationship with Core-Energy?
- How does Source-Energy manifest in this material realm, and what part do we play?
- What are the differences between energy and matter?
- What are the challenges and obstacles behind converting energy into matter?
- What role do our brains/minds play in creating our reality?
- How can we use Creative-Energy to perfect our reality?

This is exciting stuff!

Please note that the terms "brain" and "mind" both refer to our biological thought center, which is separate from thoughts channeled from our Spirit. In addition, the term "ego" as I use it here is not tied to the standard Freudian model (id, ego, superego).

Instead, the terms ego, ego-mind, and ego-self are all synonyms for the biological brain's predisposition to create an insular, brain-oriented vision of reality that places one's human mind as the center reference point for life. The ego's point of view stands in stark contrast to the view of reality emanating from our "true nature" (which exists in the realm of energy) and is identified as the Spiritual-Mind, Spiritual-Personality, Spirit, Soul, Real-Self, etc. You can find additional information in the Glossary of Terms.

$$\infty$$

Source-Energy's relationship with our material universe is complex. We human beings (along with our sentient minds) have developed to bridge the gap between the Realms of Energy and Matter. In this section, we will examine this relationship, including our ability to channel energy and to use energy to communicate with our environment.

Of course, this process remains far from complete. As you will see, however, we are heading toward an evolutionary tipping point, where there will be no barriers between our physical existence and our existence as pure energy—as Spirit.

I now believe that we are all sparks of the Divine, enjoying ourselves in this material realm. We are forging a path toward an ever-deeper experience of the sensual wonders of this universe. This is who we are as human beings, and this book is based upon this belief.

CHAPTER II:

YOU ARE LEARNING HOW TO LINK TO SOURCE ENERGY

Growing up within the framework of traditional religion as I did, I found it unnerving that the all-knowing, all-powerful Divine would create a material reality (and human beings, in particular) that is loaded with imperfections. For example, why would God "create man in his own image"[31] only to set us loose to devolve into the self-centered, destructive, warlike creatures we are? Preposterous! It wasn't until I understood that *evolution* is a fundamental characteristic of all matter that the relationship between Source and this material realm became clear.

---

31 Genesis 1:27 (NIV).

An Evolutionary Experiment

Converting Source-Energy into matter (in particular, sentient matter in the form of the human brain and nervous system) is in the throes of a dynamic evolutionary experiment. I describe this process as "matter learning to become an integrated expression of Source-Energy." We are each charged with moving this laborious process forward. In short, you are a material expression of energy learning how to use your sentient mind to form a cohesive link back to Source. This is the overarching aim, realized or not, of every person, in every lifetime, throughout history.

Perfecting Our Connection to Spirit

It might not always be apparent, but from the beginning of time, life on Earth has been working towards perfecting this connection. Starting as unicellular organisms, we have been on a slow, winding trajectory toward developing a biological structure that can host sentient consciousness. The big advancement came with the hominid brain. This novel brain structure provided a platform for matter to channel and manipulate energy in a new way. For the first time, matter gained the ability to reflect on itself and the world around it. This expanded the doorway through which Source-Energy could flow, back and forth, between our material realm and the dimensions of energy. Thus began our conscious relationship with the Spirit-World... the Realm of Energy. This not only provided a platform for communicating with the energetic realms, but it provided a channel for funneling Creative-Energy into our material existence.

While we have come a long way in our quest to form a seamless, cohesive interface with Source-Energy, we still have a long journey ahead of us. The regrettable truth is that because of the complexities inherent in synching our amazing and complicated biological brain with a non-biological Energy-Field, most people remain disconnected from Source-Energy. Like a clever bit of AI, the mind must develop its programming and learn how to build a successful interface between this material existence and our energetic Self.

This evolutionary process continues to advance with every passing moment. Step by step, we are expanding our connection to Source-Energy. There will come a day when we have developed sentient matter to where there are no barriers between the Spiritual and material worlds. This is the beginning of nirvana (of heaven); when our energetic Beings can savor all the tactile joys this material world offers, and our physical existence will reflect the love, peace, and abundance that flows from our Creative-Core.

Tools for Development

On the surface, the prospect of developing every human mind might seem improbable. Thankfully, we each possess an arsenal of tools to assist with moving consciousness forward. Foremost is the connection you have to your Spiritual-Center. You are not thrown into this, or any other, incarnation as a random experience. Instead, you placed yourself in this time and place with the specific intent of advancing the evolutionary connection between the energetic and material dimensions. As a result, your Energetic-Core is at work—placing you in situations that present you with the highest potential for growth.

This same process is playing out across the entirety of humanity. Each person's Core works to transform the sentient brain into a superconductor for Spiritual-Energy. It is your destiny—your responsibility—to engage with this process. The more progress you make, the more access you will have to the wondrous power of Source-Energy. The more progress we make collectively, the closer we will come to perfecting this material realm.

SPIRIT AND HUMANS

This diagram shows the relationship between humans and Spirit. The development of the sentient mind gave humans the ability to connect consciously with Source-Energy and choose the type of energy they wish to channel to create reality. This unique ability also necessitated the development of individual Spirits or Souls to assist each incarnated human with their evolutionary journey. Therefore, the Spirit both emerged from the advent of sentient matter and co-evolves along with each human in each lifetime.

HUMAN EVOLUTION

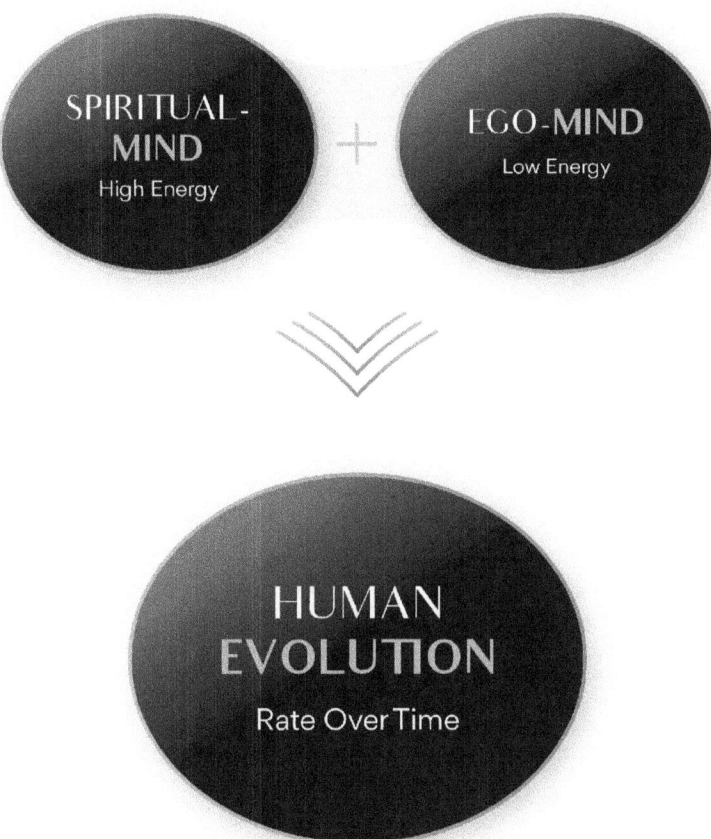

This diagram shows the relationship between the human ability to channel Creative-Energy and our ability to evolve. The type of energy we bring into reality determines whether we are advancing or hindering our progress over time. Energy generated from the ego usually stifles growth, while energy channeled from the Spiritual-Mind advances our evolution.

CHAPTER 12:

YOU ARE AN AVATAR FOR SOURCE-ENERGY

WHILE EXAMINING THE JUXTAPOSITION BETWEEN Divine energy and the imperfect human form, I realized we are the latest evolution of a developmental process that began some 13.8 billion years ago. Like a spacecraft sent out to explore distant worlds, each of us is a kind of pod that allows Source-Energy to probe the depths of material reality. Our form can also evolve—allowing this energy to grow its experiential link to the sensorial wonders of the material realm.

The revelation that each of us is an avatar for Source-Energy transformed my ideas about Self and the meaning of existence. In fact, it is impossible to overstate the impact that this epiphany has had on my life. I realize now that I am a direct representative of God—imbued with the ability to channel the Creative-Power of God! I am not only an avatar, but I am also an avatar with a mission—a mission to evolve this material existence into a harmonious, synchronic expression of the Divine.

To get a better picture of this relationship between God and avatar, let's explore the interplay between our physical bodies and the

Field of Creation. Specifically, let's address our connection to Source-Energy and our role in channeling this energy into the universe.

We Are More Than Our Bodies

From the beginning, we human beings have pondered our origins and tried to find meaning behind our unique place in creation. Why are we alone in our ability to reflect on life and our place within the greater context of existence? By way of providing context around this mystery, many religions and spiritual traditions (such as Buddhism) subscribe to the notion that our consciousness is separate from our physical form.[32] Our true self lies outside of our material form. It occupies an other-dimensional space beyond our body and mind. Indeed, that the "real" you exists outside of your brain and body is the impetus for the concept that we are physical avatars representing a greater consciousness beyond this physical realm.

The body you see in the mirror, what you refer to as "self," is a temporary material expression of the same energy matrix that created every bit of this universe. At the moment you were conceived, a piece of this energy made a conscious decision to jump into this material dimension and begin a life journey as *you*. From the moment of conception until your death, your physical/material incarnation remains connected to Source-Energy. Both your human form and your characteristic sentience are a direct byproduct of this connection. You are a physical manifestation of Creative-Energy in this material realm—pure energy converted into matter. As an avatar for Source-Energy, your unique capacity for conscious thought serves as an energy pathway that allows you to connect with Source and channel this Creative-Energy into the universe.

Let's take this concept one step further. Not only are we creations of Source-Energy and portals for channeling this energy into the world, but each of us is also a direct representative of Source-Energy

---

[32] Michael A. Singer, *The untethered soul: the journey beyond yourself* (Oakland, CA: New Harbinger Publications, 2007).

in material form. Let this distinction soak in: You are a physical manifestation of Source. You are the embodiment of God. You are an *avatar* representing Source-Energy in this material dimension!

Defining Your Energetic and Material Forms

The prospect that each of us is an avatar for the same divine force that is responsible for all creation is daunting. After all, most human beings do not behave like benevolent hosts. In fact, most of us cannot represent anything close to our imagined concept of a Divine Creative Force. To gain perspective on this gap between our human condition and our Spiritual-Core, it is important to understand the fundamental differences between our energetic and material forms.

We often refer to the energetic version of self as "Soul" or "Spirit." Broadly speaking, your Spiritual-Self is your "True-Self"— who you really are in the core of your being. You emerged into this life from your Spirit. Not only does this relationship provide a direct connection to the creative power of Source, but your Soul also sets the agenda for this lifetime and serves as the authentic (will of God) mind behind your physical representation. Your Spirit chose the *how, when, where,* and *why* of this lifetime and gives you access to the tools for accomplishing your objectives. You picked *how* you are represented in this lifetime (i.e., your body). You determined *when* on the human timeline to enter physical existence. You picked the place, family, tribe, and culture *where* you wanted to enter this life. You decided on the goals for this life—the *why* behind your existence. You chose all of this to give yourself the best opportunity to achieve your objectives for this lifetime—to take the next steps toward perfecting your link to Source-Energy.

In contrast to your Spiritual-Self, your physical form (i.e., your human body) represents your unique Spiritual-Energy in this material realm—it is an avatar designed to engage your Energetic-Self with the sensorial touch points of the material universe. We created our unique avatar for two primary reasons:

- First, the body gives our Spirit-Selves access to the cornucopia of sensual experience available in this universe. It is possible that these tactile, matter-oriented, sensorial experiences are only accessible through matter-dominated dimensions such as this one.
- Second, our physical form serves as a receiver and transmitter through which we transfer other-dimensional energy into this realm and back to our Energetic-Core. This movement of energy is the catalyst behind humanity's amazing ability to create. In every moment, we are channeling this energy to create and develop reality in this material dimension.

Our Brain/Mind Is Still a Work in Progress

The crown jewel of the material body is the conscious brain/mind. In one respect, the mind is an advanced biocomputer. It is a machine capable of storing massive amounts of data (as information, feelings, memories, etc.) and using this data to create programming that produces an unlimited array of material objects, concepts, actions, and ideas. However, the human brain serves the much higher purpose of facilitating the flow of Creative-Energy into this material realm.

Optimally, this flow of Creative-Energy would be a pure reflection of your Spiritual-Self. However, at this point in human development, our physical mind and body are still developing the ability to connect with our Spiritual-Self and to channel its energy into reality. As a result, some of the energy you channel may align with your spiritual objectives, while other energy might channel into areas that diverge from these objectives. Many of us spend massive amounts of our creative potential in the frivolous pursuit of satisfying the demands of our insatiable biological brain instead of aligning with the desires of our Spirit.

Each individual has the "potential" for establishing a seamless connection with the realm of Spirit and creating a life that is a direct reflection of Spirit. However, as we go about the business of being human, we are still developing this capacity.

Aligning with Spirit Is Beneficial

The degree to which we are aligned with our Spiritual-Self has a direct bearing on the quality of our human experience. When our thoughts, actions, and behaviors reflect our Spiritual-Core, we experience the fulfillment, peace, and happiness characteristics of Core-Energy. When we do not reflect our Spiritual-Core, we struggle against the worst aspects of being human.

As always, each of us is free to choose our path. Does your avatar evolve its connection to Spirit in this lifetime, or does it "kick the can down the road" to evolve in another incarnation? Do you experience a wondrous, joyful lifetime, or do you wallow in misery? The choice is yours.

Life can be arduous. The journey is made even more difficult when you conjoin your self-identity with your physical form. Remember, the real "you" is pure, boundless Creative-Energy. You are not your body. Job One for your avatar is to figure out a way to develop your connection to Core-Energy. This process involves a lot of hardship—a lot of trial and error—and a lot of falling flat on your face.

As you go through your day, it helps to remind yourself that your body is a platform for your Spirit to experience and create in this material realm. Viewing life through this lens makes it easier to maintain equanimity, enjoy every moment, and honor your core creative self. The fact is you chose this body and lifetime for a reason. You created this physical presence because it gives you an amazing opportunity to develop your material connection to Core-Energy. You owe it to yourself to honor every aspect of your chosen form. Everybody enters life with certain inherent strengths and weaknesses. It is your mission (should you choose to accept it) to use these gifts and challenges to advance your connection to Core-Energy.

When we approach every moment as a gift from Spirit, we can find the lessons embedded in everything. Only in this way can we maximize our evolution in this lifetime.

LINK TO MATTER

This diagram examines the process that Source-Energy is using to evolve a connection to matter. The key to this process is the evolution of the sentient mind, which gives Source-Energy the ability to use humans as an avatar gateway for experiencing the Material Realm fully. The Spiritual Realm serves as a conduit for Source-Energy to perfect our avatar capabilities.

CHAPTER 13:

YOU ARE BORN TO CREATE

Growing up in an environment of poverty, domestic violence, and turmoil, I was surrounded by chaos and desperation. Our constant efforts to survive left little energy for contemplating the root cause of our predicament. Instead, we placed whatever modest hopes and dreams we had in the hands of mysterious forces beyond our control. More often than not, this involved a ritual of supplication—of begging for God's help.

The notion that the actions of the universe are controlled by a fickle, attention-seeking deity struck me as so grotesque that I abandoned my religious tradition. True or not, I reasoned, striking out on my own was better than continuing with this absurd dysfunction. The simple act of taking agency in my life changed everything! I discovered we have complete control over the reality we create. In fact, the insertion of a third-person deity as the controlling force of life is detrimental to achieving our objectives.

Our Connection to Spirit Forms Our Reality

Most of us are unaware that our life reflects our insatiable impulse to create. You are a firehose of Creative-Energy—spewing reality into existence. However, the grind and struggle of daily life filters through our minds and creates the illusion that our reality is governed by external forces beyond our control. It is easy to feel like a rudderless ship whose direction is dictated by winds and waves. But this nihilistic viewpoint is camouflage for the uncompromising agency that each of us has over reality. Our personal creative power is always in control.

It is the quality of your connection to your energetic Core-Self that dictates the nature of your reality. If your mind and body are tuned into your Spiritual-Self, your reality will reflect the positive aspects of a developing, sentient being. If you have neglected your mind/body connection to Spirit, however, your world will be chaotic. Creative-Energy wants to create, so it is up to us to connect with the desires and aims of our Core-Self. In this way, we learn to harness our creative power for the greater good of ourselves and the world.

Your Reality Reflects Your Creative Impulse

Take a minute to ponder the concept of possessing infinite creative power. In a genuine sense, you are God, and in every moment, you create material reality from pure energy. What is your initial reaction to this notion? For most people, this thought is at once exhilarating and daunting. As you explore the landscape of your reality, ask yourself, "Am I happy with what I see? Does life reflect my highest ideals, dreams, and ambitions?" and "Have I fallen short of achieving the desires of my heart?" Do not worry if your life does not match up with how you want it to be. You can use your created reality, for good or bad, as a guide to direct you back to your connection with Spirit.

EXERCISE
UNDERSTANDING YOUR CONNECTION TO SPIRIT

The process of self-examination is a valuable tool for highlighting the kind of Creative-Energy you are channeling into your reality:

Step One:
Pay close attention to what you like and don't like about your life. There are areas you feel good about—areas in which you are channeling Creative-Energy that align with your Spirit. On the flip side, take an unflinching look at the negative, unfulfilling aspects of life. These result from misaligned Creative-Energy.

Step Two:
Next, examine the core belief systems behind both the positive and negative creations of your world. How you view yourself and the world around you has a direct bearing on the reality you manifest. For example, if you feel unworthy of experiencing love, love will always be beyond your grasp. Likewise, if you feel capable and deserving of financial abundance, wealth will flow into your life. Each belief is a signpost that can direct your actions from now on.

Step Three:
Finally, take responsibility for changing and redirecting your Creative-Energy. If you need to take action to change your attitude and mindset, it is up to you to take charge of your life and make the change.

You are a natural-born creator, sculpting life with every passing moment. If you want a positive, fulfilling life, you must align your creative impulses with the agenda of your Core-Self. For many people, this involves a long process of discovery and refinement—which is OK. After all, this is the reason you are here—to learn and grow.

CHAPTER 14:

YOU EXIST IN HEAVEN NOW

As I UNPACKED THE MÉLANGE of mythologies attached to my religious upbringing, far and away the most troubling was the Christian concept of "heaven." From its idealized physical representation (pearly gates, streets made of gold, etc.) to the notion of eternally existing in this static construct—it all struck me as a fatuous attempt to escape reality. It made no sense that there would be such a stark demarcation between the realm of God and our material realm. What is the point? Why would God go to all the trouble to create the universe, only to cull it and deposit his "chosen ones" in some sort of idealized physical existence? For sport? For fun? For ego? The whole concept struck me as asinine!

My investigations reveal a version of "heaven" that is not a future destination, disconnected from our material reality. Instead, it is an amalgamation of our Spiritual and physical existence that we can enjoy at this very moment. Far from being an abstract, eternal Disneyland, our access to heaven is fundamental to who we are right now.

We Exist in Multiple Dimensions

It seems like most people are slogging through this life in order to one day make it to heaven. This is a travesty, because just the opposite is true. We already exist in energetic form... in "heaven." There is no need to transcend this world. We are here to transform this material realm into heaven, to bring heaven to us.

Look at the iconography of the world's major religions. They all recognize the existence of dimensions outside this material realm. There are heavens with gods and angels, and there are hells with gods and demons. Interestingly, in these paradigms, these spiritual entities somehow merge into our existence and interact with us, affecting this material world. Considering these existing belief systems, I would argue that the idea that we (human beings) are tethered to other dimensions is not so outrageous.

While I find major flaws in the standard mythologies of world religions, their overarching supposition is correct. There are energy fields beyond our material dimensions where other beings live, and these entities can interact with this world. However, most religions confuse the relationship between humans and God—they separate the glorious God-realm from us, the mere mortals who occupy this lowly material world. We are already in the glorious God-realm! Your True-Self—your Spiritual-Self—is, at this moment, existing as an amazing manifestation of pure energy... as God. You don't need to wait to get to heaven because you are already there!

The challenge for each of us is to learn to use our human biology to channel the full force of God and to transform this material realm into HEAVEN on Earth!

You Are God

Walk over to a mirror and look at yourself. Make no bones about it. You are looking at God. You may not feel like God, but just know that you exist in God-form at this very moment. Let this sink in. Look at your reflection again. Now, repeat, "I am God... I am God... I Am God!" How does this make you feel? Good... ? Powerful... ? Like a fraud... ? Maybe all of the above? These mixed feelings are natural because your brain knows, deep down, that it is not God. How could it be... it is just a brain, and your body is just a body... and these things differ from a God... or so the mind will tell you.

EXERCISE
TRAINING YOUR MIND

Recognizing your Godliness may require a paradigm shift. It requires you to create an environment that will resonate with your mind. The first step in this process is repetition. At every opportunity, reinforce this concept by reminding yourself of your role as a representation of God. This will open up your mind and will have a profound impact on how you navigate life.

The next requirement for shifting the mind is to build a track record of results. To change its orientation, the logical brain requires "proof of concept." It needs to experience the effects of this new perspective, and this involves connecting to your Spiritual-Self and using your creative powers to show your mind that you can channel energy in order to reach your objectives. Take a few steps outside your comfort zone. Shifting your attention from your brain to your Spirit will unleash the stream of Creative-Energy you need to mold reality around your deepest dreams and desires. Bit by bit, as your mind recognizes the power of submitting to your Creative-Core, you will overcome any fear or reticence of reaching out with your Creative-Energy at every opportunity.

Between the use of repetition and proof, the mind will recognize your link to the Divine and serve as a help rather than as an impediment to your process of creating heaven on Earth.

CHAPTER 15:

CONNECTING TO SOURCE-ENERGY REQUIRES TAMING YOUR BRAIN

As my burgeoning theories on reality started taking shape, the confounding role of the human brain took center stage. How can the thing that sets us apart from all of creation—that allows creation to ponder its own existence, to imagine, to think abstractly, to create artistic wonders and technological marvels—also be the source of so many problems? On one hand, we are the highest expression of consciousness. On the other hand, we are merchants of personal, societal, and environmental chaos. Why? Why? Why?

When looking at this paradox, it is easy to either lean into traditional theistic explanations or to throw yourself down a rabbit hole of nihilism. However, I had disavowed both options, so I was stuck with the challenge of reconciling these desperate aspects of the human condition within the context of my emerging ideology.

Sources of Cognizance

My exploration into the form and function of our sentient brain led me to the conclusion that there is a stark dichotomy between our Energetic-Self and the biological function of our brain and nervous system. As a result, I conceptualize our cognitive abilities as originating from two separate and distinct sources.

First is our biological brain, which I also refer to as *mind*. This is the human brain and nervous system as it has developed through the ages. It is akin to a biological supercomputer that stores information and makes decisions, either consciously or unconsciously, based upon our experiences and encoding from our DNA. As a cognitive vehicle, the human brain/mind stands as separate from Source-Energy. If devoid of any influence from Source, it responds to stimuli and decides based upon its memory and hardwired instinct. Left to its own devices, the mind operates within the insular confines of our material dimension.

The second source of cognition is tied to Source-Energy. This is our Soul, our Spiritual-Self—the True-Self that is tied to the Core of who we are in the dimensions of energy. The thoughts and impulses that emanate from our Spiritual-Mind always direct us toward the evolutionary objectives of Source. This is the Mind of God.

Connecting Different Dimensions

As we have explored, forming a seamless link between energy and matter is no easy feat. This is because the dimensions of pure energy and our material world could not be more different. Pure energy can best be compared to the traditional concept of God. It is all-knowing and all-present, all the time. In the energetic realm, there are no barriers to transferring energy or communicating information throughout the system. Strangest of all, there is no concept of time or space. On the flip side, our material realm has none of these characteristics. We occupy a space replete with physical limitations.

As we contemplate the differences between a dimension of pure energy and our physical world, the challenge for Source-Energy is creating a seamless connection between these two dissimilar realms. Bridging this gap is the role of our sentient brain.

Using the Brain to Connect Energy to Matter

The evolution of our sentient brain represents a critical advancement toward the mission to create a seamless link between the world of energy and the world of matter. Somehow, it has evolved far beyond the primitive brains of others in the animal kingdom and gives us the ability to both encode and decode the information and Creative-Energy flowing between the realms of energy and matter.

First, the sentient brain is conscious, and it can conceptualize its existence beyond the material self. This allows our physical bodies to communicate with our Energetic-Self. Second, the brain lets us use thought and imagination to channel Creative-Energy into material existence. As incredible as all this sounds—and is—the human mind is far from the efficient interface with Source-Energy we would like it to be.

Our Brain Remains Tethered to Our Evolutionary Past

It took hundreds of millions of years for the human brain to develop from a primitive nervous system into the thinking machine that it is today. However, much of the encoding from this illustrious past remains hardwired into our biology. This means that the brain defaults to patterns of behavior that served our past survival needs but that don't enhance our connection to Core-Energy. In fact, many of these involuntary responses are antithetical to the objectives of the Spirit. Some of this programming emerges as rote "animal" reactions such as "fight-or-flight," stress, or aggression, but by far, the most problematic characteristic of the brain revolves around its self-centered orientation.

To help describe the brain's proclivity for self-centeredness, consider the more primitive brain of an animal whose only concerns are getting food, securing shelter, being safe, and reproducing.

These are 100 percent brain-oriented functions that require the mind to control everything. The animal is not considering that there might be a higher authority that could take part in or govern any of these activities. This brain is reliant upon its own interpretation of life—the biological brain is the sole authority for existence.

Even though we now can tap into higher states of consciousness—to look beyond our immediate survival needs, our brain is still rooted in our primitive past. This is why, to the brain, the concept of deferring to a higher cognitive authority (i.e., your Core-Self), is strange and unnatural.

As our sentient abilities have expanded over time, the mind has developed an ever-greater ability to look outside of itself and ponder esoteric subjects far beyond our basic survival needs. This capability allows direct access to Core-Energy and our ability to funnel Creative-Energy into the world. However, the egocentric features of the primitive brain remain entrenched within the modern mind. Even though we now have access to a Spiritual-Mind located beyond our material realm, this "ego" continues to fight for control of our thoughts, emotions, and actions.

The good news? We continue to evolve. Every moment is an opportunity to connect with Source-Energy, to override our primitive inclinations, and to reprogram our biology to accept a reality beyond the bounds of this material realm. Step by step, we are marching closer to an unfettered connection to our true self!

Using the Mind to Link to Matter

As far as is known, we human beings are the only creations that possess the ability to analyze the workings of our own minds. You have the unique power to occupy a psychic space outside of your biology. Many people either take this gift for granted, or never stop to ponder the full extent of what this implies. Think about it. If you can watch your thoughts, the real you, the "watcher," must dwell in a place that transcends your physical body! Each of us possesses this powerful tool that we can use to improve the link between our physical form and our Spiritual-Core. You can evolve your mind to become a more effective conduit for Core-Energy.

Meditation as a Tool

Meditation techniques take advantage of our unique ability to observe our minds. They were developed to transform the primitive brain into a useful instrument for connecting to our energetic self. The hallmark of this process involves setting yourself apart from your mind so you can view thoughts as they surface. As you observe thoughts popping in and out of your mind, two important things take place:

- First, the mind becomes accustomed to a cognitive force (a "watcher") other than itself. This allows it to accept the reality that there is a "Me" beyond the physical mind.
- Second, this process trains the mind to subordinate itself to a higher power.

EXERCISE
BEGINNING MEDITATION

To begin a meditation practice, it helps to start small. Pick moments throughout the day to take a deep breath and observe what your mind is doing. As thoughts come and go, resist the temptation to assign any judgment or to form any emotional attachment to them. Watch them surface and recede, like waves in the ocean. Over time, your brain realizes that most of these thoughts do not represent the reality of the moment. They are figments of your imagination, based on either hardwired primitive responses, or on latent programming from experiences. The vast majority of thoughts the mind produces are nothing more than fictional apparitions from the past.

Once the mind becomes accustomed to viewing itself in this way, it will orient itself toward the "watcher"—toward your true self. This enables you to tap into the desires of your Spirit and channel the Creative-Energy that will transform your reality into a reflection of your true self.

EGO-MIND

This diagram illustrates the controlling forces of the ego-mind without the influence of Spirit. It is a closed system which comprises encoded impulses and memories from historic interactions with the world around us.

CHAPTER 16:

YOUR NATURAL
STATE IS DIVINE

Many of us indoctrinated into fundamentalist Christianity are conditioned to believe that the natural state for human beings is "the state of sin"; that there is an intrinsic separation between creator and creation. Nothing could be further from the truth. This ideology is common among institutional religions because it places the institution (and its representatives) in the intermediary power position between God and humankind. As gatekeeper to the rewards of the Divine, religions place themselves in the perfect position to control and manipulate populations.

As my skepticism of organized religion grew, the notion that there is a basic spiritual separation between God and humanity was one of the first things I targeted for exploration. What I discovered turned my Christian tradition upside down. There is, in fact, a separation between God and humanity, but it has nothing to do with our intrinsic connection to Spirit. Instead, the separation has to do with a programming issue with our brain. And we don't need religion to solve this problem.

∞

Feeling Your Natural State of Being

Any time you are connected to Core-Energy, you will get a taste for the feelings and emotions intrinsic to our energetic realm. These include ecstasy, joy, peace, love, and the energy to create. These sensations show you that you have tapped into the vibrational frequency of your authentic self. This is your natural state of being. Wouldn't it be great if we could dwell in these high-frequency states? It is possible, but first we need to develop our physical connection to Source-Energy. However, at this point of human development, the greatest obstacle to accessing this natural state of being is the interference we experience from our wrongly programmed brains.

Ever wonder why certain drugs make you feel good, relaxed, ecstatic, happy, or creative? The key is not the particular chemical compound, per se. Instead, the drugs bypass the habitual patterns of programming within the mind (a phenomenon known as drug-induced ego dissolution), creating an unobstructed channel for your natural Source-Energy. The experienced "high" is the joy coming from your Soul.[33] Of course, the downside of following a drug-induced path to Source-Energy is the biochemical side effects that come along with it. Drugs are sometimes a useful shortcut, but they serve as a short-term fix for a dilemma.

The number one reason we are not living every minute in the bliss of Source-Energy is our belief that our brain expresses the self. This is akin to letting the inmates run the asylum. There can be no consistent experience of peace, joy, or love when control is surrendered to a myopic, ego-generating machine. So, can we connect with the Field of Energy without staying high all the time?

---

[33] N.L. Mason, K.P.C. Kuypers, F. Müller, et al., "Me, myself, bye: regional alterations in glutamate and the experience of ego dissolution with psilocybin," *Neuropsychopharmacol,* 45, 2003–2011 (2020), https://doi.org/10.1038/s41386-020-0718-8; D.E. Nichols, "Psychedelics: *Pharmacological Reviews,* 2016 Apr; 68(2):264-355. doi: 10.1124/pr.115.011478. Erratum in: Pharmacol Rev. 2016 Apr; 68(2):356, PMID: 26841800; PMCID: PMC4813425, https://pharmrev.aspetjournals.org/content/68/2/264.short.

Alas, because your programmed brain and nervous system are entwined with every cell in your body, you need an intervention (to expand on our drug analogy). You must take the steps to transform the brain's notion that it encapsulates the *Self*. Instead, the brain must relegate itself to a role that supports your connection with Source-Energy.

Your Mind Responds to Logic

Your neural network responds to logic-based concepts. You can use this tendency to your advantage by presenting the mind with a new idea, and then using real-world experience to underscore the new concept. In this way, your life becomes a proving ground that complements the mind's natural desire to align with logical concepts. Through observing actual results, what might start out as exotic metaphysical theory can be transformed into a "proven" reality the brain can absorb.

EXERCISE
TRAINING THE MIND TO ACCEPT A NEW REALITY

As you go about your daily life, pay attention to the stress and drama created by the feedback loop of your mind. As you absorb each negative life experience, examine its connection to your ego's sense of self. Ask yourself, "How is each circumstance attacking my mind's vision of who and what I am?" "How are my feelings, emotions, and actions being used to defend my ego's vision of self and the world around me?"

Now, draw your attention away from the brain's response to the negative stimuli and observe it, as if you are removed from it—looking from the outside—from the calm viewpoint of your Spiritual-Core.

Without judgment, observe both the experience and your negative feelings from this neutral mind space. Try not to get swept up in the emotions. Just observe.

What effect does this process have on your negative emotions? Do they fade? Do understanding and clarity emerge? Do feelings of peace, joy, and creativity replace the negative energy? This is your scientific process of discovery—your grand experiment to validate the existence of an alternate reality.

Now, for the last step, allow your brain to recognize the validity of this new vision of reality originating from Spirit instead of from the mind. Allow it to accept this new experience as reality. The reprogramming has begun!

CHAPTER 17:

VARIETY IS FOUNDATIONAL TO CREATION

THE TAPESTRY OF CREATION IS rich in variety. This is never more apparent than within the diversity of humanity. While I find multiplicity to be a marvelous component of reality, I pondered, "Why is it necessary? Why do we need such a wide assortment of human experience?"

It wasn't until the advent of computer networks that the reason became clear to me: The most efficient way to solve large computational problems is to spread the workload over many machines. Like a computer network, Source-Energy has determined that creating variety and diversity (particularly within humans) is the most efficient way for Source-Energy to solve the complex problem of connecting with matter.

Of course, we human beings are more complex than machines. The output of our creative brain serves to speed up the formation of variety and diversity—creating billions of problem-solving entities!

Creating Variety

Creating variety seems to be of foundational importance to the development of our material realm. Why else is there so much uniqueness between individuals and such a wide variety of human experience? This diversity in form and experience can make it seem that there are massive inequities built into the system. Why are some people born to wealth, while others suffer extreme poverty? Why do some people experience debilitating health problems, birth defects, and disease, while others live long, healthy lives? Why are some people subject to horrific forms of abuse, while others grow up in nurturing cocoons of love and support? Why are some individuals blessed with innate talents and gifts while others are not? On the surface, it all seems random and unfair!

To find the answers to these puzzling questions, let's start by examining energy's overall aim for manifesting into material form. As noted earlier, our dimension represents Source-Energy's attempt to gain full access to the tactile experiences that are only available in material form. The evolutionary process is long and complex: energy converts into matter; matter develops into life; life grows into sentience; and sentient life evolves into a perfect expression of energy. The most efficient way to accomplish this massive undertaking is to spread the developmental load out to as many distinct entities as possible. Much like a blockchain computer program spreading the computational load, each individual throughout history has done their part to develop the puzzle of Source-Energy's link to matter.

Evolving Our Spiritual-Personality

Recall that each of us represents a piece of Source-Energy—an individual expression of Spirit. Interestingly, our individual energetic identity (or Spiritual-Personality) is formed through the trial-and-error process inherent in this evolutionary system. This ties into Creative-Energy, which does not care what it creates—it only wants to create.

As an illustration, let's look at an individual who is progressing from lifetime to lifetime (refer to Section IV: Karmic-Force). As they travel through time (in both their present life and past lives), they not only experience a unique collection of circumstances, but correspondingly, they channel a distinctive array of Creative-Energy into this material realm. As a result, a distinctive set of obstacles, talents, and proclivities develops and emerges. These experiences and manifestations make an individual who they are. This individuality migrates into its Spiritual-Self to determine the obstacles, roadblocks, and lessons that need to be addressed from one lifetime to the next. The evolution of the individual Spirit influences the talents and gifts that each person brings into each lifetime, and the interests they develop.

This brings us back around to the query about why each of us experiences life in such a different way. The explanation is that each of us is on a unique evolutionary path. While we are all heading toward the same goal of perfecting the link to Source-Energy, each of us is a product of our individual expression of Creative-Energy. Because we are free to create, we are also free to experience the reality we have created.

Your individual circumstances in this life teach you lessons and give you the tools you need to evolve into a pure channel for Spiritual-Energy. You (your Spirit) placed yourself in this experience to learn. You are responsible for the content of your experience, no matter how glorious or vile it might be.

Take a moment. Examine your life and experiences. What challenges and barriers have you overcome? What have you learned from these experiences? Where have you let circumstances derail your personal development? Where have you fallen short of using these experiences to learn positive lessons?

We all have experiences on either side of the ledger. However, one thing is a constant: we learn more from adversity than we do from pleasure. As a result, spiritual advancement often involves placing ourselves in adverse circumstances. From this viewpoint, these negative experiences have the potential to become the greatest of blessings.

As you review your life and take an objective view of your present circumstances, be thankful for your blessings, but be especially grateful for the challenges and obstacles in your life. Resolve to use all of your experiences to increase your connection to Spirit and reach your creative potential for this lifetime. You are free to channel Creative-Energy to be the very best version of your unique expression of Source.

CHAPTER 18

YOUR LIFE HAS PURPOSE

Much of the angst behind being human is trying to answer the proverbial question, "Why am I here?" In my life, this question has hovered over me like a dark cloud. It took many years of work before I developed a map of reality that allowed me to solve this puzzle (for myself). To my continued amazement, the answer to this significant question is dead simple: I am here to advance my connection to Source-Energy.

Life with a Purpose

Your birth was not a random occurrence. Your entrance into this lifetime not only occurred in the body, time, and place of your choosing; it happened for a purpose. In fact, Spirit always manifests into this physical realm with a clear set of objectives, all of which improve your link to Core-Energy. These objectives fall into these broad categories:

- Burn off negative karma/energy from prior lifetimes (see Section IV: Karmic-Force).
- Improve your ability to consciously channel Creative-Energy.
- Leverage and amplify your strengths and talents.
- Resolve relationships from both your present and past lifetimes.
- Advance humanity's link to Core-Energy.

It's important to keep in mind that none of these life objectives occur in isolation. Each involves a complex tapestry of energy relationships that weave through time and space until settling into the present moment. Knowing that any unresolved aims will carry over to a future life, it is your mission in this lifetime to develop a conscious understanding of each aim, and to advance as far as possible. If you don't deal with your challenges in this lifetime, you will face them in lifetimes to come.

Discovering Your Purpose

Do you ponder what makes up a meaningful existence? Do you ever feel rudderless, wondering which direction your life should take? If only there were a manual for navigating through life! The signposts for directing your life are all around you. You need to train your awareness to recognize them. These cues almost always come in the form of your *emotions*.

EXERCISE
USING EMOTIONS TO DIRECT YOUR LIFE

If you pay attention to your emotional response to your thoughts and your interactions with the world, these feelings will guide your life:

- **Negative emotions** help uncover underlying pathologies caused by suppressed fear, anger, desire, insecurity, and negative brain programming. If you have a negative reaction to something or someone, try to identify the root cause for this feeling. It will point to a problem area within your psyche that needs to be resolved.

- **Neutral emotions** help answer "go or no-go" types of questions. Not sure what direction to take? Ask yourself how taking the action will make you *feel*. If you feel nothing one way or the other, or if you feel a "deadness" or lack of enthusiasm, that path is not for you.

- **Positive emotions** are great indicators to confirm you are heading in the right direction. Does a thought, idea, dream, or action bring excitement, joy, love, or inspiration? If the answer is "yes," your Spirit is confirming you are heading in the right direction.

Each of these types of feelings represents a frequency of energy that is bouncing against your Core-Self and returning to the brain as feedback. Whether consciously or unconsciously, your brain operates as a receiver, taking in information and interpreting frequencies according to its base programming. If this programming mirrors the Core-Self, you will interpret the incoming data in a healthy way that supports the agenda of your Spirit. However, if this information enters a part of the brain that is not aligned with your Core-Self, confusion, negative reactions, destructive behaviors, and the like will result.

Each emotional state, whether negative, neutral, or positive, is there to instruct you along your journey. It is healthy to embrace these feelings and respect them as the guidance tools they are. Once you learn to deal with your emotions consciously, you need never wonder about the direction your life should follow.

CHAPTER 19:

EVERY ENCOUNTER TRANSFERS ENERGY

Like many people, I was exposed to the concept of energetic communication through religion. We called it prayer. Prayer, a central feature of my faith, was used to effect a change in all areas of life—from physical healing to financial success. As my concept of God changed, so did my ideas around the ritual of prayer and transferring Creative-Energy. First, I discovered that each of us can transfer energy back and forth within our environment. There is no need for a third party "gatekeeper" (or God) to serve as an intermediary for channeling Creative-Energy. Don't believe it? Try this simple experiment. Stare at a person from across the room. In short order, they will "feel" your attention and look your way.

Since realizing that human beings can project and receive energy, I have been exploring this capability. I discovered we are (consciously or unconsciously) channeling and absorbing Creative-Energy from the world. Every physical interaction with another person is also an "energetic" interaction. By directing this energy, we can maximize the benefit of each encounter.

∞

Encounters and interactions with other human beings are integrated into the fabric of life. Some of these encounters may seem fleeting, inconsequential, or random, while others feel life-changing, timeless, or divinely inspired. However impactful it may (or may not) be, every engagement with another person is the consequence of an intricate dance among Souls. Every touch point is designed as an opportunity for each person to grow and evolve.

Consciously or not, you are exchanging energy with your environment. Every physical interaction with another person is also an "energetic" interaction. This energy falls into two broad categories:

- there is energy projected from your body; and
- there is energy projected from your Spirit.

With the energetic body, this energy radiates into the physical environment and communicates with the energy fields emanating from the people, places, and things in the material realm. The idea that our body is a channel for energy can be traced to ancient Hindu Vedas. This concept expanded later to recognize that our body exists in two parallel dimensions: one being the "physical body," the other referred to as the "subtle body" (or energetic body), characterized as psychological, emotional, mental, and nonphysical. The subtle body is composed of energy, while the physical body has mass. To advance this theory further, based on my experience, all matter (animate and inanimate) contains an energetic body that communicates and interacts with its environment.[34]

As a channel for Spiritual-Energy, your subtle body facilitates the communication between your Core-Self and the individual expressions of Spirit of the people around you. In this way, every physical interaction also involves an agreement between your Core-Self and the spiritual counterpart of the other person. The aim of this "meeting of Spiritual-Minds" is to create an opportunity for each person to grow and develop.

---

[34] "Chakra," Wikipedia, www.en.wikipedia.org/wiki/chakra.

Every Encounter Is Planned

There are no coincidental or "chance" encounters. In fact, our energy has been communicating long before we are aware that we have contacted another person. Every encounter involves a transfer of energy that is consequential for both individuals. And each interaction also harbors the potential opportunity for each person to grow. This may sound like a great deal of responsibility, especially for a momentary encounter with another, but such is the power of the energy we emit.

You have the power to change the world, a moment at a time. Every encounter with another person is an opportunity for both of you to develop your connection to Core-Energy. Of course, there is a flip side. You also possess unlimited opportunities to spread damaging negative energy. We are free to do either, but there are karmic consequences for every negative action toward another person, and for every missed opportunity to make a positive connection.

Most people sleepwalk through life, too focused on the machinations of their mind to take notice of the flow of humanity that crosses their path daily. This is a lack of awareness—the habit of a disconnected mind. How many opportunities to grow and contribute to the evolution of others do we pass up because we are not tuned into the world? As you go about your daily routine, be mindful of every interaction. Ask yourself, "What energy am I sending out to this person, and how am I receiving the energy that is coming to me?" Practice seeing other people for what they are—material forms trying to evolve—just like you. In this way, you unleash your Spirit to spread positive energy and attract the relationships that will assist with your journey through life.

ENERGETIC COMMUNICATION

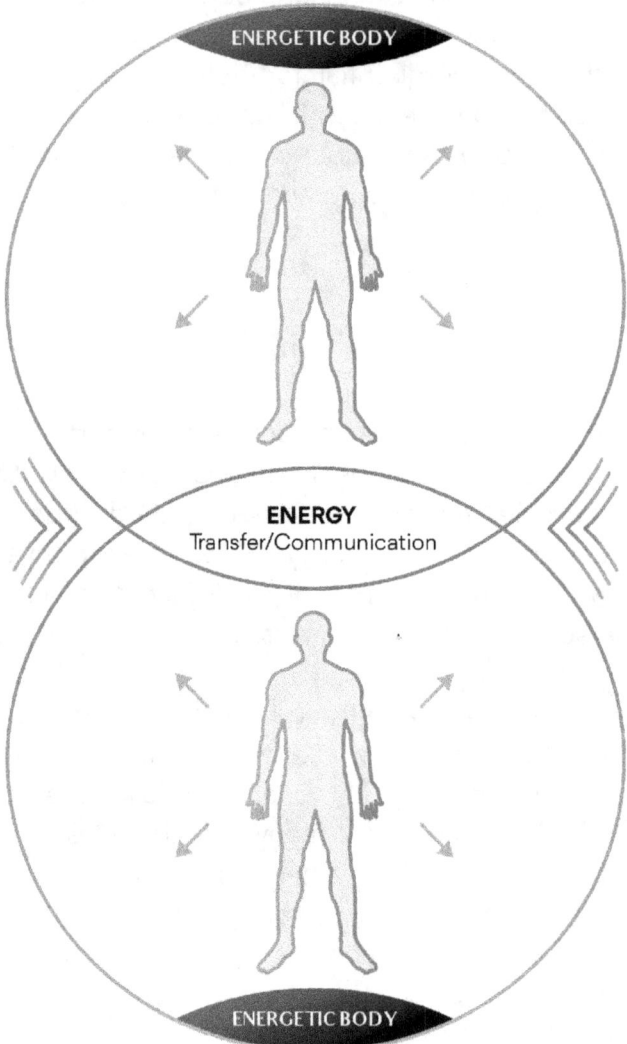

This diagram illustrates the communication that is always occurring between energetic bodies. The subtle energy transfer occurs automatically and is picked up through our feelings.

CHAPTER 20:

YOUR SOUL LOVES TO PLAY WITH OTHERS

I DON'T ENCOURAGE DRUG USE AS a gateway (shortcut) to spiritual revelation, because there is always an energetic price to pay for such behavior. However, I was tripping the first time I received a clear vision of the Soul Realm. I say "vision," but it was more than an arm's length view of what is happening within this dimension. I had the experience of transitioning all of my consciousness into my Spiritual-Self and sitting with the multitude of other Spiritual-Personalities represented by the people in my material lifetime.

To my amazement, every Soul (even those represented by the most damaged and depraved of humans) was a shining receptacle of pure, ecstatic joy and love! Like children at the pinnacle of creative play, everyone was engaged in gleeful collaboration, helping one another solve the mystery of linking this energetic realm with our material existence. To my everlasting gratitude, this portal to my

Spiritual-Personality has remained open ever since. It is a constant reminder that I am not alone on my journey. In fact, at the core of every interaction is a Soul of pure love wanting to help me grow and evolve.

Souls Having Fun

The quest for spiritual growth can take on a patina of high-minded seriousness. This is unfortunate because the nature of Source-Energy is quite the opposite. Once you tap into your Energetic-Self, you find a field of joyful (dare we say playful) dynamism, devoid of any self-important stuffiness. You realize that any attitude of decorous seriousness is a construct of the human mind. Indeed, the Soul Realm comprises souls at play, interacting with one another as we go about the business of evolving our material realm to receive the full complement of Source-Energy. You could say that our fundamental state is at play with the other Souls around it—we are having FUN!

Individual Spiritual-Personalities

In the same way that each person is both part of humanity as a whole, as well as an individual expression of humanity, our Souls are Source-Energy *and* a unique expression of Source-Energy. The gifts and talents we exhibit in this material world are extensions of our energetic personalities... our Souls. It takes a range of creative input to achieve the evolutionary objectives of our Source. As we have seen, in order to garner as broad an array of inputs as possible, each Soul develops a unique evolutionary style, which manifests in the material realm as our individual personalities, gifts, talents, and weaknesses. Once you combine this with every other individual, you get a symphony of Creative-Energy, with each Soul collaborating and playing an integral role in the development of humanity.

Of course, in the material realm, collaboration is not always a bed of roses. We often learn more from the conflicts in life than we do from our nurturing relationships. Our Spirits are aware of this and team up with one another to maximize the growth potential for everyone, in each lifetime. However, whether these interactions are pleasant or unpleasant, each relationship represents an alliance between Souls meant to foster growth and evolution.

I want to emphasize that the Energetic-Self is not bound by the familiar constraints of the material world. There is no time. There is no decay. There is no ego. Imagine operating in an environment of timeless, limitless creative expression. Nothing but *pure joy* would be possible! This drives the interactions between Spirits.

Agreement Between Souls

Gaining a true understanding of the relationship between our individual Souls will change the way you relate to others forever. If you can view every relationship as an energetic agreement you forged out of love for the benefit of yourself and the other person, it becomes impossible to extend anything but love and gratitude. This perspective enables you to detach yourself from ego-driven impulses and appreciate the "other" for participating in your evolutionary growth. It allows you to discard the negative chatter of the mind and search for the underlying lessons and truths behind your relationships and interactions.

Achieving this perspective represents a massive evolutionary leap. Imagine a world in which everyone adopted the perspective that "our Souls are at play." How different the world would be!

LIFE INFLUENCES

This diagram illustrates the elements of our Spiritual-Mind or True-Self. While the Spiritual-Mind is influenced by past incarnations (which creates our Spiritual-Personality), its sole purpose is to use each lifetime to maximize our evolutionary developmental link to Source-Energy. This includes collaborating with other Souls.

CHAPTER 21:

YOU EXTEND FAR BEYOND YOUR BODY

LIKE MANY PEOPLE, I WRESTLE with trusting my instincts and intuition. The fear and insecurity from my past left such a strong imprint on my brain that it often requires a herculean effort to make it relinquish control over my perceptions and actions. However, I have learned that there is an immense spectrum of communication taking place beyond the limited scope of my human mind. Indeed, the limited perception of my "logical" mind often inhibits my ability to access this energy-based communication.

In my life, one such example is my aptitude for energy healing. As far back as I can remember, individuals have remarked on my ability to identify points of physical pain and then to relieve this pain with a simple touch. Because this seemed preposterous, it took many years before I honored and developed this ability. Today, I have developed this faculty to where I can see, feel, and manipulate subtle energy fields far beyond the human body. Had I continued to rely on my mind to inform reality, I would never have experienced the immense and elaborate tapestry of energetic communication occurring around me at every moment.

State of Perpetual Communication

Whether or not you are aware of it, your energetic body is engaged in constant communication with its environment through the absorption and projection of energy.[35] Because everything emits an energy, you are communicating with the entirety of your surroundings at all times. This not only includes humans, animals, and plants, but it also includes inanimate objects such as minerals, chemicals, materials, even your possessions![36] In addition, this exchange extends well beyond our material dimension to include the Spiritual-Personalities of those around you and other energetic entities assigned to guide your personal evolution.

Some of this communication can be categorized as "overt"—it is registered through our body's five senses. However, most communication taking place at any moment is occurring on a nonphysical level. This "subtle" exchange takes place through transferring energy. While most of us are adept at sending and receiving communication through overt channels, we find it more difficult to deal with subtle energy.

Tapping into Subtle Energy

We, as human beings, begin life with the innate ability to identify and process all forms of subtle energy—we emerge from the womb tuned into the energy coming from our environment. Without the

---

[35] Tianjun Liu, "The scientific hypothesis of an 'energy system' in the human body," *Journal of Traditional Chinese Medical Sciences*, Volume 5, Issue No. 1 (2018): 29-34, ISSN 2095-7548, https://doi.org/10.1016/j.jtcms.2018.02.003.

[36] Natalie Walchover, "A new physics theory of life," *Quanta Magazine* (January 22, 2014), https://www.quantamagazine.org/a-new-thermodynamics-theory-of-the-origin-of-life-20140122/#comments;Yujin Nagasawa, "Where does consciousness come from?" *BBC Focus* (August 2017): 64-69.

capacity to think logically, we absorb what is going on through our feelings. This is all we can do. We *feel* the messages from our body—hunger, pain, exhaustion, joy, excitement, etc. We *feel* the input from our environment—love, stress, approval, anger, etc. All of our communication is based on subtle energy. However, as we mature, this orientation diminishes. The logical brain takes center stage. We rely on the mind to interpret the world—to categorize things as good or bad; to form judgments, beliefs, and ideologies; to build psychological walls of protection against perceived dangers; to defend our concept of self (ego). The mind dominates how we perceive our environment and how we communicate with the world. We cut off our conscious access to subtle energy.

This change in focus, from outward to inward, shifts our conscious connection away from the energetic body and toward the brain. As a result, we become desensitized to a majority of the subtle energy that washes over us in every moment. When this happens, our communication with the world constricts. All we perceive is what our egocentric mind allows us to perceive. In the meantime, the energetic body is left to knock on a door no one ever answers.

By stifling our ability to communicate, we create problems for ourselves. Not only do we miss out on valuable opportunities for growth, but we also rob ourselves of creative power. We relegate ourselves to wandering around in the dark while a resplendent landscape unfolds around us!

Signs of Ignoring Subtle-Energy Communication

To retune your brain to pick up messages from subtle energies, you need to recognize signs you are ignoring them:

1. Feelings of weariness, heaviness, or depression:
    i.   Each of us possesses an inner voice that is connected to our Spiritual-Self. If you ignore this voice (or more likely, if it is drowned out by engaging in superficial activities),

you will feel an immense weight associated with the low-energy environment you have created.

2. Feelings of stress, anxiety, or isolation:

    ii. If your brain is not acknowledging the surrounding communication, it will feel isolated and unsupported. The mind wants to be in control; however, at a deep level, it senses that it is not fulfilling its mission to connect with Source-Energy. Humanity's "sentience" evolved until Source could communicate with its Creation. As the vehicle for sentience, the mind is not designed to exist without a thriving connection to subtle energy. It feels these self-created blind spots and the dangers they present. In response, the mind panics.

Manifestations of Subtle-Energy Connections

Tapping into the subtle-energy systems in the environment raises your vibrational energy and improves clarity and balance. Hunches, gut feelings, intuition, emotional responses, excitement and expectation, coincidences and serendipitous experiences, unexplained attractions, interests, psychic visions... all are manifestations of energetic communication.

EXERCISE
CONNECTING WITH ENERGETIC COMMUNICATION

Enhancing energetic communication involves overriding the mind's natural skepticism and tuning into your feelings and the more subtle reactions and impulses we associate with inner dialogue. As the mind gains confidence that these insights are valid, your perception opens to more and more communication. This connection to your energetic body becomes your default state, which will restore your ability to communicate with the subtle-energy systems that dominate reality.

Start small. Start with where you are. Instead of dismissing hunches and intuition, stop. Recognize them. Even if you don't act on them, the act of honoring the existence of energy beyond your five senses will reactivate the neural pathways to these realms.

With practice, you will not only become more aware of the energy radiating from every person, place, and thing in your environment; you will also tap into communication from your Spiritual-Core and the realms beyond. These interactions are available to anyone. All that is required is a mind that is open and willing to receive these communications!

ENERGETIC BODY

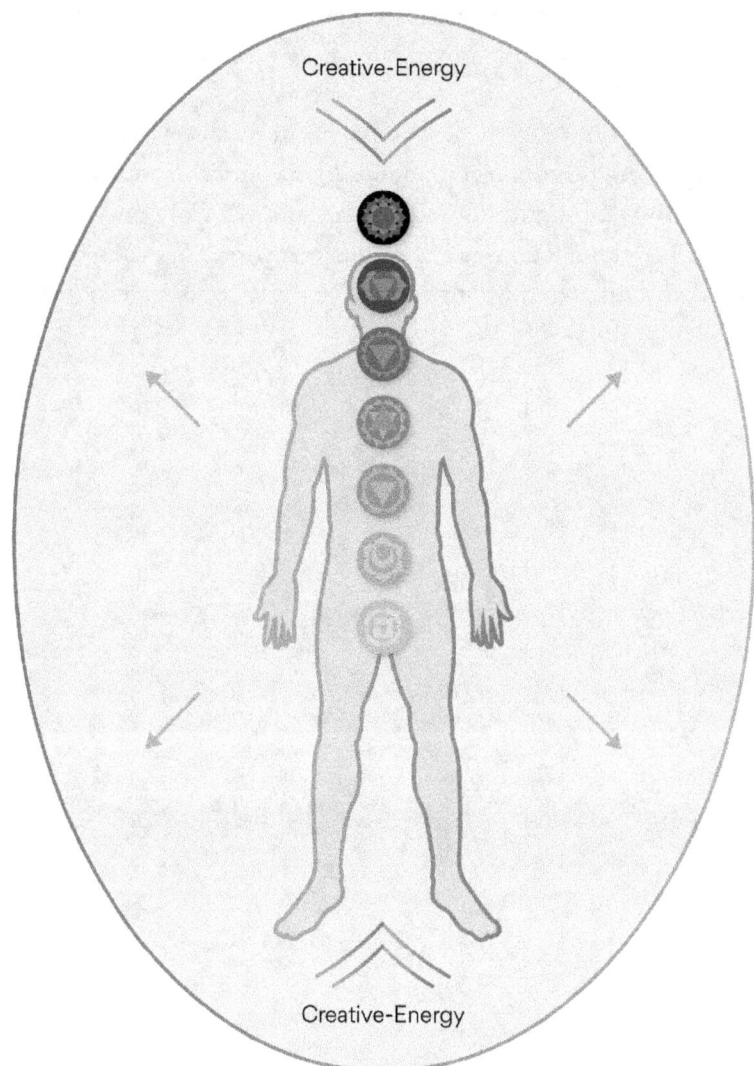

This diagram illustrates the energy flowing through
the physical body from the energetic body.

CHAPTER 22:

CREATIVE-ENERGY IS EVERYWHERE

It took many years of development to realize that I have control over the type of energy I allow into my life. This is antithetical to the natural workings of the mind, which wants to process every bit of energy (good and bad) that enters our field of consciousness. When you see a person who is ping-ponging between extreme highs and lows or experiencing anxiety because they feel they have no control over their life, it is a sign that they are not filtering the energy they are allowing into their reality. I should know. This describes my existence for much of my younger years. Over time, however, I understood the futility and damage of absorbing the endless supply of energy available at any moment. This insight allowed me to take control of my emotions and channel only the energies that contributed to my desired vision of reality.

Carried by a Stream of Energy

Imagine floating in a sea of energy, where instead of being carried along by water currents, the different frequencies of energy determine not only *how* you travel (is it fast and turbulent or calm and peaceful?); but *what* you see along the way (are you passing through war zones or fragrant gardens?); and *where* you end up (does life advance your evolution, or do you end up where you started—or worse?). Floating in this energy stream is analogous to experiencing the force behind the omnipresent Creative-Energy that permeates all of existence.

Our lives are awash daily with an unfathomable assortment of these energies. Each is distinguished by its particular frequency, and these run the gamut from ultrahigh frequencies to ultralow. The direction of your life and the nature of your reality are determined by which of these energies you absorb into your life.

As you are exposed to a particular energy, you decide (consciously or subconsciously) either to consume the energy or disregard it. By absorbing the energy, you empower it to transition into your manifested reality. In this way, you create a life that is carried along by the stream of energies with which you bond.

Creative-Energy Is Everywhere

The sources of external energy are everywhere—from the electronic media we consume, to the people we encounter and with whom we interact, to the energy emitted from the natural world around us. For good or bad, everything brings a certain type of energy into our reality. The good news is, we don't have to subject ourselves to being swept away by every type of energy with which we are confronted. We can describe not only how we will consume this energy, but how we will use it for our highest benefit. In this way, we can take control of the currents of energy and ensure they will take us where we want to go!

∞

Strategies for Managing Energy

You can develop strategies and skills that allow you to process the flood of energy entering your life. One strategy is to minimize your exposure to low-frequency energy. If you think about it, you can control a lot of the sensory input in your environment. To what types of television, social media, news, music, and movies do you expose yourself? What reading material and information are you consuming? In what social situations are you placing yourself? All of this represents energy coming into your reality that you must process. If it is having a negative effect on your emotions or outlook, it behooves you to filter out these stimuli as much as possible. Of course, it is not practical (or desirable) to remove yourself from all low-energy input, so it is imperative to develop the skills to process this energy. With personal interactions and relationships, this starts with removing your identity from your ego and understanding the other people's egocentric behavior.

As you begin separating your own self-image from the mind's ego-based definitions of self, it becomes easier to recognize the low energy, ego-motivated behavior of others. You see that defending the fragile ego-state is a universal phenomenon—and the cause of most negative behavior. Once you realize we all have this in common, it is easier to treat every individual as you would treat yourself—with love and compassion.

As for other forms of low-energy input, such as local and global events beyond your control, center on your own connection to Source. Remember, Source-Energy is working on many levels to perfect its connection to this material realm—all for the benefit of humanity and creation. As in your own life, this developmental process involves a great deal of pain. So, take a deep breath. Rest knowing that a loving creation is behind the entire grand design and that you are an integral part of this process. The most impactful thing you can do is maximize your own connection to Source. This not only helps you and everyone you come into contact with, but it also contributes to raising the average vibrational frequency of the world.

CHAPTER 23:

YOU ARE A SENSUAL BEING

IT IS FASCINATING TO WATCH very young children explore the world around them. They stare in wonderment; they touch and feel *everything*. My daughter would test every unfamiliar object by putting it in her mouth (no matter how dirty or disgusting it was). In short, children engage with their environment by using *all* their senses. For them, the world is an amazing kaleidoscope of feelings—brought to life through touch, sight, smell, taste, and hearing. They experience life moment by moment in a state of complete awareness.

Somewhere along the way, many of us lose the inclination to experience life through our senses. Instead, we turn the exploration of reality over to our rational, thinking mind, focusing on the past and the future rather than on the sensual experiences of the present moment. Slowly but surely, the connection to our sensual core diminishes and life *feels* more and more dull.

Like many people, I once found myself in this very predicament. I was so busy trying to *think* my way through life, living in the past and planning for the future, that I forsook the sensual pleasures of the present moment. Life had become so dreary that each new day brought nothing but dread and apprehension.

This journey taught me that sensuality is essential to humanity. In fact, anytime we diminish our ability to enjoy the sensual pleasures of the moment, we deny the very reason for our existence—allowing energy to experience this amazing realm of matter.

Our universe is a marvelous blend of beauty and diversity. Just ponder the profusion of sights, sounds, smells, and tactile, kinesthetic sensations available to us. Our entire material realm is designed for maximum impact on the five senses. We human beings are engineered to experience all of it... to *feel* all of it. In fact, we have transitioned into these physical bodies with the express mission of connecting with the plenitude of sensual experiences offered by this material realm. Foremost, we are sensual beings!

What a shame that many of us deny ourselves the ability to experience all this world offers. The development of more sophisticated societies and technologies has had an enormous negative impact on our conscious connection to the material world. Under the banner of "advancement," our modern brains prioritize projection and problem-solving over tapping into the plethora of sensations available in the present moment. We focus our attention on future goals and objectives, and away from what is happening around us. As a result, we go to great lengths to insulate ourselves from nature, and we structure our cultural norms to stifle the sensual contact between us.

Because all of this sensory deprivation opposes our nature and intended purpose, it causes a tremendous amount of energetic tension between our physical and Spiritual expressions of self. This suppressed energy ends up being stored in our bodies and psyches, manifesting as a plague of negative pathologies for modern humans.

The distractions of contemporary life have dulled our ability to be present and tap into our surroundings. We are so engrossed by our mental contrivances; we don't realize the immense damage we are causing ourselves and the world. If you have ever taken time to explore nature, or relish the wonder of the human body, you have experienced a taste of the peace, joy, and excitement that is available to us in every moment.

When we deny our being the visceral stimuli we crave, it shuts off a primary artery connecting to Source-Energy. Life loses its vibrancy and texture. Your perception becomes clouded, and the world around you seems dull. This leads to many problems:

- depression and other mental illnesses;
- the stagnation of the energy systems that operate the body (which results in a host of diseases);
- the breakdown of healthy interpersonal relationships (which has far-reaching social and geopolitical consequences); and
- a disconnection from nature and our biological life-support systems (which is causing catastrophic problems for our planet).

Advancing technology continues to remove us further and further from our sensorial core. Will the future bring a technological solution that will help reconnect our senses with the world? It is imperative that we form the habits necessary to nurture the connection between the sensory body and our Spiritual-Core.

Think about your daily routine. Are you running from one controlled environment to another? Are you so distracted by your thoughts that you cannot take in the sensory details of the world around you? What types of physical human contact do you engage in? What sensual desires and fantasies are you suppressing?

Most people are so removed from their sensorial core that it takes a profound effort to reestablish their connection and develop the skills necessary to nurture this crucial pipeline to Core-Energy. The key to this process is *awareness*. Train your mind to slow down. Focus on the details of the physical world around you. Engage all your senses and revel in the joy and amazement intrinsic to this physical realm. Once you integrate these habits, life will explode with color, beauty, joy, and excitement. Your mind will clear, depression will lift, and reality will take on a vibrancy you did not realize you were missing. You will once more be fulfilling your directive to serve as a sensory conduit to your Higher-Self!

CHAPTER 24:

YOU CAN HARNESS THE POWER OF SEXUAL ENERGY

FOR THE LONGEST TIME, I was puzzled by people's divergent conceptions about sex. How can sex represent the most vile and dark aspects of humanity while also representing joy, pleasure, and the greatest aspects of human connection? It is easy to dismiss these contradictions as subjective projections from culture and religion, but I discovered there are concrete reasons sex creates this dichotomy within the human condition. In fact, history is replete with literature extolling the greatness of sexual energy, while also recognizing that misdirected sexual impulse is the impetus for many of the greatest atrocities in human history.

The "high" received from sexual energy is beyond anything else we can experience. However, this same energy can also blind us from seeing the repercussions of our actions—which can cause some idiotic behavior. So, what is going on here? What is behind this dichotomy and contradiction? What is sexual energy, and why is it so wonderful and awful at the same time?

The Energy of Sex

Of all the frequencies of energy at our disposal, sexual energy is the most compatible with our biology. In more primitive times, our very survival as a species depended upon the easy access of this attractive-reproductive energy. As a result, the human brain (as well as the brains of all species) developed in a way that prioritizes reproduction over all else. We are hardwired for easy access to this frequency of energy. With a simple conscious or subconscious instruction from the brain, the body produces a biochemical cocktail that shuts down the logical thought centers of the brain and stimulates the part of the brain that controls primitive, instinctual behavior. This biochemical process clears the mind to receive a boost of Core-Energy aimed at the sexual energy receptors of the body. If you want to know what Core-Energy feels like, tap into the feelings that emanate from sexual stimulation. Excitement, joy, euphoria, motivation, boundless energy, bliss—all of this comes from Source-Energy, not from your biology or your mind.

Distorting Sexual Energy

Of course, the concept of sex also brings with it a host of brain-originated compulsive thoughts and behaviors. Some of these problems emerge from past traumatic experiences with sexual energy; however, most of the trouble derives from repressive cultural and societal norms.

Humans have a long history of trying to harness and capitalize upon the enormous power generated from sexual energy. It has long been recognized that repressing and harnessing this energy could help subjugate and extract wealth from populations. As a result, partnerships arose between religions and governments to create legal and moral structures to take advantage of this human proclivity. The first order of business was to vilify sex; to transform it from a healthy, useful expression of Core-Energy into a destructive force for evil that must be controlled. This permitted governments to increase their power through developing laws around sexual behavior, and most impactfully, it allowed religious institutions to step in as the sole arbiter of sexual conduct. All this led to a wholesale repression of what is a natural human function, and a loss of individual control over a vital pipeline of energy.

The resulting psychological damage cannot be overstated. Many of the worst individual and societal pathologies are the direct legacy of these institutional actions. Rather than learning how to work with sexual energy healthily, we have been trained to suppress this energy and view it as carnal and evil. Once pushed into our subconscious, this energy only grows in strength. It festers and mutates into a "form," which conforms to our negative concepts, and then forces its way to the surface, where it is released with dire consequences. Rape, pedophilia, pornography, prostitution, impotence, and the like are byproducts of this suppression. It also contributes to violence, anger, frustration, depression, aggression, fatigue, illness, and a host of associated conditions.

In short, the enormous power of sexual energy can create or destroy. In order to harness this power for our benefit, we must cast off the artificial conventions that society imposes and learn to direct this energy toward our healthy creative journey.

The first step to harnessing the power of sexual energy is to reject the socialized stereotypes around sex. You must reprogram your mind to view this enormous fountain of energy as coming from your very essence. It is available to give you pleasure—to strengthen your creative abilities—to enhance your awareness of the beauty and wonder of this material realm.

Once you bring this energy into your awareness, you can learn to manipulate it for your benefit. Of course, it can be directed into cathartic, interpersonal bliss. However, it can also be funneled into each of the other energy centers. You can apply it to artistic creativity; to universal love; to actions and performance; to healing of the mind and body; to insight and wisdom; and to anything that requires your energy.

The key is to open yourself to the flow of energy. Feel it. Appreciate it. Be thankful for its abundance. Then, ask it to help you achieve your purpose. You can use it to produce a mind-blowing sexual connection with another individual, or you might use this same energy to create in another area of your life. It is available at that moment to serve your highest purpose.

CHAPTER 25:

YOU ARE GOD

THE MOMENT I REALIZED I am a physical manifestation of God changed everything! This illumination granted me the authority and power to transform my life and the world around me. No longer did I need to rely on any outside source to make things happen. No longer did I need to appease a higher power. *I am it*! I am the higher authority—and I have all the tools of creation at my disposal.

Of course, this is at once exhilarating and terrifying. After all, being God is a great deal of responsibility. But I am not alone. We are all God. And every one of us is learning how to channel our Godly power into this material realm.

You really are God. This may sound trite, hyperbolic, even blasphemous. But we are each a manifestation of the same force that handles the creation of everything in our existence. It matters not what you call this *energy*. If the term "God" gives you difficulty, label it in any way that makes you comfortable. The only prerequisite is that you conceptualize this energy in an inclusive way—a way that recognizes you as an integral part of the system. Like a leaf on a tree, you are at once the tree and a useful tool for the tree. The life of the tree is flowing into you—radiating through you and you are soaking up the sun and nutrients and providing life back to the tree. Likewise, you are part and parcel of God. The energy of existence is flowing into you, and your evolutionary impulse helps drive the entire system forward.

The notion that you are "part and parcel" of the process of creation attributes a couple of significant features to your relationship with the Divine:

- not only are you a product of Source-Energy, but you also have direct access to the flow of this power. You are literally built to channel Creative-Energy into this material realm.
- it is each person's responsibility to become a creative expression for Source-Energy—to do our part to help the system grow and expand. We are integral to the full expression of God—to creating heaven on earth!

You manifested into this material realm for a reason. You placed yourself here to help evolve the conscious link between matter and energy. This is your mission and your purpose. Luckily, this quest also comes with access to the creative power of life itself. The good news is you have all the tools at your disposal. You just need to learn to use them. The not-so-good news? This learning involves an unavoidable cycle of pain that everyone must endure. Evolution is a long and complex process.

EXERCISE
EVOLVING YOUR CONNECTION TO GOD

While there is no avoiding the difficulties of life, there are steps you can take to accelerate the evolution of your intrinsic connection to God:

- The first step is to recognize that you are a representation of God in this material realm. You are elementally divine, and you have access to the creative power of the Divine.

- The second step is to identify the special gifts you have brought into this lifetime. You have chosen this unique set of tools to contribute to the evolution of reality.

- Finally, you must go through the often-painful process of clearing the channel for the flow of Creative-Energy to your gifts.

This energy is waiting, ready to be released into your life. Your Creative-Energy wants to create—it wants to maximize your personal evolution for this lifetime, and, to the fullest extent possible, it wants to contribute to the evolution of humanity.

CHAPTER 26:

YOU CAN CONTROL YOUR EXCHANGE OF ENERGY

WE HAVE ALL EXPERIENCED THE charismatic individual who doesn't have to announce their presence. As soon as they walk into the room, all eyes turn toward them. People gravitate toward them. This is an example of the power we all possess to exchange energy with our environment. In fact, whether or not we know it, we are all projecting and receiving energy from the world. This exchange occurs beyond the register of our five senses. It taps into the subtle subliminal energy systems that surround every one of us. It cannot be hidden. It cannot be faked. The energy you project is the true energy you possess. If this is low-frequency energy, it will affect your environment negatively. Likewise, if you are promoting positive energy, you will attract a positive reality—much like our charismatic friend!

The three-dimensional world around you (height, width, length) is a bit of a deception. It belies the fact that there are unseen dimensions that affect everything. Like a fish swimming in water, we are at all times immersed in a sea of energy. You may think your body is interacting with the world through your senses, but it is your energy that is interacting with the energy around you. Reach out and touch something—anything. You are feeling an illusion. Your skin is not in contact with that object. Instead, you are registering an exchange of energy in the space between the skin on your hand and the outer molecules of that object. Animate or inanimate, it makes no difference. Everything in existence projects and absorbs energy.

If you think about it, the ramifications of this concept are pretty mind-blowing. It means we are exchanging energy with everything in our environment all the time. For good or bad, each of us is having a continuous and profound effect on the people around us. We might think we are communicating or not communicating, but our energy is always interacting with the environment. On an energetic level, positive and negative vibrational frequencies are passing between everyone we encounter. Whether this is a stranger we pass on the street, or a dear friend with whom we are conversing, there is no hiding from this exchange.

The sharing of energy is a creative conversation. Without uttering a word, by projecting our energy, we can lift or lower the surrounding energy. This means we have the creative power to influence and impact everyone within our sphere of reality. Of course, this is at once an incredible gift and an awesome responsibility, and it requires careful consideration.

∞

Ask yourself, "How am I going to wield the power of my Creative-Energy?" First, congratulations! Not everyone comprehends their ability to project energy into the world. Once you realize your energy affects those around you, it becomes imperative to harness this power for the greater good. You can no longer muddle through life assuming that your emotional and mental states affect you alone. Regardless of your actions, the frequency of your energy affects others. Being aware of this dynamic is the essential first step in taming your energetic projections.

As an experiment, when you meet someone new, try to emote positive feelings. You will experience something amazing. You will see and feel a shift in the person's mood. Their eyes will brighten; they will stand a little taller; they will become more present. This is the power of your hidden energy at work. It feels magical.

Once your brain becomes attuned to the benefits of controlling and projecting positive energy, your awareness will expand. You will become more open to your environment and will seek opportunities to manipulate and enhance reality. As a result, more high-frequency energy will flow your way. This will alchemize into better relationships, more opportunities, and the manifestation of your Soul-driven goals and objectives.

SECTION III: CRAFTING REALITY

SECTION III:
CRAFTING REALITY

Framework for Section III: Crafting Reality

In Section II, we examined the connection between our material realm and the realm of energy. We discovered the sentient mind originated as a mechanism for developing a pure link between energy and matter, and that humanity's mission is to perfect this channel. We also looked at Creative-Energy and the interplay between our physical avatar form and our Spiritual energetic form.

In Section III, we continue to focus in on the role humanity plays in developing a more perfect connection between energy and matter. We dive into the role the mind plays in channeling energy and discover how to use this ability to create our desired reality. This exploration illuminates the fundamental differences between our thinking brain, anchored in the material realm, and our Spiritual-Mind, which exists in the realm of energy. We delve into the brain's role as both a help and a hindrance in creating our desired reality and explore some of the societal constructs that hamper our ability to connect with Source-Energy. Finally, we learn valuable techniques for molding the mind into a useful tool for creating our desired reality, as well as methods for transforming negative, low-frequency energy into a resource for growth and evolution.

Each of the insights within this Section build upon the notion that we (human beings) are engineered to create reality from energy. The question is, "What kind of reality are you creating in your life?" If we understand the dynamics of creation, we can harness this knowledge to create positive change in our individual lives and in the reality we all share.

CHAPTER 27:

YOU HAVE BOTH A SPIRITUAL-MIND AND A PHYSICAL MIND

ASK A CREATIVE PERSON WHERE they get their novel ideas or inspiration, and whether they are an artist, scientist, philosopher, technologist, or business executive, they will have trouble pinpointing the source. More often than not, you will get a general, vague response like, "I am not sure—it just came to me."

My own life is replete with examples of insights, inspiration, and creativity appearing "as if out of nowhere." They drop into my mind or are channeled through my body with no life experience to account for them.

One fun example is a vivid dream I had many years ago, in which I picked up a harmonica and could play the most amazing blues licks. Mind you, up to that point, I had zero musical training and had never played a harmonica in my life. The next day, I could not shake the dream, so I stopped at a music store, approached the clerk, and pointed to one of perhaps thirty harmonicas in a glass case. I took home that Hohner Blues Harp in the key of "C," put on a Stevie Ray Vaughan album, took a deep breath, put my lips to the silver cover plates, and began to blow. To my ever-loving amazement, I could not only play—I played like I had been playing all my life! Thus began my love affair with playing music.

It is impossible to filter this kind of experience through the rational mind. There is no explanation other than that this type of impulse comes from another dimension. This mystery left me pondering the validity of the notion that the brain is the originator of all thoughts and ideas. I discovered a duality engrained in the fabric of thought and creativity. In fact, we possess two very different minds. One is anchored to the material realm, and the other? It's the very expression of your Soul!

Many people go through life without realizing that their thoughts and impulses emerge from two different sources. We attribute our cognitive abilities to our brains, but a more powerful wellspring is the source of our inspiration, creativity, and grandest ideals about the world. This expression of our highest self comes from the dimension of Spirit—from pure energy—which is channeled into our mind through quantum processes.[37] Throughout history, we have given many names to this intelligence, but I refer to it as Spiritual-Mind or Core-Self.

Comparing Your Spiritual-Mind and Your Brain

To distinguish between thoughts originating from our Spiritual-Mind and those coming from our brain, it is important to understand the differences, similarities, and complementary relationship between the two. To set the stage, let's begin with a brief description of each:

---

[37] Steve Volk, "Down the quantum rabbit hole," *Discover Magazine* (March 2018).

- The Brain (Mind): The brain is a material-realm-based, biological, information-processing machine.
- The Spiritual-Mind (Core-Self): The Spiritual-Mind is pure, multidimensional, intelligent energy that is channeled into our material form from the Realm of Energy.

Now let's look at the nuanced characteristics of both the brain and Spiritual-Mind and explore the intricate interplay between the two. The brain takes external stimuli and information, which is harvested through the five senses, and packages this data in a way that helps ensure the survival of... well, the brain. Right away, we notice this circular loop is always oriented toward what psychologists refer to as "ego." Left to its own devices, the brain will create a vision of reality directed to promoting and protecting itself above all else.

In addition, the nature of the brain makes it a slave to the past. Its only frame of reference is what it has already experienced. It is incapable of generating a thought not rooted in the past. It cannot, by its structure, have an original idea. The brain may be good at problem-solving, but it can only deal with the information it has accumulated. It might appear that the mind is producing novel concepts, but if you look closely, the brain can only create from what it has learned and experienced. This differs greatly from *inspiration*, which arises beyond the mind's field of experience.

Fortunately, we humans also have access to a mind that operates beyond the constraints of our physical brain. The Spiritual-Mind provides direct access to the same creative intelligence responsible for everything in the known universe. It represents the will of our individual Spirit and serves as a channel for communicating the needs and desires of our Spirit to our physical form. This is our source of inspiration, innovation, and creativity. I conceptualize the Spiritual-Mind as our "true self" because it represents who we are beyond the bounds of our human form in this lifetime. While it is informed by our experiences in this material realm, it is our mind that always acts in the best interest of our evolutionary objectives— channeling thoughts that connect us to our highest expression of self. As a result, the Core-Self enables us to think beyond the confines of our physical mind and into an innovational future.

Of course, our biological mind does not always play well with our Spiritual-Mind. If we are conditioned to grant the brain dominion over the Spirit, then our thoughts, beliefs, and actions will align with the ego. This translates into a reality dominated by fear, conflict, narcissism, dissatisfaction, and materialism.

It is possible to let the Spiritual-Mind lead the way. This might require reprogramming the brain to accept a new vision of reality, but it also gives you access to the joy, peace, creativity, and abundance of your authentic nature. The good news is you have a choice.

EXERCISE
REPROGRAMMING THE BRAIN

It is possible to alter the way your brain interacts with your Spiritual-Mind. The aim is to use the brain as a tool for channeling more and more Creative-Energy from your Spirit. The key is to work within the context of what the brain is designed to do. Because it is a learning machine, we must go about the business of reprogramming the brain to accept a different version of reality:

Step One:
Relegate the brain from the "center of the universe" to what it is: a tool for exploring and creating this material realm.

Step Two:
Reorient your sense of self, the "I" in "I am," outside of your physical body and into your Spiritual-Self—your Soul—the one observing this very process. You are not your body. You are not your brain. You are not your feelings. You are not the roles you play. You are not your success or failure. You are not your ego!

Step Three:
As you go about your daily life, pay attention to the multitude of touch points controlled by your ego. Negative feelings such as anger, resentment, and envy are indicators you have activated your brain-driven ego. Each time you stimulate the ego, remind the brain that it is not in control and use that moment to recenter to your Spiritual-Self.

Step Four:
Exercise patience with the process. These are the same basic steps used to break any habit. Many of us have spent a huge chunk of our lives viewing reality through our brain. Because of this, the reprogramming process will require time and patience.

CHAPTER 28:

REALITY REFLECTS YOUR CONNECTION TO SPIRIT

I SPENT YEARS STRIVING TO CHANGE the conditions of my life, with little to no success. Unfortunately, I had no role models for achieving personal success, and I was far from alone. Everyone I knew was experiencing the same cycle of hope leading to despair—of taking one step forward and two steps back. I was absorbed in a culture of "bad luck." For us, nothing ever seemed to work out the way we wanted. The hounds of trouble were at our doorstep perpetually.

The most maddening part was looking out at the world and seeing people who were thriving and successful. I wondered, "Are they that much smarter than I am?" (Maybe.) "Have they been given advantages I did not have?" (Possibly.) "Are they working that much harder than I am?" (I doubt it.)

It took years of effort to discover the secret formula for manifesting my dreams. Amazingly, it had little to do with *what* I was doing. It had everything to do with *how* I was doing it. Since I realized that, I have been able to create limitless abundance in my life.

Far too many people view the world as a harsh, chaotic, and dangerous place. They move from one conflict to another, in a never-ending succession of stressful, unsatisfying life events with little hope or expectation that things will improve. No matter what they do, or how hard they work, life never seems to work out for them the way they want. In fact, they become so habituated to negativity, they develop a perverse attachment to it and are skeptical when happiness or bliss enters their field of consciousness.

On the other end of the spectrum, there are those who glide through life. For them, life is a joyous adventure filled with good fortune, fulfillment, and bliss. Reality "magically" materializes as a reflection of their dreams and desires, and abundance flows from whatever they touch.

What are the determining factors in these extremes? Why do some people live in a state of frustration and chaos, while others achieve peace and abundance? Why do some people have all the luck and others none? The answer has nothing to do with an individual's intelligence, innate talent, or luck. Instead, it all depends on the brain's ability to link to Core-Self.

As we project Creative-Energy into reality, our thoughts, emotions, and actions serve as a template for how reality should look. If this template reflects negative concepts such as scarcity, unworthiness, or a dog-eat-dog outlook, "voilà!" You manifest a less-than-ideal reality. This negativity originates from a mind disconnected from Spirit.

On the flip side, if your brain is oriented toward your Spiritual-Mind, your thoughts, emotions, and behaviors mirror the desires and needs of your Higher-Self. When Creative-Energy flows into this template, it creates a reality that actualizes the characteristics of Core-Energy: limitless abundance, ecstatic energy, boundless creativity, perfect peace, and immeasurable joy.

Each of us is somewhere on the spectrum between having a pure connection with Spirit and a being a slave to our disconnected mind. Our lives reflect where we are on the scale. If, for example, you are dissatisfied with how things are going, or you are frustrated with your ability to manifest your dreams, you must evolve your mind's connection to Spirit. You (and only you) can make changes. As you take on this responsibility, the doors to Core-Energy open, and you create a reality beyond your wildest imagination.

Let Feelings Be Your Guide

It is easy to identify the areas in which you are disconnected from your Core-Self. You need to tap into your feelings and assess how your life is developing. "Feelings" will always serve as your guidepost. Positive feelings (such as peace, joy, excitement, and high energy) are associated with the touch points where your Creative-Energy is aligned with your Spirit. These energy profiles are the hallmark of your Spiritual dimension and show that you have an open channel to your Energetic-Self.

Likewise, negative feelings such as fear, anger, jealousy, envy, insecurity, depression, and frustration point to the areas where the mind restricts or cuts off the flow of energy from your Spirit.

Left to its own devices, your brain will gravitate to that with which it has been imprinted—what it has experienced, no matter how unpleasant, destructive, or unsatisfying. As a result, when we rely on our brain to control the flow of Creative-Energy, we find ourselves stuck in repetitive negative cycles of creation. Like the 1993 movie *Groundhog Day*,[38] the same patterns of pain and drama show up repeatedly. We wonder, "Why doesn't life change for the better?" The answer is simple. It is because we are letting

---

[38] Harry Ramis (Dir/Prod.) and Trevor Albert (Producer), *Groundhog Day* (1993, United States: Columbia Pictures.)

our biological programming control our concept of self and our purpose for existence.

This is not your brain's fault. It is behaving according to its nature. It is your responsibility to learn to use this biological supercomputer for its maximum benefit. This starts with paying attention to your feelings and training your biological mind to open the clogged channels to your Spiritual-Mind.

CHAPTER 29:

YOUR BRAIN PROJECTS AN ILLUSION

My violent, tumultuous childhood created a host of psychological problems that left me wary of my mind's ability to process reality. Early on, these mental problems (depression, panic attacks, dissociative disorders) wreaked havoc in my life. In retrospect, however, I count these negative experiences as my greatest blessing. Because I knew my mind was damaged, I did not allow my mind to be the arbiter of what was true or false, real, or unreal. This mistrust prompted me to look outside of my mental framework for answers and to explore concepts and ideologies outside of my personal experience. My discoveries gave credence to the notion that the human brain is indeed the primary obstacle to personal and spiritual growth—not just for my damaged brain, but for all of humanity!

Your Subjective Mind

In the West, we have created a mythology around the mind as the seat of logic, rationality, and objectivity. We are conditioned from childhood to rely on our cognitive abilities not only to solve complex problems but also to provide an unbiased interpretation of what is true and untrue, real and unreal, fact and fiction. Over time, this sets up the mind as the definitive authority on all things *life*: on morality (what is right and wrong), on society (what is good and bad), and on existence (what is real and unreal).

The problem is the mind is anything but objective! In fact, as noted earlier, its interpretations of self and the world rely on its programming. As a result, the mind's view of reality is always self-referential and may or may not reflect what is *actually* going on. It is *subjective* and can create an illusory existence that blinds us to our greater nature.

Illustrations of these illusions are everywhere. For example, there is no such thing as solid matter. Even the objects that appear the densest, such as metals and minerals, comprise mostly empty space with subatomic particles whizzing around at incomprehensible speeds.[39] It is the vibrational speed at which these particles move (in conjunction with "quantum superposition")[40] that makes objects "appear" solid. Another brain-illusion occurs on the macro level of our daily perceptions. It might appear as though objects are separate from one another and that we, as individuals, are separate from everything around us. In reality, something else is going on. On a quantum scale, our bodies, as well as the physical forms of everything around us, are interacting and exchanging energy. Here are some examples:

---

[39] Roger Barlow, "If atoms are mostly empty space, why do objects look and feel solid?" Phys.org (Feb. 16, 2017), https://phys.org/news/2017-02-atoms-space-solid.html.
[40] Rafi Letzter, "There Is a Giant Mystery Hiding Inside Every Atom in the Universe," *Live Science* (Jan. 03, 2020), https://www.livescience.com/mystery-of-proton-neutron-behavior-in-nucleus.html; *Caltech Science Exchange,* "What Is Superposition and Why Is It Important?" (2022), https://scienceexchange.caltech.edu/topics/quantum-science-explained/quantum-superposition;"Radioactive Decay," United States Nuclear Regulatory Commission (March 09, 2021). https://www.nrc.gov/reading-rm/basic-ref/glossary/radioactive-decay.html.

- What is radioactive decay, except a mineral/element changing form and throwing off subatomic particles which are then absorbed by the environment?
- Experiments have shown that isolated plants can gather life-sustaining energy from other plants without the need for physical contact.[41]
- Water crystallizes (freezes) into either beautiful geometric fractal patterns or chaotic random patterns, depending on whether it is subjected to positive or negative emotional stimuli.[42]
- Experiments in quantum physics have proven that the act of observing an experiment (or even the thought of observing the experiment) changes the form of a quantum particle;[43]
- ... The list is limitless.

The bottom line is, we live in an interconnected universe, and our thoughts and actions are intermingling with all of creation to co-create our environment in real time. The mind's illusion that we are separate is just that... an illusion.

If your aim is to expand your consciousness, never let your mind dictate the parameters of what makes up reality. Serving as a gatekeeper, it will always default to a vision of life that is supported by its past programming. So, the greatest gift you can give yourself is the gift of curiosity. By remaining open to new ideas and experiences, you bypass the built-in biases of your mind and allow for a direct exchange of energy from your Spirit. This flow of Source-Energy creates a crucible for change and transformation.

---

[41] Olga Blifernez-Klassen, V. Klassen, A. Doebbe, et al., Cellulose degradation and assimilation by the unicellular phototrophic eukaryote *Chlamydomonas reinhardtii, Nat Commun* 3, 1214 (2012), https://www.nature.com/articles/ncomms2210.

[42] Masaru Emoto, *The hidden messages in water* (New York: Beyond Words Publishing, 2004).

[43] Paul J. van Leeuwen, "Experimenter effect in parapsychological experiments?" *Quantum Physics & Consciousness* (Nov. 09, 2019), quantumphysics-consciousness.eu/index.php/en/2019/11/09/experimenter-effect-in-parapsychological-experiments/.

Instead of being a slave to habits, dogmas, and ideologies, you can create a life that reflects the desires of your Core-Self. Instead of perpetuating the illusions of your mind, your life can become an accurate reflection of the transformative power of God.

CHAPTER 30:

YOU CONTROL YOUR REALITY

Many of us are conditioned to believe that our reality is beyond our control—that our circumstances are governed by the mysterious force of God, or fate, or chance. As I tested the idea that we are each the author of our own reality, I came face-to-face with the proof that we (not some mysterious force), are manifesting the details of our existence. As if through magic, my desired vision of reality unfolded everywhere I directed my creative attention. From the transformation of health to the accumulation of wealth, it became undeniable that each of us is the author and architect of our reality. The mind and body are conduits for creative power.

Born to Create

The essence of our Spirit is dynamic creativity. Our Soul is driven to build, to grow, to innovate, to develop, and to create. We are born with the ability to channel Creative-Energy into life and to use this force to create reality on a grand scale. This includes the creation of physical things such as art, technology, medicine, and buildings; concepts such as ideals, philosophies, and systems; and more esoteric conceptions such as developing our mind's ability to interface with Core-Energy.

Human beings have come a long way in developing the basic mechanisms both for transferring Creative-Energy and adapting this energy to our material environment. The most important tool at our disposal is our mind, which provides us with the power of imagination. We take imagination for granted, but the capacity to conceptualize a reality beyond our field of experience is the motivating force behind our creative impulse and the alchemy of applying Creative-Energy in new, exciting ways.

Compounding Energy

There is also a universal "compounding force" behind the act of creation. This can best be described as a "Fundamental Law of Nature," which states, "through the act of creating, you increase your access to Creative-Energy." You can see this principle play out in prolific individuals. They often experience an overwhelming flood of ideas and inspiration, along with a sense that they cannot create fast enough to keep up with the wellspring of Creative-Energy flowing through them. This boundless energy is available to anyone who commits themselves to responding to their Creative-Impulse.

The opposite is also true. If we shut off our creative output, we receive less and less Creative-Energy. This affects every area of our life, from sexual energy to the ability to think creatively. If we are not exercising our creative muscles, our experience atrophies. In the most extreme case, existence becomes dull, meaningless drudgery, and we descend into nihilism.

The choice is yours—you can either exercise your creative potential and reap the benefits that accompany your alignment with your creative nature, or you can choke off your creative power and live a stagnant, low-energy existence.

EXERCISE
RECOVERING CREATIVE POWER

The first step in recovering your creative power involves tapping into your Energetic-Self. Your mind and body have developed the ability to do this. There is a simple but powerful trick that allows you to create a direct link between your biology and Source-Energy. This process offers miraculous results and can be useful anytime you want to channel Creative-Energy. It involves the Eastern traditional concept of the "energetic body." In this view, the body comprises energy centers (sometimes referred to as "chakras") that facilitate the flow of energy between our physical bodies and our environment. In many spiritual teachings, this energy network is conceptualized as an energetic extension of the "flesh and bone" body (i.e., our energetic body).[44]

Begin by finding a quiet place to sit. Breathing in through your nose and out through your mouth, fill and then empty your lungs. With each inhale, let your mind reflect on the blessings in your life and your feelings of gratitude and joy. In your mind's eye, envision areas of your life that support these feelings (such as loved ones; blessings you have experienced; or perhaps, the simple gift of life).

As the feelings come in with the breath, open your heart to receive this energy. With each exhale, project feelings of gratitude and joy from your heart outward to all corners of the physical world. Visualize a continuous loop of this positive energy coming into your body and projecting out into the world.

Now express these feelings: Smile. Laugh. Expand your chest. Raise your arms. Whatever the impulse, respect your body's expression of appreciation.

---

[44] Anodea Judith, *Wheels of life: A user's guide to the chakra system*, 2nd ed. (Woodbury, MN: Llewellyn Publications, 2018).

After several deep breaths, and with a smile on your face, bring the energy of thankfulness and joy up to the core of your brain where the small, almond-shaped amygdala lives. Feel this energy lighting up the amygdala.[45] You might even feel a warm vibration. Now bring that energy forward and project it out of the "third-eye" chakra at the center of your forehead.

You have now established an energy circuit which channels Creative-Energy into the chakra of the solar plexus (below the diaphragm). The energy gets charged by the heart chakra and moves through the brain and back out through the third-eye chakra.[46] You have transformed your body into an antenna and a transmitter that allows you to take in Creative-Energy and focus this energy on whatever you would like to create for yourself.

Next, while still breathing deeply, still feeling thankfulness and joy, still projecting from your amygdala through your third-eye chakra, visualize what you want to create *as if* you have already created it. Use ALL your senses. How does this creation look, feel, and taste? How does it smell? What does it sound like? What is your emotional response to this creation? What is your reaction—how does this make you feel? The more detail, the better. The more specifics, the better. Dwell on the feelings—dwell in the details.

End your meditation by expressing gratitude for your creative power. Then go about your day *as if* you have manifested your dream.

---

[45] Lisa-Maria Schonefeld and Lars Wojtecki, "Beyond Emotions: Oscillations of the amygdala and their implications for electrical neuromodulation," *Frontiers in Neuroscience* (April 18, 2019), https://www.frontiersin.org/articles/10.3389/fnins.2019.00366/full; E. Mohandas, "Neurobiology of spirituality," National Library of Medicine, *Mens Sana Monogr* (2008) Jan;6(1):63-80. doi: 10.4103/0973-1229.33001. PMID: 22013351; PMCID: PMC3190564, https://www.ncbi.nlm.nih.gov/pmc/articles/PMC3190564/.
[46] Alethia, "The ultimate guide to third eye chakra healing for complete beginners," *Loner Wolf* (Sept. 23, 2022), https://lonerwolf.com/third-eye-chakra-healing/.

ENERGY CENTERS/
CHAKRA SYSTEM

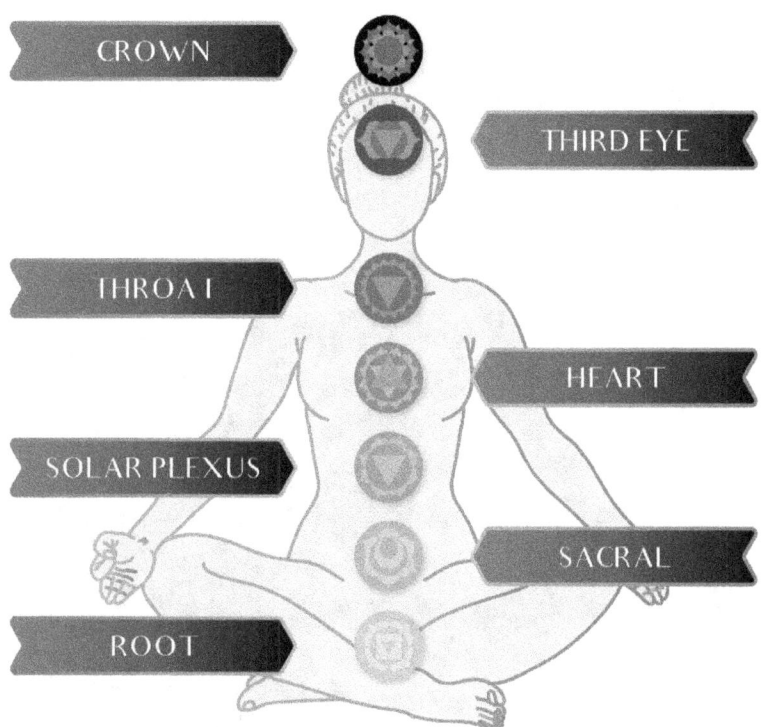

CROWN

THIRD EYE

THROAT

HEART

SOLAR PLEXUS

SACRAL

ROOT

Eastern religions acknowledge the existence of energy centers within the human body that connect our physical form to the ever-present Field of Energy that permeates reality. This diagram illustrates the most commonly referenced seven chakras and their locations within the body.

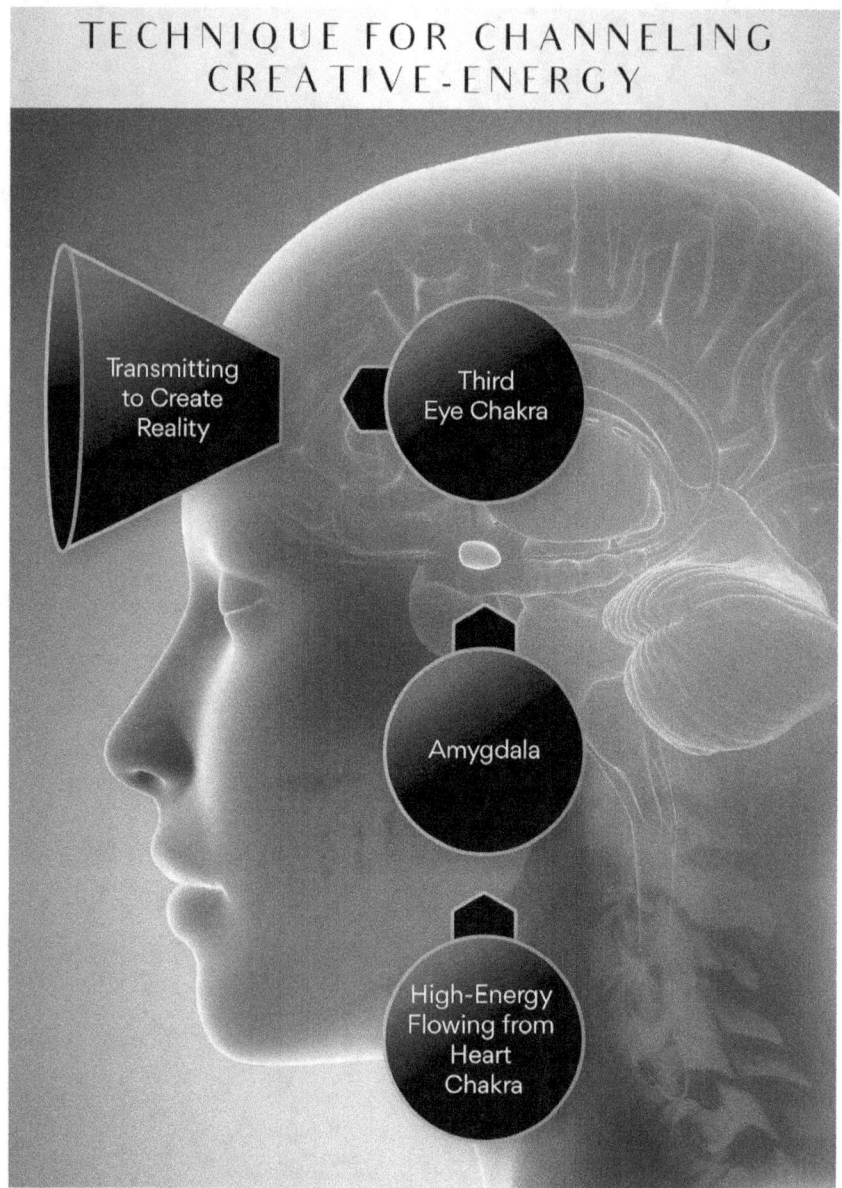

TECHNIQUE FOR CHANNELING CREATIVE-ENERGY

Transmitting to Create Reality

Third Eye Chakra

Amygdala

High-Energy Flowing from Heart Chakra

This diagram illustrates the author's technique of using the high-vibration energy of gratitude to channel creation. Creative-Energy is absorbed through the heart chakra; amplified by feelings of thankfulness and gratitude; directed to activate the amygdala in the brain; and finally, transmitted through the third-eye chakra to manifest reality.

CHAPTER 31:

AVOIDING PAIN IS DAMAGING

Much of my life serves as a cautionary tale about the dangers of repressed energy. Like many people, I never received the tools to process negative experiences healthily. I was not taught to identify the host of harmful pathologies that arise from stored negative energy. As a result, my reality unfolded as a maelstrom of sickness, mental illness, self-destructive behavior, and poor decision-making. These trials and tribulations helped me discover a simple axiom: "If you can't control the flow of energy into life, then the flow of energy will control you."

Once I understood the dynamics and effects of repressed energy, I developed techniques for locating and eradicating pockets of this energy from my mind and body. This is a lifelong process, but the work I have done so far has transformed my life.

Life Is Painful

Life bombards us with painful and unpleasant energy. From the moment of birth, when we are extracted from the warm, safe confines of the womb; to the trials and tribulations of childhood; to daily interactions with our fellow human beings; there is hardly a break from the flow of low-frequency energy in our lives. It is natural for us to feel pain and discomfort when encountering this negative energy. However, there are healthy and unhealthy ways to deal with pain, and the decisions we make determine the level of impact pain has on our life.

The complex human mind is a wonderful tool. Among its many attributes is the ability to manipulate the complex web of feelings that emerge from our interactions with daily life. Because many of life's touch points are painful, our minds develop a host of defense mechanisms to help guard against negative feelings. These strategies often involve trying to avoid pain by damping it down, compartmentalizing it, or otherwise burying negative emotions. On the surface, this might seem reasonable. However, as we shall explore, most of these defensive measures end up causing more harm than good.

Humans have a unique ability to evade psychological pain. We can bury our response to negative stimuli deep within our neural network. The trouble is, any time we block unwanted thoughts or impulses, whether unconsciously (repression), or consciously (suppression), we risk trapping this energy within our body, psyche, or both. Unless this trapped energy is excised in the proper way, it festers and grows into an even greater destructive force.

It might help to think of negative energy as being like the electricity that powers your home. Once channeled into your house, electricity can take one of three different paths: You can use it to power something, it can return to the power grid, or you can store it in batteries for use later. Repressing or suppressing negative energy is akin to storing this energy for later use. However, instead of using a battery, we bury the feelings associated with negative events within the physical body or deep within our psychological framework (or both).[47] Unlike our electricity analogy, stored negative energy does not just sit there, passively waiting for us to bring it into awareness. Instead, it engages in a constant struggle to release and manifest itself. It wants to be set loose so it can fulfill its mission and create reality. So, it rises to the surface as reactionary behavior, emotional outbursts, and negative emotions. Of course, if you are trying to avoid this energy, this can create genuine problems.

Compounding Repressed Energy

What is our natural response when these energy gremlins bubble to the surface? Well, our logical mind would have us pour even more energy into keeping these unwanted feelings submerged. As an example, let's assume you experienced a traumatic childhood event with which, for various reasons, you do not want to deal. Instead, you bury these negative feelings deep within your psyche. As you mature, this energy bubbles to the surface as sadness, anger, or rebelliousness. Each time this happens, you apply force to avoid the painful feelings. Over time, as the original pain absorbs more and more energy, it morphs into ever-more-extreme negative emotions and behaviors. Sadness becomes depression, anger becomes violence, rebelliousness morphs into self-destructive behavior, and so on. This describes the compounding process of repressed energy. It takes an acorn of pain and nourishes it so that it grows into a mighty oak of uncontrolled pathological reactions.

The Effects of Repressed Energy

In the real world, the effects of repressive and suppressive energy can be extensive and extreme. In fact, they are the primary contributing factors for most of the horrible behavior we see in the world. Just look at your own life and at the world around you. We are awash in reactionary anger and violence, in rabid materialism,

---

[47] Stuart Wolpert, "UCLA Biologists 'transfer' a memory," *UCLA Newsroom* (May 14, 2018), https://newsroom.ucla.edu/releases/ucla-biologists-transfer-a-memory.

in psychological diseases, and in a cornucopia of pathological behaviors, most of which are because of repressed pain. With repressed Creative-Energy, there is no "free lunch." You cannot bury it or hide it. Creative-Energy will always express itself.

To a lesser or greater extent, every life bears the burden of repressed pain. As storage facilities for buried thoughts, feelings, and memories, we are at the mercy of this unresolved energy bubbling to the surface and taking control of our lives. In fact, repression is baked right into our culture and institutions. Many of us are taught from childhood to compartmentalize or to deny our negative feelings outright. We are encouraged to tuck them away and move forward with no guidance on how to process emotional pain.

Even our religious institutions provide an unhealthy response for dealing with destructive energy. Instead of taking personal responsibility for engaging with pain, they provide a proxy in the form of deities or saints. It is all well and good to "give your pain to God," but if you have not taken the personal steps to process this energy and learn the lessons embedded within the pain, then you are back to square-one—*repressed energy*.

We all have negative behaviors that stem from our failure to process negative energy healthily. As we examine our lives, it behooves us to examine this history and take responsibility for confronting the pain at the root of these behaviors. These issues do not resolve themselves. They require overt action and our willingness to face our darkest fears. Only then can we hope to free ourselves from their oppressive grip.

EXERCISE
STEPS FOR DEALING WITH REPRESSED ENERGY

So, how do we deal with our stored, repressed energy? How can we avoid repressing fresh energy in the future? Luckily, there is a simple three-step process: Step 1. Identify; Step 2. Burn; Step 3. Release.

- The first step is to IDENTIFY and bring forward each repressed feeling or episode in your life. This might take psychic digging as well as therapy (from a qualified mental health practitioner), but it is essential that the event be brought into the light of your conscious mind. Once in the open, it is of vital importance that you understand how this energy affects you in the present moment... how it influences your thoughts, decisions, relationships, career path, and station in life.

- The second step, BURN, is often the hardest. You must do what you have been avoiding (i.e., you have been repressing). You must immerse yourself into the past event. You must feel (fully and completely) the sadness, anger, betrayal, hurt, guilt, inadequacy, torture, or doubt. This might involve weeping, stomping, screaming... do whatever you feel like doing to fully embrace every aspect of the event. This is the BURNING of the energy. Crucially, you must express the totality of the energy—all of it—or you will not be rid of it. A critical part of this process requires that you take 100 percent responsibility for the event in question. You create your past, current, and future reality. There is no room for blaming anything or anyone... the buck stops with you and *you* alone. I realize that this may not be a pleasant or popular notion, particularly with those who have experienced massive trauma. However, my experience has shown me that unless you take full responsibility for your reality, you cannot clear the pain completely. Any blame or responsibility placed on someone else carries with it an equal measure of negative energy as resentment, sadness, fear, or anger. If you take control of *all* the energy, you give yourself total control over BURNING *all* the energy. Otherwise, pockets of repressed negative energy will remain... festering... waiting for cleansing actions that may never come.

You are now prepared, once and for all, to RELEASE the negative obstacle. For this step, it is important to realize that the Field of Creative-Energy has an infinite capacity both to transmit and receive energy. Once you dig repressed energy out of its hiding place and expose it to your full complement of feelings, the harmful energy transmutes into a higher frequency that flows away from the mind and body. As the energy releases back to the Field, it helps to visualize the event and all the drama evaporating into elemental energy and drifting off into the universe. You will experience positive emotions emerging to replace the long-harbored negative ones. You will feel joy, forgiveness, compassion, understanding, and maybe even humor. Let "release with joy" be your mantra.

CHAPTER 32:

RELIGION IS A GIFT AND A CURSE

Over the years, I have come to view the world's religious institutions as the primary impediment to humanity's evolution. Because of my personal experience with Christianity, I am hypersensitive to its negative impact on personal growth and societal transformation. However, it doesn't take much insight to recognize the carnage wrought under the banner of "God," no matter what your religious persuasion.

I also recognize the real value of our religious traditions. They offer community and an efficient way to convey culture and tradition. However, if we want to achieve our evolutionary goals, the structure of these institutions must undergo fundamental change. Instead of an autocratic "top-down" approach, which operates as an inflexible, power-hungry authoritarian regime, they must open up to cede power to the diversity of the masses. In addition, organized religions must recognize the fluid nature of spiritual evolution and eliminate the notion of uncompromising doctrine. As pollyannaish as this sounds, I believe that all our institutions (whether religious, governmental, or societal), must shed their inflexible dogma and embrace the ever-changing environment that defines reality.

The Good and Bad of Religion

Discussing religion is polarizing. This is because the world's major religions represent both the best and the worst of humanity. The primary impetus for their formation was a quest to provide form and context to both the mysteries of the physical universe and our innate connection to its creative source. By formalizing this information, religious institutions have provided precious benefits to society:

- First, religion offers a common axis around which cultures coalesce. Throughout history, religious communities have been a primary driver for advancing trade, innovation, and creativity.
- Next, religion provides a unified explanation for the mysteries of life. The human mind hates uncertainty. By offering a culturally understandable explanation for the complex and unpredictable world around us, we are better able to stay focused on advancing civilization.
- Finally, religion delivers a standardized process and procedure for accessing the Divine that is transferrable to future generations. This is a great leap forward for the human connection with Spirit. It serves to focus the collective mind on the Spiritual Realm, thus raising the average vibrational energy of humanity.

Of course, there are also negative sides to religion. Instead of focusing on the plethora of atrocities and abuses proliferated in the name of God, let's touch on the two core issues that represent the biggest obstruction to our spiritual advancement:

- One: A static model for spirituality and the concept of God. The idea that God, the realm of God, and God's relationship to the universe is perfect, fixed, and unchanging. This belief permeates all the major religions. However, it does not synch with the evidence of creation itself.

Contrary to many religious beliefs, everything in the known universe is in dynamic flux: cosmology, biology, technology, societies. Yes, even our Spiritual-Energy is evolving. If we are indeed a product of an other-dimensional creative force, it stands to reason that God is evolving right along with humanity. Based on this logical supposition, a static model for spirituality cannot be valid.

With this understanding, adherence to a fixed concept of spirituality is problematic. If your belief system does not allow for change, it becomes outdated the moment you subscribe to it. So, what if your static religious dogma is anchored to a belief system that is thousands of years old? Well, this means your viewpoint is thousands of years removed from reality.

- Two: The accumulation of power. Over time, religious institutions can devolve from beacons of spiritual exploration into power structures focused on accumulating wealth, control, and political influence. Many theologies become corrupted and directed toward harvesting community assets to feed the ambitions of institutional bureaucracy.

This change represents a huge decline in the vibrational frequency of the energy in which these systems operate. Because of this decline, religious institutions can no longer channel high-frequency, God-source Creative-Energy into this material realm. Instead, to maintain control, they rely on the lower vibrations of fear, greed, and oppression.

As we examine the conflict and divisiveness inherent in society today, the fingerprints of our dysfunctional religious institutions are everywhere. Those who have anchored their view of the world in damaged ideologies are fearful when reality does not match their expectations. Their fear produces anger, judgment, anxiety, discrimination, and tribalism. This helps explain why some groups are so resistant to change—to anything that threatens their outmoded way of looking at the world.

Likewise, religion's emphasis on regimented conformity and imposed morality causes individuals to repress feelings and creative impulses, which is a huge contributor to psychological problems and harmful behaviors. In addition, by controlling and manipulating the flow of information, religious institutions can create distrust of any unsanctioned ideology. These echo-chambers can stunt a person's ability to learn, grow, and evolve.

Of course, these characteristics, both good and bad, are not the sole purview of religion. They apply to any institution: religious, governmental, or otherwise. Therefore, it behooves each of us to always maintain a critical eye toward the motivations and agendas of our institutions. We must glean what is beneficial and leave the rest behind.

Identifying Valid Teachings

Despite how it might sometimes appear, there is spiritual "truth" behind all our religious traditions. Like mining for precious gems, finding these truths often requires sifting through a great deal of debris. That being said, the distinguishing characteristics of a valid teaching are recognizable because they mirror the characteristics of Source-Energy itself. Here is what to look for:

- The teaching is based in love.
- The teaching is inclusive.
- The teaching promotes personal responsibility.
- The teaching advocates tolerance and forgiveness.
- The teaching recognizes a Spiritual-Self beyond the physical body.

These five characteristics are foundational to every great religion and religious tradition. However, many of these ideals have long since mutated into a form that only serves the institutional power structures. It is our responsibility to "separate the wheat from the chaff" and develop these original principles into a form that aids present-day humanity.

CHAPTER 33:

YOU ARE RESPONSIBLE...
FOR EVERYTHING

SOMEWHERE ALONG MY JOURNEY, AFTER many years of soul-searching, I recognized the greatest obstacle to my personal development: I had appropriated a worldview that I was a passive participant—that life's circumstances forced me to respond to influences beyond my control. Some of this passiveness was because of a religious culture which ceded power to a third party (God), and some was a reluctance to hold myself accountable for the misery I was experiencing.

The moment I took *complete* responsibility for *everything* was the single most liberating and empowering moment of my life. I no longer had to rely on anyone or anything to craft the reality of my dreams. The power was now in *my* hands!

This decision set off a chain reaction of creation that transformed my life. It left no doubt in my mind that each of us is the author and architect of our reality.

∞

You Are the Architect of Your Life

Coincidence, luck, happenstance, and fate are some labels we give to life events that we deem out of our control. However, for the formation of reality, there is no such thing as randomness, good or bad luck, or the like. You can think of your reality as a giant billiard game of colliding Karmic-Forces, where the actions of each moment have an irreversible influence on the game at play. Life events unfold the way they do because of the energy we funnel into each moment along our path.

As a result, each of us is the architect of our reality and 100 percent responsible for everything (good and bad) that happens to us in life. For many people, this concept will sound like heresy. They will ask, "What did I do to deserve all the bad things that are happening to me?" Or they will look around at the good fortune of others and ask, "Why do they deserve their success… health… abundance?"

Reality is the product of an energy (Creative-Energy) that makes no moral judgment about what materializes. There is no good or bad, right or wrong, deserving or undeserving. Creative-Energy responds to our thoughts, actions, attitudes, beliefs, and feelings, to make our vision of reality come true. You can think of Creative-Energy as similar to a computer language—raw code that can be directed into creating something. It takes a programmer to format the language into something of substance. Here, you and I are, individually and collectively, programmers. We spend every moment crafting Creative-Energy into the reality we see around us.

We all know people who possess dueling realities. They may succeed in one area of life and fail in another area. This is no accident. Their reality mirrors how and where they place their Creative-Energy. Let's look at a common example of someone who is gifted at creating wealth and financial prosperity but whose personal life and relationships are a disaster. Here, the individual's mind is programmed to accept a reality of personal wealth and abundance, and their actions corroborate this vision. They believe in their ability to create wealth, and their work ethic and attitude support this belief.

However, this individual has deep-rooted negative pathologies associated with relationships. Perhaps they grew up in a hostile environment and erected walls to protect their feelings from the outside world. These wounds are carried into adulthood and continue to manifest in unhealthy relationships.

In this example, we can see that the same individual is using Creative-Energy to manifest two very different outcomes. To reiterate, it is the same Creative-Force—the same "programming language!" They are channeling this energy through a mind that filters it to reflect the brain's view of reality.

EXERCISE
CONTROLLING YOUR REALITY

Each person experiences an ever-changing landscape of positive and negative events. What remains constant is your influence over your personal surroundings and your power to change your circumstances moment by moment. The key to changing the world around you is to learn how to change yourself: how you think, how you view yourself, and how you react to positive and negative forces in your environment.

The first step in this process is to take ownership of how things are right now. Look at your reality. What do you like? What do you want to change? Understanding that you are responsible for all of it—not only does it provide a sense of the Creative-Energy at your disposal, but it also gives you the power to change things.

For the things you want to change, the next step is to take an unflinching look at your belief systems and actions that support these negative aspects of life. This might be harder than it appears. Many of our creative mechanisms (positive and negative) result from hidden pathologies that have accumulated over a lifetime (or even past lifetimes).

Each of these underlying belief systems must be brought forward into the conscious mind. From here, you can craft a new vision of reality by reprogramming your mind to reject old beliefs and accept a new worldview.

This is the process of renewal—of learning how to use Creative-Energy for your highest benefit. You are taking control of your reality!

CHAPTER 34:

AWARENESS IS THE KEY TO CHANGE

THE PRACTICES OF MEDITATION, BEING aware, and being ever mindful are not natural to the human brain. For years, I beat myself up trying to achieve these states of consciousness through the application of thought. As nonsensical as it sounds, I was trying to use my thoughts to achieve non-thought.

I am far from alone. This is because the thinking brain dominates our daily existence. Our mind feels most comfortable when we are processing a steady stream of images, memories, and projections. It feels most vulnerable when it is not engaged in processing information, dredging up the past, or planning for the future. This is how it has evolved. It wants to control the action, so it bucks against the idea of "letting go" and is wary of a moment with no projections beyond the here and now.

You can learn to overcome this barrier, but it requires you to discern the difference between the actions of the mind and the inner voice originating from your Spiritual-Core. The ancient techniques for meditation are helpful, of course, but they require practice and diligence. More than anything else, they require patience—patience with your progress and patience with your obstinate mind.

Spiritual and meditation communities emphasize "awareness" and "mindfulness." These terms are used to represent a confusing array of thought-based and even non-thought-based states of consciousness. It is best not to get hung up on semantics and instead to focus on the various states of consciousness that are useful to your spiritual journey.

Mindfulness and Detachment

The techniques of mindfulness and detachment attempt to create a distinction between the thoughts swirling around in your biological brain and who you are beyond those thoughts. They point to the fact that the real "you" does not live in your brain; that your "authentic self" is located outside of your physical presence. Because of this, you can rise above the limitations of your brain and connect your physical presence to the realm of Spirit and energy.

We achieve our ability to observe our thoughts in a balance way through the technique of *detachment*. The term *detachment* can be confusing because it implies an uncaring or indifferent attitude toward what is happening at any moment. However, this is not the case. Instead, detachment allows you to observe life from a conscious perspective. This is a bit like watching a movie: You have an emotional and physical reaction to what you are watching, but because you know it is a movie, you can choose how you react to what you are witnessing.

In real life, detachment allows you to assume the role of "the witness." Your brain has a natural response to what is going on around you, but because you have adopted the role of an impartial bystander, you have control over how you react. While the feelings and mental imagery remain the same, you can make a conscious choice about how you want to respond.

Once you develop the ability to become "the witness," the reactionary mind loses control over your thoughts, emotions, and actions. Since most thought is tied to past events, or projections of the future, this new perspective also allows you to be present in the moment.

Many of our emotional responses to life have nothing to do with what is happening in the moment. Instead, they are affected by the wounds of the past and our fears for the future. By witnessing these false narratives, we become grounded in what is happening in each present moment.

In its most advanced form, the practice of mindfulness can supersede your mental process altogether. As the mind becomes accustomed to being observed, it will relinquish its dominance and quiet down. This is the key to achieving states of consciousness in which there are no thoughts, or in which one is in a state of total awareness of the present moment. The Buddha achieved the purest form of this state when he became enlightened.[48] For most of us, enlightenment may not be in the cards. However, with practice, we can use this process to (at least temporarily) align with Source-Energy and experience what the Bible describes as "the peace (of God) that transcends all understanding."[49]

The bottom line is that the practice of awareness allows you to gain control of your reactionary mind, and gain control of your life. It allows you to transform your mind from an obstacle into a useful tool for channeling the energy that reflects your highest self and the reality you wish to create.

There are myriad techniques for achieving mindfulness. However, they all begin by focusing your mind on a particular action (such as your breath, feeling sensations in your body, or chanting a mantra)

---

[48] Qiango Xiao, "The mindful self: A mindfulness-enlightened self-view," *Frontiers in Psychology* (Oct. 13, 2017), https://www.frontiersin.org/articles/10.3389/fpsyg.2017.01752/full#:~:text=Principally%2C%20mindfulness%20in%20Buddhist%20teaching,no%20self.%E2%80%9D%20According%20to%20Buddhism.
[49] Philippians 4:7 (NIV).

in order to move the mind from its natural state of chaotic thought into a calmer state.

Concentrating the mind's attention toward a simple benign thought helps to prevent the mind from being bombarded with the emotional stimulation that characterizes its "normal" condition. This allows for an easier transition into being a dispassionate observer of your thoughts as they occur. In spiritual parlance, you "witness" your brain's activity. You bypass the sense that your mind is the seat of your being and can view your thoughts from the perspective of your Spiritual-Self, which is located outside of your physical form.

Once you achieve the perspective of Spirit and can observe the mind, "you" realize that you are something and somewhere other than your brain. This becomes the impetus for taking control of the mind and training it to become a pure conduit for channeling Creative-Energy from your Spiritual-Core into this material realm.

CHAPTER 35

DIFFICULT RELATIONSHIPS ARE YOUR GREATEST TOOL FOR GROWTH

WHEN IT COMES TO UNHEALTHY relationships, I have had some doozies. In fact, when I look back over the years, I have had as many negative interactions as positive ones. Not only that, but I've often repeated the same relationship mistakes. Difficult relationships ALWAYS represent an opportunity for personal growth. They are white-hot flares pointing to lessons we need to learn, and they will continue to blaze until we learn our lesson. As unpleasant as it might be, I have learned that it is best to embrace the challenge of these connections and discover the wisdom embedded within them.

Every one of these hard-earned experiences has enhanced my ability to form positive, loving connections in life. Without them, there is no way I could have cultivated the nurturing relationships with family and friends that serve as my greatest source of joy.

∞

Interpersonal relationships are the number one tool our Spiritual-Self uses to help us develop. Every relationship in life represents an agreement between Souls to help one or both parties develop their connection to Core-Energy.

As is so often the case, we learn more from experiencing hardship than we learn from being comfortable. The difficult relationships in our life are important because each one represents a golden opportunity to make giant strides in our development. And, like it or not, the more difficult the relationship, the more potential it has for teaching us valuable lessons. This does not mean, however, that we should remain in destructive or abusive relationships. It means we must learn to manage negative energy.

Navigating difficult relationships is an unavoidable part of life. We view these challenging connections negatively. We find relationships annoying, stressful, harmful, or worse. However, viewed from the perspective of Spirit, every personal encounter is a choreographed dance between your Soul and the Soul of another individual.

While the scope and structure of this relationship dance is dictated by each individual's needs, the outcome depends on the mind's ability to actualize the lessons embedded in each relationship. Many conflict-riddled relationships are slow to resolve. They can carry on over the course of a lifetime, and we can even carry them forward through multiple lifetimes. Unless their energy is resolved through an evolutionary step forward, you will encounter these dynamics repeatedly!

Each new lifetime brings with it a new opportunity and strategy for evolution. As the architect of this strategy, your Core-Self knows the evolutionary path you are on. Relationships are organized on a Spiritual level to help you achieve these objectives. While nobody wants to be involved in a conflict-based relationship, these connections are often the key to unlocking the most significant wellsprings of Spiritual-Energy. The brain often is not programmed to process this type of negative energy, and as a result, individuals establish karmic cycles that might continue from one lifetime to the next, or until one person (or both people) absorbs the cosmic wisdom and breaks the cycle.

The bottom line is all relationships provide an opportunity for growth. Either you learn those lessons now, or you must learn them later. The choice is yours.

EXERCISE
LEARNING FROM RELATIONSHIPS

Think about the most significant relationships (both good and bad) in your past. How did you handle these connections? Did you accept the positive energy offered? How did you process the negative energy the other person/people subjected you to? Did you internalize the anger and violence or convert this energy into a positive force in your life?

Now, consider the positive and negative relationships in your present moment. Recognize that you have brought each one of these into your life for a purpose. What is there for you to learn that will enhance your connection to your Core-Energy? Is it unconditional love, forgiveness, tolerance, or acceptance of self? Perhaps you need to learn to use your creative power in a more effective way?

These are often hard realities to analyze. In particular, it's difficult to accept the fact that the most challenging people in your life are your greatest teachers. It's true! Until you can understand and appreciate even the most damaging relationships, you will not be open to learning the lessons embedded within them.

It is essential that we open our hearts and process everything we face. Otherwise, we will relive the same cycles—over and over again.

CHAPTER 36:

YOU ARE A GATEWAY TO BLISS

IF OUR PRIMARY AIM IS to perfect the link between energy and matter (as I propose), then the question becomes: "What would this experience be like?" When our sentience evolves into a pure channel for Source-Energy, how will our human experience change? We can only imagine, but I do occasionally get to experience a small taste of what this must be like. I call it "dropping in" because the sensation I get is like a bliss bomb has been launched from a great altitude into my mind and body.

I believe these moments represent a foreshadowing of our potential destiny—and it is amazing! The power of these experiences keeps me hungry to grow; to move forward and evolve as quickly as possible; to place my consciousness in a position to access the full power of my Spirit.

The Spiritual-Self is always striving to perfect its conscious connection to this material dimension and propels us forward on our individual and collective journeys as sentient beings. Because we are happiest and most fulfilled when our brain and biology serve as a gateway (rather than an obstacle) to this process, we must gather the tools and experience we need to move our consciousness from our brain to our Core-Self.

This is a bit like establishing a master-student relationship, whereby the brain is subordinated to a supporting role that allows our Core-Self to take control. This movement of the brain stepping aside and allowing the high-frequency energy of Core-Self to flow into your physical form is often accompanied by an amazing physical sensation. It feels as if all of your senses go from black and white to technicolor in a blink of an eye. When pure consciousness has "dropped into" your avatar-human form, everything becomes more "alive" and ecstatic, and Creative-Energy is abounds. In a sense, this is exactly what is happening. You are allowing your Core-Energy to take over your physical form and do what it does.

The extent to which you can open this energetic channel affects every aspect of your experience in this physical realm—your emotional state, your physical state, your interactions with others, and even the form and function of the creative power you can bring into the world.

EXERCISE
LEARNING TO "DROP IN"

The key to opening and expanding your channel to Core-Energy is *awareness*. You start by understanding what you *are not*. You delete any concept of "self" attached to your physical form operating in this material life. Instead, recognize that *you are* pure Creative-Energy that is using your life to perfect its access to this material dimension. You are using this life to enhance your ability to manifest your unique creative impulses. The real "you" wants nothing more than to unleash ecstatic, creative joy into this world. All the "physical you" needs to do is learn how to be a channel for this energy.

Once you understand the dynamic between your physical form and your Core-Self, you can bypass your thinking mind to allow Core-Energy to flow into your body. The exercise of "dropping in" to your body can involve any action that takes your brain out of the equation and raises the frequency of your energy. This might include meditating, playing music, dancing, exercising, making art, praying, chanting, writing, performing, having sex, closing a business deal... anything that manifests the hallmark characteristics of Source-Energy—which is the joyous impulse to create.

It might seem counterintuitive, but you can also activate your connection to Source-Energy through a host of actions that have the potential for negative consequences. These might include drug use, extreme sports, violence, criminal activity, or gambling. The "rush" achieved from these activities comes from the same Source, and the flow of energy activates the same biochemical compounds (such as adrenaline, serotonin, and dopamine). In this way, Creative-Energy is agnostic as to social norms and morality. Unfortunately, these behaviors (like all actions) have direct karmic consequences that can never be avoided... for good or bad.

CHAPTER 37:

YOU ARE INDEFINABLE

I FIRST ENCOUNTERED THE CONCEPT OF "equanimity" when I began my exploration of Eastern Religious practices. Equanimity is often described as the ability to remove oneself from a situation emotionally so that it no longer has power over your state of consciousness. As I have had major struggles with burying emotional trauma in the past, equanimity sounded like a dressed-up version of suppressing and repressing negative energy—which I wanted no part of!

It took time to realize that the Eastern idea of equanimity is more nuanced and positive. You don't shield yourself from the pain of life. Instead, you place yourself in a position to process the pain in an objective and healthy way.

I now use this practice every day of my life, and it is an essential component of my spiritual growth. I still experience the pain of the world—in fact, I feel it more because I am no longer deflecting or suppressing it. By establishing this viewpoint, I can remain calm, stable, and composed, especially under stress. It empowers me to respond to the trials and tribulations of life objectively, rather than from my base emotions.

The practice of equanimity is a characteristic feature of many Eastern religions, but modern Western culture tends not to emphasize it. In Eastern traditions, equanimity involves the ability to process life's events in a calm, positive manner, without being overrun by the chaotic, self-serving machinations of the mind. Fundamental to this process is the understanding that the True-Self lives somewhere outside of your physical form and brain.

The real "you" is not defined by life's circumstances or by the roles you play in this lifetime. However, this viewpoint is in dramatic opposition to the perspective of most modern human beings because today's societies believe that an individual's *ego* is synonymous with *self*. In this modern paradigm, a person's defined identity is connected to the *brain's* assessment of what makes up self, such as:

- the roles we play within our family, tribe, and society;
- our physical appearance and the health of our body;
- past events embedded in our memory;
- feedback from society; and
- our occupations and interests; etc.

The practice of equanimity is based on the notion that in this physical realm, the real you is indefinable. When you recognize that your mind is not the seat of your authentic self, as noted earlier, you gain a powerful tool for achieving dominion over the mind-induced ego-state. As events unfold in life, the mind's natural inclination, moment to moment, is to process these events through the filter of one of the many "identities" it has established for you. These identities are stories (both positive and negative) you tell yourself about who you are and your place in the world. They are labels your brain uses to help it process the waterfall of stimuli coming in at every moment. When our mind-constructed labels and ideas about self are challenged, the mind goes to work, trying to protect our sense of self. We revert to our "fight-or-flight" instinct and either lash out against the challenge (fight) or bury the pain within our psyche so we don't have to deal with it (flight).

By separating yourself from your mind's chatter, you realize that the events of life are only happening to your physical form, not to your True-Self. This allows you to respond to life from a position of strength and to make conscious decisions that contribute to your highest expression of self, instead of reacting to the whims of your emotional confusion. This is the gift of equanimity!

Daily life is chock full of events that challenge our ego's definition of self and deliver pain to our doorstep. It can be a rebellious child that undermines your sense of authority; it can be an economic situation that challenges your role as provider; it can be a health issue that diminishes your physical capacity; it can even be a one-finger salute from a fellow motorist that exposes your fallibility as a driver. Your ego wants to defend against these intrusions by attacking or repressing. But you can learn to use *equanimity* instead.

EXERCISE
ESTABLISHING EQUANIMITY

As with many paths to spiritual growth, practicing *awareness* is the key to using equanimity in your daily life. Through awareness of your thoughts and reactions, you become conscious of your ego attachments and can take the steps to move your mind beyond those attachments:

Step One:
Step back and *observe* the situation and your mind's reaction to it.

Step Two:
Examine the mind's motivation for its reaction objectively.

Step Three:
Process the emotions attached to the reaction.

Step Four:
Correct the mind's behavior consciously.

Step Five:
Choose a healthy course of action and/or reaction.

This process might seem complicated, and at first, it will feel clunky. You will use these steps after the fact to evaluate a situation. That's OK. With practice, your brain will become more responsive to the process and allow equanimity to serve as your default reaction.

CHAPTER 38:

YOU HAVE THE POWER OF ATTRACTION

Dallas, Texas is not on the front line of innovative spiritual thought. Early in my spiritual journey, I felt stifled and frustrated by the lack of any sort of like-minded community that could support my spiritual-exploration efforts. I had already planned my basic theory on the mechanisms for creating reality, so I put them to the test. By aligning my intentions and expectations, I resolved to manifest a beacon of light within the spiritual wasteland. Having stated my intention to the universe, I sat back and awaited a response.

The universe responded almost instantaneously—and in a most unexpected way! To make a long (dull) story short, a situation arose where legal mediation was required for an unresolved dispute with a home repair contractor. Against all odds, the lawyer heading up the mediation was none other than a spiritual pioneer who has served as my mentor since that day. An improbable set of circumstances led to an impossible outcome: a New Age spiritual lawyer?... in Texas? *Please—the odds are beyond absurd!*

This is just one example of a multitude of improbable serendipities that were orchestrated in my life through an alignment of Creative-Energies. It seems to make no difference how outlandish or fanciful the request; if I align my creative power with Source-Energy, help always comes riding in!

A big part of our creative arsenal is the power to draw in connections to help construct our vision of reality. Within the realm of our Spiritual-Self, there is a limitless well of Souls willing to forge alliances and lend a hand toward actualizing our dreams and desires. We have direct access to this resource; however, far too often we view this power as fanciful and discount it as chance or coincidence—or as only accessible to a lucky few. This negative attitude becomes a self-fulfilling prophecy. Once we deny ourselves the power to attract what we need, the world conforms to the energy of our negative expectations by placing a cap on the connective energy coming into our life.

The Power of Attraction

If you survey the world around you, you notice certain individuals seem to attract the help they need to accomplish their goals. As if by magic, doors open, opportunities present themselves, and just the right people show up to aid in their creation process. Some may attribute this success to "hard work." While our actions play a huge role in our success, we are all familiar with examples of individuals who "work their fingers to the bone" yet make no progress toward actualizing their dreams. So, hard work alone cannot account for this apparent good fortune. There must be other forces at play that contribute to our ability to attract what we need.

Indeed, tapping into the power of attraction involves focusing on several energetic tools to support a common, creative theme.

It requires that our thoughts, feelings, and actions work in unison to deliver the same energetic message to the universe. If your thoughts and beliefs are not aligned to support your objectives, you will toil forever with no hope of making progress. Likewise, you might possess a grand vision for your life, but if you are too insecure or lazy to let your actions reinforce those dreams, then you are stuck in a state of "wishful thinking."

The ability to leverage your "attraction" powers requires that all of your creative forces be aligned. An apt analogy is a rowboat in which the paddles row in opposite directions. The boat rotates in a circle, going nowhere. Likewise, if your thoughts, beliefs, and actions are misaligned (i.e., are not rowing in the same direction), you will never attract the resources you need to manifest your dreams and desires.

If you feel "stuck" and are not accomplishing what you want, it might be time to evaluate how you are channeling your Creative-Energy. Are the energies of your thoughts, feelings, and actions supporting one another and uniting to attract the resources you need? If not, you need to recognize that you are creating competing energy patterns. These energies can cancel each other out and lead to personal stagnation. When this happens, life can become monotonous, predictable, or boring.

If you find yourself in this predicament, take risks. Reach outside your comfort zone. Work on the creative forces that are not supporting your needs, desires, and visions. This does not have to mean a radical overhaul of your life. In fact, it is better to start with small experiments in growth and build your new reality, bit by bit, over time. For example, perhaps you have a persistent habit of expecting the worst from the people around you. When you understand that you are "creating" this situation by drawing out the worst in people (or attracting negative people into your environment), you can change the narrative. When you focus on the positive aspects of those around you and expect that others who possess positive, supportive energies will enter your life, your reality will conform to your higher-frequency outlook. It will amaze you!

You can apply this same experimental process to every area of life. Pick an area of weakness in your thoughts, feelings, or actions that is not aligning with where you want to go and figure out a way of reversing the energy 180 degrees. In short order, miracles will take place. Seemingly "random" individuals will enter your field of view with just the right skill, information, or connection to actualize your vision. Circumstance will drop in "out of nowhere" that provides the important missing pieces of your puzzle. It is all the result of aligning your creative tools.

CHAPTER 39:

YOUR EXPECTATIONS BUILD YOUR FUTURE

I AM ETERNALLY BLESSED TO HAVE found a life partner who is a magnificent example of turning passion, determination, and hard work into material reality. Indeed, she embodies the process of channeling Creative-Energy into existence. She is also an extraordinarily talented businessperson, marketer, and charismatic leader.

As our relationship grew, we discovered that our unique talents and gifts blended in a way that compounded our ability to manifest our dreams and ambitions. Together, we are an unstoppable force! This realization eventually led us to join forces and build a highly successful marketing agency.

Our intention was to sell our agency one day. After twenty-two years of hard work and extraordinary business growth, we felt the time had come to find the right suitor. Of course, we put our Creative-Energy to work and set the stage for bringing this intention to reality. Sure enough, potential acquisition partners began appearing.

If you have ever bought or sold a company, you understand the unfathomable time, effort, stress, due diligence, and legal documentation that comes with the process. Within the next three years, we explored four different acquisition opportunities—each ending in our decision not to proceed for an array of reasons.

The acquisition process was both frustrating and exhausting. Our desire to sell had not waned, but we wondered why the perfect partner had not yet materialized. So, we became even more specific about our expectations by setting an aggressive valuation for the company and visualizing the specific characteristics of our "perfect" acquisition partner. Within two months, two potential suitors emerged. A bidding war erupted. We closed the acquisition with the "perfect" partner within an unprecedented time period of ninety days. Now that is some reality-creating power!

Like a painter stretching and priming a canvas, preparing it to receive artistic expression, or like a builder, erecting a frame on which to construct a building, you too can lay the foundation on which to apply your creative impulse. You can use the present moment to project your desires into your *future* reality.

Before we explore the mechanisms of projecting reality, realize that the physics of energy are not bound either by *time* or *place*. Energy can be expressed anywhere and everywhere, and in the past, present, or future. As beings comprising energy, we can learn to harness these characteristics to our advantage. Take a moment to evaluate your expectations. Are you a "the glass is half-full" or "half-empty" person? Do you expect daily life to work against your efforts or support them? Do you have confidence in your talents and abilities, or do you feel fear or insecurity? Are you comfortable with who you are, or do you require validation from others?

Now, ponder how your day-to-day reality matches up with your expectations. Do you wonder why bad things happen to you, or are you amazed at the blessings that flow your way? In fact, reality always reflects our beliefs and expectations, and this phenomenon is far from coincidental! The road to our future reality is paved with our expectations in the present moment. Keep in mind that for energy, time is relative. There is no difference between our present and the future. What we project will always take form, either in the present or the future.

Harnessing the foundational power of energy can seem almost magical. The creative power of setting a clear intention allows you to reach into the future and set the stage for receiving your desired reality. As an example, imagine this scenario: You have an important meeting scheduled. While you have a desired outcome for this gathering, there might be antagonistic personalities involved who have the potential to derail the proceedings and create an undesirable outcome. You can head down one of two paths.

On Path One, you can obsess about the possible unwanted outcome by imagining the influence of the negative personalities and all the potential obstacles you might encounter. Many will tell you that this is the "prudent" course of action... that it is wise to flesh-out every conceivable problem so you are prepared to address them if and when they arise. In effect, however, this approach risks setting up a negative expectation for the proceeding—creating a foundation that supports a scenario of failure instead of success. Your negative expectations can "pre-wash" each of the participants with a wave of negative energy that reinforces their antagonistic positions. You might indeed be prepared to address potential problems and concerns, but if your preparation turns into "fear of the unknown," you risk subverting the overall desired outcome.

On Path Two, you use your energy in advance to manipulate a positive outcome for the meeting. It is not wrong to recognize the potential opposing forces and to prepare to overcome objections, but you must establish a set of expectations that conform to your desired outcome.

EXERCISE
CREATING YOUR DESIRED OUTCOME

- The first step is to visualize your success. Hold fast to a vision of your desired result. What does it look like? What does it feel like? What impact will this outcome have on your reality?

- Next, visualize the proceedings of the meeting. How do you want it to progress? How do you want the participants to receive your information?

- Now, reach out through your Energetic-Self to the energetic forms (the Spirits) of each participant. Solicit their participation to help with the proceedings and your desired outcome. Agree to accept their help in achieving your objectives.

You have now laid the groundwork for reality to build upon your vison. All of creation is aligned to help you achieve your objectives!

There is, however, one last step to this process. This involves the *release* of the specific outcome. How many times have you desired something but later either regretted receiving it or were grateful it did not come to pass? It happens all the time, right? The fact is our limited perspective does not always provide a solution that represents the highest benefit to us and those around us. You can take control of this potential conflict by releasing your expectations to the universe. Once you establish your desires and expectations, release the outcome to the Field of Creative-Energy by expressing the additional desire, "I am thankful that my intention has been fulfilled, or for another manifestation that serves my greatest benefit."

Once released, your Core-Energy will achieve the very best scenario for you, whether you use this process for a business meeting or for any other area of life. Allow the wisdom of your Spirit to work for your highest good!

CHAPTER 40:

UNIQUENESS IS YOUR SUPERPOWER

My HEROES AND ROLE MODELS always have one thing in common—they are *creative rebels*. I am most attracted to those willing to buck against staid conventionality and chart their own course, to pursue their unique brand of individual expression fearlessly, and to let their "freak flag" fly in all its idiosyncratic glory! This explains my love for modern art, experimental music, and art-house movies—any creative articulation of *uniqueness*, no matter the medium. This also explains the attraction I have to my wife—she is a fearless badass who marches to her own drummer.

So, what is going on here? Why am I so attracted by these expressions of uniqueness? Why are some people so repulsed by them? Well, using my emerging theory of reality, I find there is a simple explanation. As usual, it all comes down to the flow of Energy.

As we have explored, Source-Energy prioritizes diversification (among humans) as the most efficient way to perfect our evolutionary link with Source. High-frequency Creative-Energy is predisposed to flow through channels that support this diversification. As a result, when we tap into a new or novel mode of expression, we align with the objectives of Source-Energy and open the floodgate for Creative-Energy to flow through us. We are rewarded energetically for exploring our individuality—our uniqueness!

When we encounter an original expression of Self, whether through the arts, literature, business, technology, or personality, we can feel the flow of energy. It is palpable, and it is attractive. We connect to it energetically, not intellectually. It is not until after we connect that our mind can process the energy as information. This is why we respond emotionally to creativity—we are processing the energy through our feelings.

Of course, sometimes we interpret unique expression negatively. We find it frightening, threatening, or unsettling. Two people can have an opposite reaction to the same thing. It all comes down to energetic alignment. If we harbor a worldview that restricts growth, change, or personal evolution, we will feel threatened by energy that pushes beyond those boundaries. Because of this, our response to uniqueness is a great litmus test for our alignment with the evolutionary nature of Source.

Your uniqueness is your superpower. Your innate gifts, combined with your unique life experience, provide an original perspective through which you can assist the evolution of humanity. In fact, the ability to actualize your distinctive abilities drives your life-force. To express them brings joy, increased energy, and fulfillment, while not expressing them leads to frustration and depression.

In every moment, you possess a well of Creative-Energy just waiting for you to focus it on your mission—to express your uniqueness. The key to this process is to celebrate what makes you different from everyone else. You must filter out the pressures to conform and resist any impulse to be mediocre. You must learn to follow your inner voice and pursue your dreams, no matter what the reaction from others might be. You must choose to follow the impulse that paints your dreams and fantasies. You must let your unconventional, non-conformist "freak flag" fly in all its glory. Once you do this, your natural Creative-Energy will flow, and life will transform into a reflection of your unique imagination.

CHAPTER 41:

YOUR SPIRIT WILL GUIDE YOU TO FULFILLMENT

So MUCH OF WHAT WE do in life seems to be disconnected from our Spiritual-Core—from who we are and from our true evolutionary mission for this lifetime. From careers to relationships and leisure pursuits, our energy is directed by the expectations of others, whether they be family, society, culture, or the media. Is it any wonder we feel lost, misdirected, and unfulfilled?

I spent a big swath of my life in this very situation. I toiled, worried, and obsessed over goals that meant very little to me. This led me down some dark paths and took me in directions antithetical to the desires of my Core-Self. Regardless, I am grateful for these mistakes because they each provided a valuable lesson I needed to learn in order to get to where I am today. One of the hardest things I had to learn was *to allow* things to happen in their own time and in their own way. Often, the more we push, the more mess we make. It comes down to trusting your connection with Spirit and having confidence that the universe has your best interests at heart.

∞

In the West, we are conditioned to control every aspect of life. We are planners. We set up expectations for how our life should look—and we want this vision to happen "yesterday." However, our mind lacks the perspective for perceiving the optimal path and timing for the channeling of Creative-Energy. Because we cannot see "the big picture," we force energy onto paths that may not match the objectives of our Spirit. This leads to frustration (when events don't transpire in our timeline), or we force things to happen, often with disastrous consequences.

If you are not living consciously (if you do not understand the proclivities and limitations of your mind), you are throwing Creative-Energy toward desires separate from the objectives of your Higher-Self. Because Creative-Energy is agnostic, it will go about the business of manifesting your desires even if they do not line up with the evolutionary goals of your Spirit. As a result, you risk accumulating karmic energy that works against your Spiritual objectives.

The opposite experience occurs when your energy follows the mission of your Higher-Self. You can picture the flow of Creative-Energy like the flow of water, which seeks the path of least resistance. For us, this path corresponds to the objectives of our individual Spirit. When Creative-Energy is following the will of our Spirit, creation feels smooth. Effortless. Opportunities appear. Healthy relationships materialize to give help. Abundance flows into your life.

When you direct your energy *outside* the purview of the Spirit, you activate a karmic chain of events with negative consequences. Instead of flowing, energy becomes constricted. Stifled. This creates stress and feelings of anxiety, hopelessness, or frustration. The resultant creations might seem great in the short run, but they always harbor negative consequences.

Learning to rest in the belief that there is a greater plan beyond your mind's ability to conceptualize it is difficult. It requires you to have faith in your Higher-Self and to understand that there is a force at play that is designed to actualize your best self.

Aligning with Your Spiritual Objectives

Think back on your life. Sometimes things have come easily, and sometimes everything you touched seemed to go bad. This is not good luck or bad luck. This is not because you are chosen as "special" or have been cursed. The simple explanation is that sometimes you are aligned with your Spiritual purpose and sometimes you are not. There are no boundaries around your creative abilities. In fact, your Spirit wants you to create as much as you desire. The more, the bigger, the better! There is, however, a way to create that optimizes not only your personal evolution but the evolution of the rest of humanity. This process involves aligning the intentions of your mind with the intentions of your Spiritual-Self.

Step One: The first step in this process subjugates the goals of the ego to the objectives of higher consciousness. For example, you might want financial abundance, but to what end? Are you gratifying the ego's craving for status, material possessions, and security, or is there a higher aim for this wealth? This does not mean that we can't enjoy the benefits of wealth. In fact, we should! However, your Spirit has greater aspirations for this lifetime. Once you tap into these Spiritual objectives, wealth creation transforms into abundance that no longer carries negative karmic repercussions. This same viewpoint can be carried into every area of life, from relationships to artistic expression to business and financial success.

Step Two: This step involves releasing expectations back to your Spiritual-Self. The perspective of your brain is so limited that it cannot conceive the most beneficial way to actualize your dreams. Therefore, once you set an intention, it must be released to the wisdom of the Spirit. This permits Core-Energy to work on your behalf to create events and circumstances to serve your cause and to attract individuals that can assist with your journey. This also means that you surrender your expectations regarding timing. Your intentions will actualize at the perfect moment. Rushing this timetable out of impatience serves only to shortchange your capacity to create.

Step Three: The ultimate step entails recognizing present and future creative outcomes. The energy of gratitude is powerful. Its frequency synchronizes with creation and provides a kind of scaffolding upon which creation can form. Being thankful in advance for achieving your intention releases the energy to the Spiritual-Realm and supports the brain's link to this process. Expressing gratitude once you witness creation in action helps reprogram the brain to accept the existence of a higher power, which assists the flow of Creative-Energy for the future.

By allowing the Spirit both to set your intentions and take part in their creation, you can transform the process from a struggle into a joyful expression of who you are. This is the only way to ensure that you achieve your potential for this lifetime!

CHAPTER 42:

CREATIVE-ENERGY MUST BE FILTERED AND CONTROLLED

THE OLDER I GET, THE more I realize the importance of controlling the energy coming into my environment. I recognize now that all the energy swirling around me has the potential to affect my reality. This becomes even more critical today because we are in constant contact with electronic media. If I watch the nightly news, or pull up certain social media sources, I come away feeling stressed and anxious. Make no mistake, this is an example of energy transforming into material reality!

Our general lack of awareness around the potential effects of the energy in our environment stymies our ability to control how it affects our lives. As a result, we can find ourselves ping-ponging between anxiety and euphoria, depending on what enters our field of perception. Until we learn to filter this energy, we remain slaves to any energetic breeze blowing our way!

Daily life is awash with the energy of innumerable frequencies. In and of themselves, these frequencies cannot be classified as good or bad. Some are of a higher frequency, and some are lower, but they all have the potential to create something in this material realm. The energy itself is benign; however, it is the intention behind the energy that determines its creative direction. As an example, think of the plethora of radio waves associated with the multitude of communication devices that we use every day—from radios and televisions to mobile phones and Wi-Fi. This electromagnetic radiation is always streaming around us and through us. If we tune into a particular frequency, we might find some of this communication inspirational or educational, while other radio waves contain violent or hateful content. The energy is the same, but the intent behind the energy governs its creative content. The same is true for all the energy we encounter in life. Some energy is helpful, some is harmful, and some is neutral to our growth and wellbeing.

We are bombarded by Creative-Energy with differing frequencies and intentions. Unfortunately, many people stumble through life being thrown around by this chaotic input. By absorbing the surrounding energy indiscriminately, you can create an existence that swings from one extreme to the other. One moment you are feeling up; the next moment you are feeling down. *Unless you take control of your energy intake, you will never have control over your life.*

Filtering Energy from Media

The good news is we can learn to filter the type of energy we absorb. Of course, much of this energy comes from the media and entertainment we consume. Make no mistake, everything you view, listen to, and read comes with an energetic signature. Unless you learn to process this information in an active, healthy way, you leave yourself open to its effects, whether positive or negative. The nature of these interactions may seem impersonal, but your mind is conditioned to accept and internalize this energy. Ask yourself, "What external sources of information am I consuming that are having an adverse effect on my emotional and mental wellbeing?" You must make a conscious decision to restrict, block out, or avoid these stimuli.

Filtering Energy from People

Another major source of energy comes from our interactions with other people. Of course, we are always going to encounter individuals spewing negative energy, but unlike electronic media, it is much harder to avoid confronting this kind of energy. The first line of defense is to avoid or remove yourself from harmful energy exposure, but much of the time, this is not possible or realistic. Instead, we can learn how to process energy from personal interactions in a way that does us no harm and might even raise the energetic frequency of the other individual.

For many people, employing this technique means overriding their socialized compulsions to please and solve problems for others. You can have compassion and empathy without allowing someone's destructive energy to have a negative impact on you. We can train ourselves not to respond to stimuli. Through awareness, we can override our brain's fight-or-flight instinct and take a considered approach to the energy to which we are exposed. We can develop the skills to use any form of energy (even negative energy) for our highest benefit. We can learn to become masters of all the energy in our environment.

To manage any energy, it is important to take stock of the legacy programming from your past, particularly the profusion of subconscious messaging that governs your reflexive actions. For interacting with others this includes the myriad dysfunctional behaviors labeled as "caring," "empathy," or "love," but that involves taking on someone else's problems or inappropriate behavior. For many seekers, this is the single greatest impediment to spiritual growth. Your evolution is contingent upon your ability to set boundaries around the energy you will accept from people around you, as well as from other stimuli coming in from your environment.

EXERCISE
PROCESSING ENERGY FROM PERSONAL INTERACTIONS

There is a way to be caring, empathetic, and loving, while not internalizing unwanted energy:

- The first step is to understand that each person is on their own special journey of evolution, which comes with their own unique set of challenges to address and obstacles to overcome. Your role is not to solve every problem, and not to serve as a repository for any negative energy. The most compassionate thing one can do is to insist that a person take responsibility for their own life and teach them how to handle their own problems. In this way, you are not internalizing the negative energy but transforming it into a useful form and reflecting it back to the individual.

- Next, it is helpful to bypass an individual's material form and visualize communicating with their Spiritual-Self. The Spirit expresses pure love, has no human hang-ups, and wants to strengthen the individual. Once you view another person from the perspective of Spirit, it is impossible to harbor any negative feelings.

All energy, even low-frequency energy coming from malicious sources, can be used for your highest creative purpose. A good example of this is using the negative feedback someone gives you to motivate you to change. The same energy could destroy your self-confidence and derail your motivation. It all depends on how you filter the information coming in. Instead of focusing on the intention of the energy source, you can flip the script, focus on your own intentions, and use any energy coming your way to uplift and inspire you. Like an alchemist, you can turn lead into gold—it is all available for your creative purpose!

CHAPTER 43:

POLARITIES ARE ESSENTIAL TO YOUR EXISTENCE

We human beings assign morality to things based on whether we perceive them as painful. For example, light seems safer and more secure than darkness, so light is *good*, while darkness is *bad*. We breathe air and we get burned by fire, so air is the domain of God and fire is the domain of Satan. You get the picture. These ascriptions are nothing but subjective constructs from our biased brains. Does an astronomer fear the night, or a chef think fire is evil? Of course not, but this is how the mind works—it wants to make sense of its environment and it wants to avoid pain, so it uses polarity as a convenient cheat sheet for interpreting the world around it.

This process is no more apparent than in today's polarized world. If we allow our mind to control our perceptions, we gravitate to one extreme view or its opposite. Anytime we do this, we shut ourselves off from the joy to be found in the opposite viewpoint, which creates friction between our "fixed" mind and a reality that does not play favorites. Your Spirit wants you to enjoy every experience and use it to develop your connection to the universe!

Material existence has a built-in paradox. It is a realm of opposite extremes—of polarities. For starters, the universe is formed from eternal energy, but in our material world, death and decay are a certainty. The existence of matter is finite. From this overarching paradoxical truth, opposing conditions can be observed everywhere: particle and wave, darkness and light, heat and cold, good and evil, suffering and bliss, and, of course, life and death. In fact, everything in this realm has an opposite, and these opposing forces are a natural source of tension for the human mind.

To illustrate this tension, let's examine our universal desire to ease suffering and achieve bliss. After all, nobody wants to suffer— right? Of course not! So, we put our life's energy into removing every potential for suffering—we accumulate material comforts, we achieve financial security, we obsess about health and nutrition. The list goes on and on. But then what happens? Every step we take to eliminate suffering brings tension—a fear, a dread, a paranoia, a desire for more! It creates an endless cycle of striving and craving. You are never satisfied, never at peace. The promise of achieving bliss is always just around the next bend, always just out of reach. "If only I could achieve this success… or, if only I had this much money… or that relationship." You spend your entire life chasing this elusive fantasy into the future. And then what? You die!

So, what happened to your choice to ease suffering and achieve bliss? In fact, it brought you nothing but dissatisfaction and misery. Worst of all, it interfered with your ability to enjoy this life. The point is not that we shouldn't strive to create a better life for ourselves and the world—in fact, we should—but we cannot deny the nature of our material realm. It comprises polarities—opposites.

Our dissatisfactions come not from life but from our inclination to choose one extreme over its opposite. We must learn to accept this material realm for what it is and savor its extremes and everything in between. Until we learn to embrace the totality of life, we amplify that which we are trying to suppress. Our mission as avatars is to enjoy all this world offers. This means embracing all of it and learning to enjoy life for the gift that it is.

Finding enjoyment in the totality of life—through good times and bad times, happiness and sorrow, success and failure, love and loss—is all about perspective. Through the perspective of the finite mind, it is an impossible task. However, from the perspective of your infinite Soul, everything becomes an experiential wonderland.

As a thought exercise, imagine being a child at an amusement park for the first time. As soon as you walk through the gates, your senses come to life! You take in the bright colors of the tents and the flashing lights of the rides. You hear the barking of the carnies, the whoosh and whiz of the rides—the screams of joy and laughter all around you. The air is filled with the scents of delectable treats of every variety. Your heart races. You are almost levitating with anticipation, joy, and excitement as you head right for the biggest rollercoaster in the park. Now, imagine being seated in the front seat of the rollercoaster as it begins its slow, *clack-clack-clacking* assent to the top. As you realize what is happening, the joy you were feeling just moments before transforms into anxiety—and fear. As you reach the top and look out over the sheer drop ahead of you, terror grips you—and you are in freefall. In an instant, the anxiety, the fear, the terror merge with the joy and excitement— you are screaming, laughing, and crying all at the same time!

What just happened? Well, you just experienced the same enjoyment from the danger as you did from the beauty. In fact, an argument could be made that the anxiety, fear, and terror experienced on the rollercoaster enhanced your joyful experience in the amusement park. It would not have been as enjoyable without these negative experiences. This is the beauty of the polarity engrained in our material realm. Without the darkness, you cannot appreciate the light. In fact, you could not experience the light because you would have nothing with which to contrast it. From the perspective of your Spiritual-Self, it is ALL exciting. Like the dive-drop on a rollercoaster, the beauty and fear, the happiness and anxiety, and the joy and the terror are all exciting experiences that should be enjoyed to the fullest!

CHAPTER 44:

MISTAKES ARE A BLESSING

LOOKING BACK OVER MY LIFETIME, it is easy to cringe at the monumental mistakes I have made along the way. It took a long time to realize that each of those failures highlighted a weakness in my development and gave me a chance to learn a valuable life lesson. Likewise, when I remember the harm others have perpetrated along my path, I can see now that each of these mistakes not only highlighted a weakness within that individual but provided me with an opportunity to grow and develop. As cringe-worthy and damaging as they may be, mistakes, errors, and failures are nothing more than a compassionate response from a universe nudging us toward perfection.

Mistakes (decisions or actions that led to behavior harmful to you or others) are an inescapable part of the human condition. In fact, the process of trial and (frequently) error is essential, both for our personal growth and for humanity to develop its connection with Source-Energy. From this perspective, mistakes are our greatest teachers and should be viewed with gratitude rather than condemnation. Things we might consider mistakes result from one of two sources. They occur when we follow a path that is not supported by Source-Energy, or they surface out of blind ignorance to the root motivation behind our actions.

There is an axiom that recognizes that "each of us does as much as we can do." Every person is on a path of growth that produces different conditions, challenges, obstacles, and different levels of enlightenment. Believe it or not, we are each doing the best we can within the circumstance of our existence. If we could behave differently or better, we would. What we might consider as faults or flaws are attributes highlighting an area for future development. Of course, the timeline for this development is unique to each individual.

Sometimes our harmful choices are intentional, and we "make a bargain with the devil" to satisfy the demands of our ego. However, often we do not know why we behave the way we do. These unconscious behaviors emerge from negative energy buried deep within our psyche. This energy lives as scars and wounds that were suppressed during this lifetime or during previous lifetimes. Our "bad behavior" (our mistakes) brings negative energy to light so we can resolve it.

Because we don't understand the cause of our behavior, our reflex is to deflect blame onto our external environment or stew in a pot of self-loathing. Instead, it is better to take responsibility for our actions and use the experience as a lesson for the future. Rejoice in knowing that you have been enlightened, pay the karmic price for your actions, and move forward, intending to resolve the negative energy that precipitated the action.

How we handle our mistakes makes all the difference in determining their impact, not only for our lives but the lives of those around us. This process starts by flipping the way we view our regrettable behavior. Most of us are conditioned to dread, fear, and fight against making a mistake. We see our blunders as shameful, as indictments of who we are, and as proof of our inadequacies. As a result, we experience our errors as direct assaults on our fragile egos. We need to learn how to transform shame into tolerance and appreciation. The transformation starts with the recognition that everyone is learning and developing. Supporting every person's life is an agreement between Source and a person's Soul, that their physical form will navigate the challenges necessary to learn certain lessons. The larger the challenge, the more significant the lesson is. The more significant the lesson is, the harder it is to learn.

Of course, this same principle holds true in our daily lives. The largest achievements require the greatest amount of effort and risk. As a result, some of our hardest spiritual lessons require us to overcome some tough situations. If this describes your life—congratulations on having the fortitude to attempt a huge evolutionary leap during this lifetime! However, know that this leap will cause a lot of corresponding failures. You will make a bunch of mistakes along the way. When you look at your life (and at the lives of those around you), give yourself a break. Evolving is hard work, and if you (or someone else) are dealing with a host of difficult obstacles, it becomes even harder. As you experience your mistakes (or the mistakes of others), understand that *we are all doing the best we can*!

SECTION IV:
KARMIC-FORCE

SECTION IV:
KARMIC-FORCE

Framework for Section IV: Karmic-Force

In SECTION III, WE DID an analysis of how each of us creates reality. We learned the sentient brain not only provides us with the ability to access the will of our Divine Spirit, but it also serves as an obstacle to us expressing this will in the material world. This insight allows us to mold our mind into a tool for healing low-energy creations and actualizing reality according to our highest self.

In Section IV, we pay special attention to the fundamental force that governs all human action—Karmic-Force. Actions have lasting consequences, and this is incorporated, in one form or another, into every wisdom tradition. However, it is the Eastern traditions (particularly the Hindu and Buddhist traditions) that provide a detailed map of the cycle of cause and effect. These traditions offer logical insight into the ramifications of our actions, and they formulated the concept of "preservation of energy" thousands of years before modern science recognized it. These traditions also show that the preservation of energy is woven into the fabric of existence. In short, we must always account for the energy channeled through our actions.

In this section, we examine the energy generated from our actions (called karma). We define the Law of Karma and delve into the role karma plays in each of our lives. We examine its effect on the reality of the present moment, the future, and even the past. We also dive into controlling and transforming karmic energy to heal the past and to minimize its negative effects on the future.

Our discussion of karma also takes us to some unexpected places. We see its influence on our personal relationships, and we discover its impact through the existence of hyper-evolved beings (people whose connection to Source-Energy far exceeds the general population's) that walk among us.

Karmic-Force is the inseparable energetic link between our actions and the reality we create. An understanding of this corollary allows us to leverage karmic power for our highest good.

KARMIC-FORCE

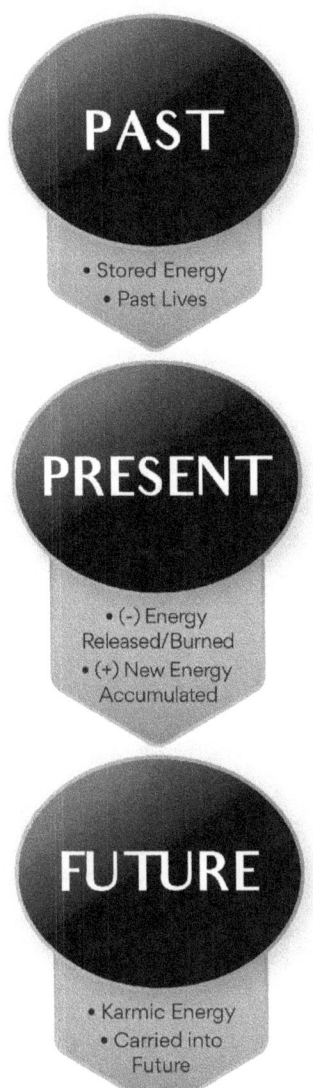

PAST
• Stored Energy
• Past Lives

PRESENT
• (-) Energy
Released/Burned
• (+) New Energy
Accumulated

FUTURE
• Karmic Energy
• Carried into
Future

This diagram shows the component parts of Karmic-Energy. Everyone begins with a pool of legacy karma from past lifetimes and spends each subsequent life both adding to and releasing stored energy. The net balance of Karmic-Energy is carried into future lifetimes.

CHAPTER 45:

HUMANITY IS GOVERNED BY THE LAW OF KARMA

My HISTORY WITH ABUSE, ABANDONMENT, and poverty left me shattered—a mass of fear, insecurity, anger, and self-loathing. It makes sense I developed an intense mistrust of life. I had no context for processing all the negative experiences dished out to me, and I sunk into a pit of despair and depression. It took many years and a lot of work to dig myself out of that pit, and my exploration into the concept of karma was a primary driver of this renewal. Once I came to the full understanding of the Law of Karma, the turmoil, the chaos, the violence, the crazy people in my life—the whole shooting match—made sense. It gave meaning to all of it!

The Law of Karma

The Law of Karma is fundamental to the inner workings of creation, but it is often misunderstood. To help conceptualize karma, its characteristics, and how it affects our life, it is important to understand how we interact with Creative-Energy once it is channeled into existence.

As we bring Creative-Energy into our material realm, it is absorbed into our overall "energy profile," which is all the energy accumulated from our past living within our material being in the present moment. You can think of this process as similar to how the body uses food. As we eat, our body absorbs the components of the food (both good and bad), and they become an elemental part of every cell. Likewise, when we channel Creative-Energy, it becomes an element in our energetic profile. We are an accumulation of all the energy (good or bad) we have channeled into existence through our thoughts, feelings, and actions. Our material self, in this moment, is a direct reflection of our accumulated energy.

Karma represents the Creative-Energy channeled through our *actions*. This energy has the same profile as all forms of Creative-Energy:

- it is agnostic as to intent (it creates whatever we direct it to create, without preference);
- it cannot be destroyed (but only converted into another form of energy); and
- it attracts other energy of the same vibrational frequency.

The adages "You reap what you sow" and "You cannot escape your past" are both commentaries on *karma*. If your actions project love, kindness, and generosity into the world, your reality will reflect the same. Then again, if your actions project fear, anger, greed, and violence, this energy will materialize in your life. There are no exceptions to the Law of Karma. It is the great cosmic "scale of justice." All the chickens come home to roost—whether in this lifetime or the lifetimes to come.

For some people, this is reassuring. There is a certain comfort in knowing that good works will lead to a reward in this material realm. Likewise, it's satisfying to know that a perpetrator of atrocities will pay the price. For others, however, the concept that we are responsible for the energy spawned from our actions is daunting.

Negative Karma

Keep in mind, with karma, *behavior* is the driving force. When our actions channel low-frequency energy, low-frequency reality is created. The form this creation takes might vary over time, including:

1. Negative events or consequences;
2. Negative feeling or emotional states; or
3. Negative physical conditions for the body (i.e., disease, malady, etc.).

This may strike us as unsettling, but there is no getting around it. We will always experience the consequences of our actions, whether intentional or unintentional.

The effects of negative karma will continue in a form, time, and place of their own choosing. However, there are ways to influence how our karmic justice is doled out, and we can take measures to ensure negative energy does not compound in the future.

As you might imagine, karmic energy manifests itself in myriad ways. For starters, it influences how and where you emerge in this lifetime. For many of us, the karma from our past lives contributes to the circumstances in which we are born. Our family, physical form, socioeconomic origins, as well as our innate talents, abilities, and handicaps are all influenced, not only by the desire for spiritual growth but also by our karmic legacy.

As an example, perhaps you were born into a turbulent family, hard socio-economic conditions, or the like. These challenges and difficulties might be a direct legacy of actions from past lives. These hardships allow you to pay the price for these actions and prevent this negative karma from following you any further.

Burning Off Negative Karma

This brings us to the concept of "burning off" negative karma. All negative karma originates from a place of ignorance. We channel low-frequency energy into life because we are not yet developed enough to do otherwise. Therefore, at the heart of negative energy is an opportunity to evolve—to learn a valuable lesson for connecting to Source. You can view karmic energy as "tough love" from the universe. It might be painful, but it is there to help you learn. Negative karma will remain in place until we progress out of it—and learn the lesson!

"Burning off" negative karma means taking harmful negative karmic energy and turning it into high-frequency energy that is beneficial to evolving our connection to Source. Once this alchemy takes place, you can process the karmic effects in a manner beneficial to you and those around you!

The cornerstone of this process is to stop avoiding the consequences of trapped karma and to embrace the pain and unpleasantness. In short, before you can change negative energy, you must *pay your karmic debt*. By bringing complete awareness to the pain and suffering caused by your actions, and experiencing all of this pain for yourself, you bring this energy to a place where you can identify the ignorance that caused the action in the first place.

Unfortunately, there are no shortcuts. The karmic debt must be paid (you must suffer) and then you must learn the lesson embedded within the suffering. Through actualizing the lesson, you have transitioned the negative energy into high-frequency energy aligned with Spirit.

As you can see, ridding yourself of negative karma does not prevent you from facing the consequences of your actions. In fact, you might experience the repercussions of your actions throughout your life. But it gives you control over how you accept the consequences, and the ability to use this energy to improve your future.

As you mature in your spiritual practice, you will view the Law of Karma not as something to dread, but as a blessing. It serves as a trusted advisor, pointing the way to a fuller, more complete expression of your Spiritual-Self.

Identifying the Source of Karmic Energy

Our aim is to manage the effects of negative karma and avoid carrying this energy into the future. Somewhat ironically, we can learn to use actions in the present moment to transform the low-frequency energy originating from past actions. The key to this process is identifying these Karmic-Forces. Once brought into the full light of consciousness, this energy can transform into another form of energy, and we can burn it off in a controlled manner. This process starts with recognizing the Karmic-Forces around you. They are often obvious, but sometimes they hide in plain sight. Karmic-Energy originates from three sources:

1. Actions from past lives;
2. Past actions from this lifetime; and
3. Actions in the present moment.

Each of these sources express karmic energy differently, so let's take a quick look at some of the less obvious manifestations within each category:

- *Actions from Past Lives:* For many people, the trials of life (particularly the beginning stages of life) represent the best opportunity to burn the negative energy from past lifetimes. This energy manifests in several ways, including health and physical challenges; problematic relationships with family, romantic partners, and business relationships; being born into a poor socio-economic environment; experiencing difficult or tragic events; and the challenges associated with the place and time of your entry into this life. It is tempting to write off these negative experiences, especially of your formative years, as originating from forces outside of your control. However, they all represent either repercussions from your prior actions, predetermined avenues for evolutionary growth, or both.

- *Past Actions from This Lifetime:* In your journey through life, every action is consequential. As a result, there is a karmic consequence for every negative action you take. Sometimes this karmic debt is paid through so-called "instant karma." Other times, this negative energy manifests as a stream of trials and tribulations throughout life. The karma that is not burned off in this lifetime accumulates and is carried forward into future lives.

- *Actions in the Present Moment:* By far, the most efficient (and least painful) way to deal with negative karma is to (as soon after the occurrence as possible) identify and then rectify the energy from negative actions. Even the most enlightened among us stumble from time to time. We react to the world through our ego or through sheer ignorance to create a wave of destructive low-frequency energy. It should be noted that this is OK and natural. It is how we learn, grow, and evolve. The important thing is to recognize these situations as soon as possible and take steps to reverse the damage to yourself and others.

EXERCISE
THE PROCESS OF BURNING OFF NEGATIVE KARMA

The key to managing all energy, whether from past lives or the present moment, is awareness. Unless you can develop the skills to bring karmic energy into your conscious mind, you will be buffeted by the effects of your past inappropriate behavior—and you won't be able to remove the negative karma. Burning karma revolves around your ability to bring this negative energy into the reality of the moment.

Step One:
Take responsibility for every negative thing in your life. Not only are you 100 percent responsible, but these things are also in your life for your benefit—to teach you an important lesson—and to help you develop.

Step Two:
Identify the negative energy circulating in your life and determine the root source. Often, your present reality is influenced by events from your formative years. These formative events might be linked to your actions in this lifetime, or they might be linked to actions from past lifetimes. Other times, your negative karma can be traced to your actions and decisions. It is important to distinguish between these two sources because your discernment has a bearing on how you will deal with the energy.

Step Three:
Bring the trapped energy forward and transform it. This process will vary depending on whether the energy originated from this lifetime or from a past life. For past-life karma, it is essential to bring any suppressed pain to the surface. You must face all the pain and hurt. It is imperative you feel all of it! Bring yourself back to the moment— back to the hurt child; back to the tragic event; back to the abuse, neglect, or failure.

For karmic energy originating in this lifetime, you must do the same thing. Bring yourself back to the action. Feel the shame, uncontrolled anger, fear. You must feel it all in a real and tangible way. Start by picturing the damage you caused, not only to your own life, but to the lives of others. Feel the hurt and pain that you caused. Embrace the pain and suffering. Take responsibility for all of it! Now you are converting this trapped energy into the energy of your thoughts, emotions, and physical reactions. You are transforming the energy into a form that you have control over.

The more you allow yourself to experience the negative energy, the more converted energy you can carry into the next steps. So, let go, feel—suffer, cry, moan, scream, writhe in pain—burn that negative karma! Also, if possible, attempt to make amends for your actions. Admit your wrongdoing and express genuine remorse. Take responsibility for the damage you caused and seek forgiveness.

Step Four:

Bring yourself to equanimity. Once you have exhausted the negative energy, you are ready to step back and view the event from the compassionate perspective of your Spiritual-Self. Recognize that your physical form is a developing work in progress. Realize that everyone around you (past, present, and future) is a developing work in progress. From this perspective, view each karmic event as an opportunity to learn and grow; improve and evolve.

The key to this step is understanding and forgiveness. Forgive yourself and forgive those who have hurt you. Understand that each of us has obstacles to overcome.

Step Five:

Release the karmic energy. The last step is to release the transformed energy back into the universe. Once this energy is no longer of use—once the lesson has been learned—it should be delivered back to Source. Feel thankful for your experience because it has led you out of ignorance and into wisdom. Feel grateful that your Spirit has guided you into this transition. Now you are ready to carry this insight into the present and future.

The progression of Steps 1 – 4 takes the negative, low-frequency energy resulting from harmful actions and converts it into high-frequency energy represented by understanding and forgiveness. The last step, Step 5, transforms and raises this energy into an even higher frequency of gratitude and thankfulness.

Take a moment to feel thankful for the lessons you receive and send this energy back to the universe with feelings of immense gratitude. The miracle of this process is the alchemy of turning pain into joy.

It ensures that you will not carry bad karma into the future. As you integrate this practice, it will have a dramatic, transformative effect on your life. Instead of experiencing an ongoing cycle of negativity, your life will blossom with positive creativity. The trials and tribulations of life will no longer have a hold over you, and you will gain the certainty that comes with tapping into the great wisdom of karma.

CHAPTER 46:

REINCARNATION IS NECESSARY FOR HUMAN DEVELOPMENT

IN THE CONSERVATIVE CHRISTIAN ENVIRONMENT of my formative years, the concept of reincarnation was viewed as heretical, preposterous, and even satanic. It wasn't until my twenties that I recognized the reason that most mainstream religions had such a powerful reaction to the notion of rebirth: it is a threat to the mechanisms they use for control. After all, the promise of a utopian "heaven" is a powerful lever for controlling behavior! Once I gave myself permission to explore the idea of reincarnation, it amazed me to discover that it provided some essential missing pieces to my emerging view of reality. Not only does it offer context to our birth into this lifetime, but the concept of karma also delivers a sound scientific account for the energy generated by each of us.

A Logical Framework for Reincarnation

In physics, the Law of the Conservation of Energy states that energy cannot be created nor destroyed; it can only be transferred or transformed from one form to another. While this scientific theory was first proposed and tested in the eighteenth century by French natural philosopher and mathematician Emilie du Chatelet,[50] ancient wisdom had postulated the practical applications of this scientific notion for millennia. One such application focuses on the transition of the energy drawn into our material realm during a particular lifetime. What happens to all the energy (generated through thoughts, emotions, and actions) that has accumulated during a lifetime? When an individual dies, this energy cannot simply disappear. According to science, it must be transferred or transformed into another form of energy. This is the logical framework for both the Law of Karma and the concept of *reincarnation*.

Each of us generates and burns off a certain amount of karmic energy during our lifetime. However, every person leaves life with accumulated energy that does not just disappear magically. When you die, transitioning from your body back into the realm of pure energy, this amassed energy becomes attached to your Spirit. However, the low-frequency karmic energy generated in our material realm is not compatible with the high-frequency energy of our Spiritual-Self. As a result, there is no way to burn off this energy in the afterlife. Karmic energy generated in the material realm must be burned off in the material realm! As a result, we bring these karmic debts into subsequent lives with the expressed intent of burning off as much of this stored energy as possible.

Negative karmic energy is not some kind of spiritual punishment. Instead, it represents lessons that need to be learned in order to advance one's connection to their Spiritual-Core. This is part of the logic behind how, when, and where you entered your physical form. You placed yourself in the best possible position to experience

---

[50] Ernie Tretkoff et al., APS News, "This month in physics history: December 1706: Birth of É'milie du Châtelet," *American Physical Society Sites*, Volume 17, No. 11 (Dec. 2008), https://www.aps.org/publications/apsnews/200812/physicshistory.cfm.

the negative repercussions of your prior actions—providing yourself with the opportunity to transform (or burn) the negative energy.

For your Core-Self, this energy represents the potential for growth and evolution. These are lessons, long deferred, that we must learn in order to grow into our best selves. We must first pay for the consequences for our negative actions (past and present), and this is always painful!

In ignorance, many people attribute the manifestations coming from negative energy as misfortune. However, without exception, every one of these troubles is rooted in the negative energy an individual broadcasts into their life. This is apparent with the reservoir of negative energy accumulated from past lives. Each of us entered this life with a strategy for transforming as much of this energy as possible. In order to accomplish this aim, it is essential to bring this process into conscious awareness and to learn the lessons attached to this pool of negative energy. You must take complete responsibility for every painful event and embrace the process of clearing low-frequency energy from life.

EXERCISE
CLEARING NEGATIVE PAST-LIFE ENERGY

The process for clearing negative karma generated from your past lives is the same as clearing out any other low-frequency energy. It starts with identifying the source of the energy and bringing it into your awareness.

To begin this clearing process, first take stock of the myriad of troubles and problems you have faced from childhood through to the present moment. Ask yourself, "Which of these can I attribute to actions I have taken during my lifetime? Which were imposed upon me as a condition for entering this life?" Not that this distinction makes a vast difference, but it is easier for your mind to dismiss past-life energies as "not your fault" or as being beyond your realm of control.

Once these root energies are brought to the surface, you must realize the negative consequences derived from this energy, and also the habitual patterns of thought, feeling, and behavior that continue to feed the energy. This level of awareness will bring you to where you can take the steps to ensure that this negative karma no longer controls your life—or the next life:

Step One:
Take 100 percent responsibility for the root cause of the energy. You chose this life, and you chose your actions. Nobody is responsible for your problems but you.

Step Two:
Face the repercussions from the energy. For example, did your karma place you within a tough family dynamic or social environment? What effect did this have on you? Did it create pathologies around anger, self-worth, or fear? Whatever the effects, you must face them head-on.

Step Three:

Relive the trauma. Most likely, you have suppressed the negative feelings associated with the root energy. To burn this energy, you must express it through your feelings and psyche. You must feel every bit of the fear, anger, rage, guilt, or pain. This process is agonizing. It hurts... a lot. Paying a karmic debt is never a pleasant experience.

Step Four:

Forgiveness and release. Once you express the pain, it is time to forgive everyone involved, including yourself. Forgive the actions, forgive the ignorance, and send/release the memory into the void. Surround the transmuted energy with peace and liberate it back to Source.

Note: It may take going through the steps many times to complete this process. You will know you have completed burning the karma and learning the associated lessons when you can no longer feel the trauma—you only experience the forgiveness and peace. From here forward, this energy is transformed and will no longer follow you on your path!

CHAPTER 47

YOU CHOOSE EVERY RELATIONSHIP

WE CHOOSE OUR RELATIONSHIPS. EITHER they originate from our Spiritual-Self, or they originate from the needs of our ego-oriented mind. Because they emerge from our actions, they are linked to our karmic profile, which always results in karmic ramifications (for good or bad). This karmic energy does not disappear because you no longer have physical contact with an individual, but continues on, from lifetime to lifetime (until the energy is processed in a way that benefits each individual involved).

My life has been full of extraordinary relationships I could not have predicted or expected. There is no greater example of the power of karmic connection than meeting my wife. An entire book could be written on the improbable, serendipitous nature of our relationship. We met in a random encounter from opposite sides of the world. Battling unimaginable odds, we forged an amazing life—a successful business—and raised incredible children. All the while, our love story has been governed by the invisible hand of karmic energy. From our initial attraction to the indispensable role we play in each other's development, it is apparent that our Souls have been connected for many incarnations. Our relationship is a manifestation of our karmic legacy and our mutual desire to guide one another to a greater connection with the Divine. This is a beautiful thing to behold.

Like my relationship with my wife and children, some relationships impact life sublimely—while others create chaos. Over time, I have gained the insight to recognize that every relationship (both good and bad) represents a path to personal growth. I have learned the hard way not to avoid these lessons but to embrace them. I honor each individual as a valued teacher interested in my greater good.

Relationships have the biggest impact on the programming of our minds, which also makes them the primary determinant of how our lives unfold. Because of this, there is no such thing as an inconsequential relationship. Every connection has an influence on how the mind interprets and interacts with the world around it.

Forces That Drive Relationships

For the mind, connections with others may seem like random coincidences, or even well-thought-out collaborations. However, every interaction is rooted in the realm of energy and can broaden our connection to Source. Using relationships as a tool for growth requires understanding the fundamental forces behind these connections. These forces can be delineated into three broad categories, each of which comprises three sub-categories:

Spiritual-Force

- Karmic legacy relationships: These are relationships from past lives that follow us into this life. They represent either unlearned lessons in how to process certain energies or a collaborative agreement between Souls to support growth and development in this lifetime.

- Life lesson relationships: We come into this life with certain objectives for evolution. To assist us in this process, we prearrange partnerships with other beings. These Soul-Partners include our parents, family members, and many other relationships in our personal domains.

- Adaptive growth relationships: As we progress through this lifetime, we encounter obstacles and opportunities that require the help of other Souls. This is an agreement between Soul-Partners to provide mutual help.

Mental Force

- Subconscious relationships: Many of our relationships result from various unrecognized pathologies of the human brain. We create these relationships to fill subconscious holes in our frail psyches. Because these connections originate from the *ego*, they almost always create additional problems and obstacles. As an example, perhaps, based on psychological damage from childhood, you have trouble expressing love and affection. To fix this, you might gravitate towards partners that are overtly loving. Of course, no one but you can repair this damage, so the union will create tension.

- Reactive relationships: If your brain is controlling your responses and reactions to life, you will gravitate toward relationships that serve your mind instead of the greater evolutionary needs of your being. As a result, these interactions can be destructive or counterproductive. As an example, suppose you have a domineering and controlling personality and feel most comfortable entering relationships with weaker, submissive individuals. This imbalance results in pain for both parties.

- Analytical relationships: We often rationalize the dynamics of our relationships with others without tapping into the wisdom of our Spiritual-Self. As a result, we often make relationship decisions that end in disaster. For example, take a scenario in which you lack the confidence to express yourself artistically. To compensate, you attach yourself to a creative individual and find yourself feeling jealous or envious of their talent. Perhaps, to compensate for these ill feelings, you take advantage of their skill and expertise, learn their creative secrets—and then discover that the relationship no longer serves you.

Collaborative Force

- Conscious relationships: In order to make informed decisions, we must bring all our hidden wounds, fears, insecurities, and desires into the light of the conscious mind. Once identified, these pathologies can be processed through the lens of the Spiritual-Mind. This enables us to override our ego-based impulses and pursue relationships that are healthy and mutually beneficial.
- Coordinated relationships: Through a partnership between the mind and our Spirit, we can view other individuals from the perspective of our Spiritual-Self. This means seeing beyond the physical form to the other individual's Spirit. Nurturing relationships always involves a beautiful collaboration between Spirits. Our minds give us the ability to bring this glorious spiritual connection into our corporeal reality.
- Developmental relationships: The very nature of life is dynamic. We are not slaves to a fixed template but have been blessed with minds that give us freedom of choice. As we progress through life, the conscious collaboration between the brain and the Spirit offers unlimited possibilities for growth and evolution. Inspired thought can lead us to relationships that will assist us in our journey.

All the forces that drive relationships exist for our benefit. Whether they are positive or negative, nurturing or destructive, permanent or transitory, they represent opportunities to enhance our personal evolution and the growth of those around us. As we move through life, it behooves us to embrace this generative process and develop sincere gratitude for every relationship we have.

We all want a life filled with healthy, nurturing relationships. However, much of our personal growth is facilitated through our association with challenging and difficult individuals. In every case, the pain associated with these encounters serves as a marker that helps direct us to areas in the psyche that remain controlled by our brain-dominated ego state. You can change your perspective from one of conflict and avoidance to gratitude and openness.

It is important to recognize that your growth is not contingent on the growth of the other person. We are each responsible for our own progression. If the other person in a relationship is not open and ready to learn, the most you can do is heal yourself and extend your love and forgiveness. As you continue along life's journey, you can glean wisdom from negative relationships and cultivate the spiritual power offered by healthy interactions.

CHAPTER 48:

YOU ARE SURROUNDED BY CONNECTIONS FROM PAST LIVES

Hᴀᴠᴇ ʏᴏᴜ ᴇᴠᴇʀ ʜᴀᴅ ᴛʜᴇ experience of encountering certain people who elicit an immediate, overwhelming emotional response in you? Sometimes these interactions stir up negative feelings, but it is more common to experience intense feelings of love, caring, and joy. Whatever the case, there is usually no logical basis for the impulsive flow of emotion. It originates from a deep memory that somehow connects you with the other individual. You can sense the same recognition in the other person—they experience the same inexplicable connection with you!

I used to be skeptical of these encounters. Before I understood the relationship between our emotions and the flow of Source-Energy, I labeled these feelings as hysterical and would not act on them. I have come to recognize these experiences as beacons from my evolutionary past. They identify legacy relationships that have followed me into this lifetime for my benefit. As I have grown to honor these relationships, I now identify them as the greatest gifts to my spiritual development.

Have you ever had a "chance" encounter where there was an immediate sense of recognition—of familiarity—maybe an inexplicable love connection? Are there individuals within your family or local community with whom you feel a strong connection? These are powerful indicators that you have a historic, soul-level connection with these people.

Just as life sends difficult relationships to help us evolve, it also infuses each lifetime with relationships that offer healthy, positive energy. Many of these relationships have developed over countless lifetimes and the individuals involved share powerful energetic roots with our own Spiritual-Core. Often, these roots stem from a legacy of friend-and-family relationships that are played out by a group of souls who have committed to helping each other along the evolutionary path.

Individual expressions of Spirit may play different roles from one lifetime to another. For example, a child in one lifetime may play the parent in another, a spouse may become a close friend or relative, and so on. These legacy relationships represent a reservoir of interconnected energy. For this reason, they are the most important and impactful connections in our lives.

Legacy connections play different roles within a particular lifetime. Some exist as a pervasive guiding force throughout life, while others might manifest for a short period or for a particular purpose. These connections can be positive, or they can offer challenges designed to help each soul evolve. Whatever the role or purpose, these relationships originate from a place of love and caring. They represent an ongoing agreement between souls to help guide and nurture their material connection to Source.

Legacy connections are easy to identify. They often manifest as direct family members and/or interactions (perhaps serendipitous encounters) throughout life with individuals with whom you feel an intense "direct connection." Even within this group of longstanding relationships, there are those that are more or less prevalent or that show up with more or less regularity as you evolve through multiple lifetimes. If you can tune into the energy profile of each legacy connection, you get a sense of how much they influence your personal journey.

The key to examining the legacy relationships in life is to move your thought process from the logical mind to your intuition. You perceive these deep connections not through the brain, but through your feelings. You "feel" an inexplicable sense of connection to another person. You know you are, somehow, kindred souls. You may find it easier to feel love, caring, and compassion for these individuals. You find it easy to anticipate and respond to their needs because you can sense them. You feel a shift in your own energy when you are around them. This is how energy communicates—through feelings.

You can even take this process further by paying attention to the more subtle energy shifts within each relationship. For example, long-term legacy relationships have a different feel than more recent connections. There is more depth and gravity to ancient energetic connections.

In addition, you can even sense the role that a particular individual is to play within this lifetime. Is the encounter temporary, for a specific purpose, or will it span this lifetime? Is the primary focus for your development, the other person's growth, or both? Even the closest of relationships from a prior lifetime can manifest as a peripheral encounter in this one. The key to analyzing all of this is to move your mind from logic to emotion. Assess how the relationship *feels* to you. If you are open and honest about what you are feeling, the nature and purpose of the relationship will become obvious. Once you understand the purpose of each relationship, it is your mission to act on this information. You are not only working to develop yourself, but you are also working for the benefit of every relationship in your life.

CHAPTER 49:

TO HEAL THE PAST, YOU MUST TRANSFORM THE ENERGY OF THE PAST

I would never have thought it possible, but I no longer harbor ill will toward anyone. This capacity for tolerance and forgiveness does not stem from my own benevolent nature (Ha!) but from recognizing my capacity for horrific behavior. Not only do I regret many of my actions, but I also know that given the right set of circumstances, I am capable of even worse. In short, I can forgive others for their transgressions because their behaviors are a projection of my potential self.

In addition, I find comfort in the notion that everything in my past represents an opportunity for growth. If I so choose, the energy from even the worst events can be transformed into tools for growth. In fact, my greatest insights have come from the most miserable episodes of my past. This perspective fills me with gratitude and allows me to heal.

Understanding the Energetic Nature of the Past

Some people will claim that the past does not exist as a form, nor can the effects from the past be changed. But that is not true. Just as we can manipulate life by projecting energy into the future, we can also manipulate the present moment by moving energy into the past. To comprehend this phenomenon, we must first understand our role in transitioning energy in and out of material form.

Before it "becomes" something (such as a thought, feeling, event, or material object), pure energy begins as a frequency "wave" with no fixed position in time or space. In this state, energy has boundless opportunities to become anything that matches its frequency profile, and it will remain in this state until it is acted upon by an outside force from our material realm. Once this happens, it is no longer free-form energy that exists in a state of unlimited, creative possibilities. Instead, it becomes fixed, possessing known characteristics. We know from scientific research that when energy "breaks down" into this state, it changes from a wave into a particle and transitions from its exotic quantum form into a form governed by our standard model of "Newtonian" physics.[51]

When we channel energy through our thoughts and actions, our physical form becomes the external force that causes energy to transition from wave to particle—from a quantum state to a material state. Once this transition takes place, the energy remains trapped in its material form until it is acted upon by another force which can transmute it back into pure, free-form energy.

As an example, consider an action from your past that you regret. That event represents a transfer of pure energy into a fixed

---

[51] *Quantum Physics Lady*, "Collapse of the wave function" (March 10, 2019), http://www.quantumphysicslady.org/glossary/collapse-of-the-wave-function/.

form. That form will carry forward into the present moment for as long as the repercussions, memories, and associated emotions remain circulating through space and time. This could be a short time, a lifetime, or several lifetimes. To add to the complexity, there may be many stakeholders involved in your action—all keeping the past alive in the present moment. So, in this way, the past is "real." It remains in existence as a form that has material weight and energetic repercussions in the present moment. We are dealing with a "quasi-material" form, a sort of ghost reality propped up by karmic consequences and mental projections. The past is at once material and non-material.

Not to despair, because this example also gives us a clue as to how we can use energy in the present moment to heal the past and bring that healing energy to bear in our present life. Simply put, we can't change the past, but we can change how the past affects us. We cannot alter the karmic consequences of the past, but we can change the energy into a form that serves our highest good. Thankfully, we can transform low energy from the past into higher frequency energy that will have a positive effect on ourselves and the world.

EXERCISE
HEALING THE PAST

As we look to transform damaging low-frequency energy from the past, it is important to recognize that we might not effect positive change for all stakeholders in a particular past event. Once energy materializes for an individual, it becomes their responsibility to manage it. Just as you are the only one who has the power to manipulate your own stored energy, you cannot, despite your best intentions, heal the low-energy deposits of another person without their participation. Many times, the best we can do is concentrate on our own healing.

Healing the past begins with the same karmic-cleansing ritual used to clear any stored negative energy:

- Identify the memory and bring it to full consciousness.
- Relive the negative experience and associated feelings.
- Release these feelings back into the Field of Energy.
- Forgive yourself and all others involved.

It is not always possible, but if you can change the consequences of past actions and/or atone with others affected by the actions, consider doing so. Remember, the karmic energy propping up the memory of the past will persist as long as it continues to circulate throughout the whole of consciousness. This process involves trying to repair as much of the damage as possible:

- Take action to repair any *physical/material* damage you have done through your past behavior.
- Take action to repair any *emotional/psychological* damage resulting from your past behavior.
- Forgive and ask for forgiveness.
- Release this energy back to Source.

The aim of this process is to change negative energy, held in the past, into healthy energy we can use to fulfill our goals in the present moment. Without this alchemy, you risk bringing problems, pathologies, and negative karma into your present endeavors and perpetuating a cycle of creating a low-energy reality. Remember, there is no way to run from the past. It is a material form which must be reckoned with... in one way or another.

CHAPTER 50:

THERE ARE SAINTS AMONG US

WHEN DISCUSSING MY IDEAS ABOUT reality, I am asked about the horrible things happening to the most innocent of beings in our midst. I don't pretend to have all the answers, but I know the suffering of these beings is not a random occurrence or some kind of sadistic game played by gods and demigods. There is reason behind all suffering. Many times, it is the reflection of karmic energy, but sometimes it reflects the magnanimous actions of some evolved creatures.

Within every earthly time period, there are advanced souls who commit their physical presence to aid the advancement of others. Sometimes they materialize in the grand form of gurus, prophets, martyrs, or spiritual leaders. However, most walk among us as simple (but shining) examples of love, perseverance, tolerance, and courage. These individuals are often presented as the most unfortunate among us—such as a terminally ill child; a person born with birth defects or disabilities; or perhaps, a person who sacrifices their own safety and comfort for the benefit of others.

Regardless of the form they take, each of these *Saints* is here to make a positive impact on the spiritual evolution of those within their sphere of influence. It is our job to absorb these lessons and use this knowledge for the greater good of ourselves and humanity.

∞

Can you identify the Saints in your own life? Sometimes their presence is an immediate source of comfort, joy, and bliss, but often their presence is cloaked in pity, grief, or tragedy.

Regardless of the form they take, these individuals emerge to shake you out of your ego-oriented mind and connect you with your Spiritual-Core. They manifest for your benefit, so it would be a tragedy if you failed to use their offering to advance your connection to Source-Energy—and learn your intended lessons!

These lessons are designed through a partnership between your Soul and theirs, to give you access to higher frequency energy. If you move in the opposite direction, you are not yet getting the point. Perhaps their sacrifice connects with your ego to produce feelings of sadness and anger. Ask yourself, "What is the trigger for these negative emotions? Could it be the immense, unconditional love I feel for this person?" Maybe you have never experienced this level of love. Well, BINGO! This is the high-frequency emotion you can carry into the world. This is a part of the intended lesson— to experience the highest form of love possible! In this way, you honor that Saint in your life—they will not have appeared in vain.

So, lift your eyes. See beyond the sacrifice to the benevolent lessons given by the Saints in your life. Honor their existence by incorporating their lessons into your life and becoming the best you can be!

SECTION V:
HUMAN
NATURE

SECTION V:
HUMAN NATURE

Framework for Section V: Human Nature

In SECTION IV, WE DOVE into The Law of Karma, exploring how energy generated from our actions can take on a life of its own, dominating our existence and creating obstacles to achieving our objectives. We also explored how to manipulate karmic energy to enhance our personal development and evolution.

In Section V, we use the accumulated knowledge from Sections I through IV to provide insight into a variety of topics that represent some of the more curious and perplexing aspects of our human condition. It is fascinating to discover that the quality of life, for good or bad, is tied to how we channel Creative-Energy into this world.

What is our primary mechanism for channeling this energy? Is it our ego-oriented mind, or our Spiritual-Self? Are our thoughts, actions, and emotions governed by awareness or ignorance? Are we pursuing our evolutionary impulse, or are we stumbling through life? The answers to these questions have a direct bearing on the quality of our life experience—and on our ability to reach our evolutionary potential for this lifetime.

CHAPTER 51:

CURIOSITY IS A PREREQUISITE FOR SPIRITUAL DEVELOPMENT

Someone asked me, "What is the single most important factor that contributes to a person's evolution?"

This might seem like one of those broad questions that has no definitive answer. However, I did not hesitate to answer, "The gift of curiosity!"

Our purpose in this life is to explore the best way to link the body and mind to Core-Energy. How can you accomplish this with a closed mind? You cannot!

As sentient beings, we are tailored to poke and prod our way through each lifetime to discover a new path—a fresh outlook that might get us one step closer to perfection.

From the moment of conception, we are tasked with using our minds and senses to explore the world, to question the failed notions of the past, and to blaze a trail into a brave new future!

We often refer to children as sponges, soaking up everything in their environment. This is an accurate metaphor for a new, infantile human brain: a dry sponge. We are born with a yearning to make sense of the world. However, there comes a point where the "sponge" is saturated, and the brain feels satisfied with its created version of reality. When this happens, our temptation is to transition from a state of openness—to being insular. We restrict the flow of information that threatens our precarious equilibrium. Unfortunately, because growth and evolution are integral to the fabric of existence, stifling these processes creates an extreme amount of tension.

As the mind erects more and more barriers, it restricts the inflow of Creative-Energy. For an individual, this results in a host of negative pathologies: fear, paranoia, and aggression. In group dynamics, these feelings reinforce the need to gather with other "like-minded" individuals for additional protection. This is the process behind the proliferation of rigid belief systems, dogmatic ideologies, tribalism, and radicalism.

The bottom line is that anytime you take action that inhibits your ability to grow or evolve, you also create negative consequences for yourself. From your first breath to your last, life should be approached with a childlike sense of wonder and curiosity.

Observe any small child and you will see irrepressible curiosity and wonderment. This is our natural state of being—children learn and explore in the world around them. Unfortunately, over time, this predilection becomes overshadowed by our mind's penchant to conform to its environment. Our evolutionary impulse gets tamped down by the expectations of family, community, and society—all of which favor the safety of conformity over the risks of exploration.

To reach your evolutionary potential in this lifetime, you must reconnect with your childlike instinct to embrace growth and change. You must open your heart and mind to become a clear channel for Creative-Energy in life—and have the courage to follow this energy wherever it might take you.

CHAPTER 52:

REALITY DOES NOT MAKE VALUE JUDGMENTS

My young mind was molded from a rigid and myopic viewpoint. I was taught to see the world through a religious lens that dictated what was true and false, right and wrong, moral and sinful. Free-thinking was discouraged. In fact, anything that contradicted the doctrinal view was deemed evil—"of the devil." As I branched out and explored the world outside of my ideologic bubble, I encountered ideas that challenged the validity of these ingrained views. Because my mind was programmed to defend these ideologies, it took me quite some time (and a host of regrettably judgmental interactions) before I recognized that each of us is subjected to various types of cultural brainwashing in our formative years.

I also came to realize that these cultural traps possess a type of gravitational pull. To escape this pull requires a lot of energy. Like a rocket trying to escape earth's gravity, it takes a huge amount of effort to achieve "escape velocity" from our dominant ideologies—to become a "freethinker."

The social mores that govern belief and behavior are subjective. The things we consider "right" and "wrong," "acceptable" or "unacceptable," "moral" or "immoral" are all influenced by a host of factors that may or may not align with Source-Energy.

From the point of view of the logical brain, it is far easier if our thoughts and behaviors are governed by a bunch of fixed rules than trying to figure things out on the fly. Call this a propensity for efficiency or just laziness, but either way, when this happens, you cede control of your worldview to someone else.

In contrast, *reality* does not make value judgments. It is governed by the fundamental relationship between cause and effect. This objective process is agnostic and makes no moral assessment of behavior. Simply put, "you get back what you give out." Channeling energy of a certain frequency will always create a reality that matches that frequency. Low-frequency energy leads to negative outcomes, and the projection of high-frequency energy produces positive outcomes. This isn't subjective morality; it is simple cause and effect.

When we adopt a subjective viewpoint as truth, we place our ego in charge of defending our opinion—we attach our fixed position to our sense of self! This requires the ego to wage war upon (or suppress) any information that threatens our viewpoint. The ruinous consequences of this phenomenon are everywhere we look. It drives our political and religious discord, and it contributes to our epidemic of mental health problems.

Rather than blindly tethering your "moral code" to tradition, or some other pre-packaged code of conduct, it is far better to observe the actual karmic effects of your thoughts, feelings, and actions and allow this information to inform your views on morality. In this way, you free your mind to learn the unbiased truths behind channeling various forms of energy into this material realm. It is better to think for yourself!

So many of today's problems are linked to the subjective morality dictated by governments, religions, cultures, and families. These institutional imperatives stifle creativity, impair personal growth, and foster a host of destructive behaviors. The only solution to this predicament is for each of us to take personal responsibility for creating our own moral framework. For many people, this requires deconstruction of the ingrained belief systems that interfere with their ability to achieve their goals. Some of these roadblocks come from society; some from tribe, religion, family, or interpersonal relationships; and others from experience. Once you understand the source of the impediments in your life, you can go about the work of reprogramming your brain to accept a new vision of reality.

On a personal level, your ability to create your best self is never contingent upon being "good enough" or upon any other subjective moral construct. Rather, your creative power is determined by your mindset, your own definition of self, and the belief that you are worthy and capable of actualizing your creative impulses.

This means that you cannot look to a so-called "higher authority" to define who you are, or to tell you about your purpose for this lifetime. Instead, you must take responsibility for how you view the world and your role in it. In this way, you can take back control of your life and grant yourself the power to mold it as you see fit. The only limiting factor is between your ears.

CHAPTER 53:

YOU CAN USE DREAMS TO HEAL PAST TRAUMA

IT TOOK MANY YEARS BEFORE I learned the technique of using dreams as a tool for healing past trauma and stored negative energy. Like everyone, I experience my share of nightmares and troubling dreams, but it was my constant experience of "five o'clock terror" that drove me to explore what was happening during my sleep. Virtually every morning at five o'clock, I would awaken, drenched in a cold sweat, having a panic attack. It was my custom to try to "meditate" myself out of this painful stress state. As a coping mechanism, I focused on controlling my breath and directing my mind to think pleasant thoughts until my mind and body regained control.

Even though I was developing my spiritual practice, these nightly episodes of sheer terror and anxiety remained relentless. It dawned on me that my Spirit might use my subconscious dream state to communicate with me. Sure enough, the next morning, I woke up terrified. Instead of damping down my feelings, I dove into them! I lay there. I focused on actualizing every bit of the abject pain I was experiencing. It was awful, but I sunk into the underlying fear at the root of this experience. Sure enough, its source was a group of past traumas I had long ago hidden away within my subconscious mind and energetic body. These suppressed wounds had been stewing for years, accumulating strength as they absorbed new fears that came their way, compounding to where I could contain them no longer. They burst through their subconscious prison to affect my mental and physical health.

This was a *Eureka!* moment. I realized I could use my dreams as a tool to identify and eradicate stored negative energy.

Much of our negative energy is suppressed, buried deep within the fortifications of our subconscious mind and energetic body. This trapped energy represents the pain, anger, fear, guilt, and anxiety from all the memories and emotions that were not processed at the time the events occurred. The longer we harbor this energy, the more damage it does, and the harder it is to extract.

The gatekeeper and defender of this energetic realm is the mind. Its natural inclination is to protect you from pain and to fortify the concept that your mind is the center of the universe. As a result, it is difficult for the mind to hand over access to what it views as harmful energy. Fortunately, it is possible to use dreams as a technique to access the suppressed energy locked away in our subconscious mind.

Dreams can bypass our gatekeeper brain and delve into our most deeply hidden karmic storehouse. During sleep, this energy, either as a symbolic or literal representation, bubbles up to the surface and connects with the emotional centers of our body in the same way it would during a waking moment. We experience all the same negative emotions—the anger, fear, stress, anxiety, etc., that we suppressed. We label these as "nightmares" or "bad-dreams," but they are a cry from our deepest self to heal—

to deal with these suppressed energies, to bring them to our conscious mind, to process what should have been processed long ago, and to heal.

The exercise of transforming dream energy into karmic healing is the same as processing negative energy during your waking state. The only added step is: You must wake up! In order to burn karmic energy, the energy must be brought into the light of the conscious mind. For dream energy, this means transitioning out of the sleep state and bringing all the negative feelings into consciousness. When we have nightmares and bad dreams, we wake up. This is no accident! Your Core-Self is begging you to rid yourself of this energy.

The process might lead to some sleepless nights, but it is imperative that you wake up and bring the feelings forward. You must drill down to the root cause of the negative feelings and experience them—all the pain, hurt, fear, and anger. Only then can you forgive others. Only then can you forgive yourself. Only then can you heal and release the energy back to the Field.

CHAPTER 54

EACH SOUL IS ON A UNIQUE EVOLUTIONARY PATH

I ACCEPTED LONG AGO THAT I am a classic "late bloomer." I have discovered that the defining characteristic of this lifetime is a mad dash to achieve as much spiritual evolution as possible. This also involves setting up as many obstacles as I can reasonably overcome. All of this requires a great deal of effort... and takes a lot of time.

For those in a similar situation, it may feel like the pace of personal growth and your ability to actualize creative visions are under constant attack—like you are taking one step forward and two steps back. It is tempting to get frustrated, especially when you see others living with much less stress and drama while achieving more in a shorter time. Just keep in mind that we are each on our own unique journey. If you chose this life to speed up your growth, your reward will come in the lifetimes to follow!

As we look at the condition of society and examine humanity's influence on our planet, it can be disheartening. It sometimes helps to take a step back and meditate on the bigger picture. On an individual level, the progress of spiritual evolution is all over the board. Some people have a developed connection to Source, while others seem to be dominated by destructive, low-energy chaos. But regardless of where someone is on this spectrum, each life is heading toward the same goal. Some of us are taking the long way around!

Of course, advancing one's energetic connection involves creating the conditions necessary for taking the next step, for learning the next lesson, for burning off negative karma, and for developing the mind-Spirit connection. For some, this is a slow process that will take lifetimes. For others, the conditions may be right to make tremendous leaps toward a connection to Spirit in this lifetime.

Every lifetime is an exercise in managing potential and opportunity. Therefore, as you look at your own progress and the progress of others, remember, the optics can be deceiving. For some people, serious obstacles (such as poverty, health issues, abusive relationships, etc.) are presented to provide an *opportunity* for large advancements. Because these conditions cause an extreme amount of psychic trauma, it might take the better part of a lifetime to deal with the trauma positively... or it might not happen at all.

The point is you cannot judge someone's spiritual evolution without considering what the person's Soul is trying to accomplish in this lifetime. Because every journey is unique, it behooves each of us to be patient and tolerant of every individual's journey (including our own) and do whatever we can to assist the process.

EXERCISE
EVALUATING YOUR JOURNEY

As a point of context, consider your own journey and ask yourself these questions:

- "What obstacles was I born into?"
- "What additional challenges did I create for myself along the way?"
- "What problems and adversities do I still face today?"

Now, examine the progress you have made.

- Are you the same person you were as a child?
  - As a teenager?
  - As a young adult?
  - As a mature adult?
- How have you grown?
- What lessons have you learned along the way?
- How did the obstacles and challenges benefit you in the growth process?
- What growth opportunities lie ahead of you?

You are a work in progress. Tolerate your mistakes and be patient with the pace of your evolution.

Now extend this analysis to the relationships in your life. Then to society. Then to the world. Recognize that we are all going through the same process. Rather than judging yourself, be patient and tolerant. Ask, "What can I do to enhance the evolutionary process of myself and others?" It behooves each of us to focus on the aim rather than the behavior, and on helping rather than condemning.

CHAPTER 55:

HABITS DRIVE REALITY

THE COMPLEXITIES OF LIFE ARE so overwhelming, there is no way the mind can go through a logical evaluation of every moment. To help ease this problem, we establish habitual responses to certain kinds of stimuli. These habits allow us to respond to our environment with little to no critical thought. While these split-second reactions may come in handy when we are dealing with any kind of perceived danger, most of these rote tendencies do much more harm than good.

Most of us have no clue our lives are dominated by habits. Once I started looking, I was floored to see that much of my life was controlled by habitual responses. Indeed, most of the negative energy in my reality was channeled through my habits. I discovered that our own habits are both the greatest impediment to crafting our desired reality and the single greatest obstacle to spiritual growth.

If we examine our lives, we recognize that much of our behavior, attitudes, and emotions emerge from a well of subconscious, habitual patterns. In fact, our brains and nervous systems are hardwired with some of these patterns. Some are passed down from our family or tribe, or by society. Some are the products of defensive strategies. Still other patterns form because we extract benefit or reward from our habitual behavior.

These behavioral tendencies not only color how we see and respond to the world, but they also affect how we absorb and project the energy we use to create reality. If your goal is to control your life and ascend to higher frequencies of Creative-Energy, you must gain dominion over your unconscious behavior patterns (i.e., your habits). There are several reasons this is not a simple process:

- The brain is a product of evolution: Our brains have developed over millions of years to help us survive in a hostile world (and it is still suitable for cave dwellers running from saber-toothed tigers). However, much of the "fight-or-flight" impulse built into our minds is not applicable to modern society.
- The brain loves forming habits; establishing patterns of behavior as an efficient way to exist. However, problems arise when these habits do not align with the energy we want to bring to reality.
- The brain is self-oriented: it relies on past experience to interpret the world around it. On its own, it has no frame of reference beyond what has happened in the past. As a result, it is inclined to orient itself as the center of your human experience. This impulse supports the dominance of the ego.
- Your mind chases pleasurable experiences. It is attracted to instant gratification, but it also responds to your being's desire for a greater connection to Source-Energy. When you are connected to Source, you feel good! You feel joy, peace, love... bliss. The brain wants to tap into this energy.

However, coming from its limited perspective, your mind derives many ego-oriented shortcuts for tapping into these higher frequencies. As an example, it learns to use thoughts, behaviors, and substances to stimulate the "feel-good" chemicals in our biology, such as dopamine and serotonin. This includes the use of drugs, sex, wealth, fame—even chocolate—anything to provide a temporary "rush" of feeling good. The trouble comes when these behaviors are self-destructive or turn addictive. Unconstrained, our minds will chase these sensations, forming deep-seated negative habits along the way.

The only way to transform a habit is to bring conscious attention to it. Therefore, the only way to overcome your destructive patterns of behavior is to gain control over how your mind channels energy into the world and to replace your brain's dominion over thought and awareness with a conscious connection to your Spiritual-Self. In this way, you can identify and root out the subconscious behaviors that are creating turmoil and misery in your life.

Your level of spiritual evolution is contingent upon your ability to shift your brain-originated, counter-productive behavior and reestablish new patterns of behavior based upon your connection to Source-Energy. This starts with an assessment of the motivations behind your actions, thoughts, and emotions. Are they based upon the egocentric machinations of the mind, or are they grounded in the higher ideals of the Spirit?

There is no shortcut for this process. To transform, you must identify hidden negative habits and bring awareness to them over an extended period. In this way, you can replace negative habits with new (healthy) reactions and responses. By practicing consistent awareness, your mind will sidestep the ego and reorient itself to responding in a way that aligns with your Spirit. As this happens, you will gain more and more control over your creative power. Life will feel less chaotic and reactive, and a new you will emerge that reflects your inspired, creative impulse.

CHAPTER 56:

THERE IS NO SUCH THING AS "TRUTH"

Boy, do we like to think we know what *truth* is! Nothing, and I mean *nothing*, lights a fire under the ego like the notion that we know what is right. Looking back over the years at all my varying concepts and classifications of *truth* makes me laugh and cringe. I have been willing to go to war (metaphorically) over many idiotic beliefs: From religious exclusionism to the sin of homosexuality (Yikes!)—my ignorance knew no bounds.

But such is the nature of growing and maturing. Or at least this is supposed to be the case! Too many people accept a static view of reality that tethers ephemeral concepts like *truth*, *right*, and *wrong* to their identity. They make no distinction between their rigid beliefs and who they are. For them, any disagreement on *truth* is a direct assault on them as a person. Of course, every day we see this playing out around us—it creates a polarized society.

The phrase "a closed mind" is not just figurative. When we fix our viewpoint, we close off our mind to the flow of Source-Energy. This restricts our ability to evolve and creates tension between our life and the rest of the evolving world. The solution to this problem seems obvious. However, it requires that your ego relinquish control over your concept of self, which can be arduous.

Truth Is a Fabrication of the Mind

Everyone is searching for the *Truth*, but the only truth is... there is none! The concept of absolute truth is a fabrication of the human mind, designed to bolster the ego on multiple fronts.

- First, the label of *truth* creates a logical shortcut which bypasses the need to spend energy evaluating the environment. Slotting life into ready-made categories makes complete sense from an efficiency standpoint, but the cost is high. By necessity, it requires transmuting a complex world into a thin, superficial veneer that fits within predefined categories. Your worldview also becomes superficial—devoid of nuance and empathy.
- Second, a fixed concept of truth feeds the mind's natural craving for uniqueness and superiority. As a closed, self-referencing system, the brain's natural inclination is to achieve dominance over its environment. The ego uses its concept of truth to set itself up as superior to others who possess differing views of reality. Of course, this leads to many problems, from religious wars to racism.
- Third, a static ideology offers a false sense of stability and security in an ever-changing world. This is a natural response from our minds, which are hardwired to avoid surprises. It is comforting to think we have all the answers.

The concept of truth provides a shield of protection around our fragile concept of self. As the mind goes about trying to apply fixed definitions to who you are as an individual, it must, by necessity, construct an infrastructure of beliefs that supports those definitions. In their static form, these beliefs become ensconced as truths. However, these truths are much like a fortification built upon shifting sands. Life is in a constant state of flux and dynamic evolution. To withstand these changes, your fortress of truth must be isolated, fortified, and defended. As a result, we shut down our ability to be open-minded, we curtail communication, and we become less empathetic. All this stunts our creative abilities.

For truth to have any value, we must recognize its transitory and subjective nature. Truth is personal and subjective. As a result, it should never be grasped—or forced upon anyone else.

The problem with a concept like TRUTH is that it sounds so positive and nice. From the time you were born, you have been socialized to tell the truth, to seek the truth, to run toward the truth. The underlying assumption is that there is such a thing as "universal truth." I challenge anyone to give an example of a fixed universal truth. It cannot happen because every example will be conditional, qualified, and contingent upon this or that.

There are not even universal truths associated with science—not one! The entire field of science is set up to find universal truths, and it has yet to find one truth that is infallible and undeniable. This does not mean that our search for truth is in vain, or that it is a meaningless exercise. It is not meaningless to seek knowledge, to search for answers. In fact, this drives the evolution of humanity. The problem comes with holding on to any piece of knowledge or insight, as if it is the end of the quest. Every discovered truth should be held lightly. It should be viewed as nothing more than a steppingstone to the next discovery.

How has the insidious concept of "truth" tainted your own perception of reality? To find out, ask yourself a few simple questions:

- "What truths have I incorporated into my life?"
- "What are the origins of these truths?"
- "Do my truths serve me, or do I serve my truths?"

Your answers to these questions will illuminate your relationship to the fixed ideologies that cause difficulties in your life.

Once you identify the various dogmas that influence your behavior and worldview, the next step is to disassociate your definition of self from these concepts. Ask yourself:

- "What if, at this moment, I discovered that this 'truth' is indeed false?"
- "How would this make me feel?"
- "What would this do to my sense of self?"

Your emotional response to these questions will define how much of your self-identity is tied to these erroneous concepts.

So, free yourself! Free yourself from having to have all the answers... of being right. Free yourself from having to defend your bogus ideas of "truth."

CHAPTER 57:

SPIRITUAL GROWTH REQUIRES CRITICAL ANALYSIS

IN MY YOUTH—BACK WHEN I was immersed in hard-core Christian ideology—I used to obsess about the concept of wisdom. Probably due to how wisdom was depicted in the Bible compared to the utter lack of wisdom I saw around me. My mind was a jumbled and confused mess. I craved clarity—I wanted to progress through life with a sense of certainty. Somehow, I knew that wisdom is the most valuable thing one can possess in life. Because of this obsession, my prayers were always directed toward achieving wisdom. I beseeched God to free my mind—to give me the ability to make clear, proper decisions.

As I look back, this focus on wisdom set the course for my life. I now know that the hunger for this quest comes from my Spiritual-Core. It defines my purpose for this lifetime and serves as the foundation for everything I have achieved.

To walk an evolved path requires both the drive to make new discoveries about reality and the openness to explore concepts outside of our comfort zone. We need to maintain a critical eye and resist accepting any ideology until it is filtered through our own experience. I refer to this balancing act between healthy skepticism and curiosity as *divine wisdom*. The skeptic puts on the airs of someone engaged in discerning wisdom. Most skepticism is based in fear or laziness. The easiest thing in the world is to be a closed-minded skeptic. It takes no courage or imagination to navigate the world from an outlook based on rejection.

If you assume that any new concept or idea is false until proven otherwise, life will validate your negative expectations. In effect, the skeptic constructs a gilded cage for themselves to protect their preconceived notions from challenges. This brings with it developmental stagnation along with a host of psychological pathologies that revolve around narcissism and the fear of change.

At the other extreme, we have those who accept any shiny new concept that crosses their path. These individuals are susceptible to the influence of their external environment, taking up one cause after the other as they bounce around through life. A prime example of the damage caused by this outlook is the conspiracy theory culture that proliferates society. These individuals chase after stimuli that feed their low-energy existence of confusion and insecurity.

There is a middle way that taps into the notion of *divine wisdom*. In this context, "divine" refers to your creative connection to Core-Energy, and "wisdom" is the process of first analyzing, accepting, and then using information in a way that supports the initiatives of your Core-Self.

Life should involve a constant refinement of your connection to Core-Energy. If this is your focus, reality will provide a continual stream of new information to help you achieve this aim. This means that your beliefs and notions about life will be in a perpetual state of flux. This process requires you to be open to receiving new information and to have the skills to discern whether this data will further your personal evolution.

Often, the only way to determine the validity of an idea is to use your life as an experimental testing ground. Based on experience, if a concept bears fruit, incorporate it into your worldview. If it does not, discard it.

As a thought exercise, ponder the environment in which you were socialized:

- Which of your belief systems has been transferred to you by your religion, family, tribe, or society?
- Which of these have you tested in your own life?
- Which have you taken at face value as truth?

You should test everything. That which is a personal truth for someone else may or may not be a personal truth for you. At first, this experimental process might feel like an act of rebellion. In a sense, it is just that. You are rebelling against the notion that someone else holds the keys to your vision of right and wrong, of good and evil, of truth and fiction. You must not only question everything, but you must also try it on for size. Does it fit? If a concept does not create a benefit for you, reject it. Search for a truth to replace it.

This same process for testing legacy beliefs applies to your ongoing journey of discovery. Read, research, seek information, explore new horizons. Screen these new ideas through your Spiritual-Mind:

- Do they seem positive?
- Are they helpful?
- Do the ideas raise or lower your energy?

Then apply these new ideas in your own life. What happens? Maybe nothing. Maybe a miracle! At least *you* will know. Your new knowledge will become *your* personal truth—*your* Divine Wisdom—that is... until you replace it with something better.

CHAPTER 58

WISDOM EMERGES FROM SPIRIT; INTELLIGENCE IS A PRODUCT OF THE BRAIN

I<small>T IS ALWAYS A JOY</small> to come across someone who might be described as "an old soul"; someone who possesses insight about life far beyond their years, experience, education, or social status. These unique individuals are living examples of the true nature of *wisdom*, which comes from a source other than this material world. Wisdom is not connected to time, place, education, wealth, or any earthly pursuit. Instead, it originates apart from the mind and represents an energetic channel leading to Spirit.

Because the origins of wisdom are separate from the brain, it is difficult for the mind to distinguish between wisdom and brain-oriented thought. As a result, it is easy to confuse wisdom with intelligence, and vice versa. This is why it is so perplexing when we see "smart" individuals (or groups of individuals) espousing ignorant concepts and ideas.

As the world becomes increasingly interconnected, it is imperative that we distinguish between information originating from wisdom and information sourced from ego-oriented thought. Fundamental to this process is understanding the difference between *wisdom* and *intelligence*.

It is easy to conflate intelligence with wisdom, but they are distinct concepts governed by different processes. In short, intelligence is the purview of the logical brain, while wisdom manifests from our connection to Spirit. Intelligence emerges from the brain's ability to manipulate data. The mind is suited to absorb information and strive to logically use it. This is all fine, except that this information is filtered through the mind's programming, which includes a perplexing mishmash of emotional scars, hidden pathologies, and miscellaneous environmental influences. These influences color how the mind interprets information and can create an illusion of reality that may support the ego but is not an accurate reflection of what is happening.

From the mind's viewpoint, its interpretation of incoming data makes logical sense. However, if the mind is isolated from Source-Energy, it might not recognize the biases built into its programming. When this happens, it will tend to reach erroneous conclusions about processed information. So, an intelligent (smart) person can reach some ignorant conclusions about data presented to them. In fact, it can be difficult for someone who is "smart" to rise above ignorance. This is because they have prioritized their biased mind, over their Spiritual-Mind, as the ultimate authority on the reality they see around them.

In contrast, *wisdom* originates from our Spiritual-Mind. This does not mean we disregard our physical mind. Rather, we use our thoughts to root out ego-controlled programming so the mind is no longer influenced by corrupt information. Wisdom can only emerge in the parts of life where the ego is not in control of filtering incoming data.

As a unique "work in progress," each of us has areas where wisdom can flourish and areas where we allow ego to remain in control. For example, one can be wise in interpersonal relationships but ignorant in business and financial matters—or vice versa. These types of inequities can occur in any area of life. Ignorance flourishes anytime you absorb only information that confirms your existing biases and you discard any thought that challenges those beliefs.

So, intelligence is the purview of the brain. Wisdom exudes from Spirit. While each of us comes into this life with a certain propensity for intelligence, there are no limitations to our access to wisdom. As a result, a child can exude more wisdom than the smartest person in the world.

We should all strive to move through life in a state of wisdom. The first step in this process is to recognize that the mind can be clouded by its own self-serving interpretation of reality. This is easy to identify because the brain will always attach negative emotions to your egocentric concepts. For example, how do you feel when your ideas are challenged? Do you become hurt, upset, resentful, or angry? Use these emotions as telltale signs that your "truth" is tied to your rigid definition of *self*.

Spirit-based knowledge (wisdom) does not require a defense. It simply "is." Your path of wisdom is synonymous with your personal truth. Indeed, your insights might be useful to the world, but the value of your truth is not contingent upon others accepting it. Do the work to root out the influence of the ego. Process life through the lens of your Spirit—and then rest in your wisdom!

CHAPTER 59:

IGNORANCE HAS NO CORRELATION WITH INTELLIGENCE

Anytime you get frustrated with the ignorance of others, it helps to remember the ignorance on display in your own life. For me, this is easy because of the embarrassment of misinformed stances I have taken over the years. Whenever I feel exasperated with the wrong-headed activity swirling around me, remembering my own foibles helps me extend compassion and understanding rather than condemnation to others. We all can grow and change, and someone's attitude today does not determine (thankfully) their spiritual trajectory for the future.

The proliferation of ignorance, even among intelligent, well-meaning people, can be both confusing and frustrating. Why do all these nice, smart people have views and opinions that appear so very ignorant? This peculiarity emerges from the fact that there is no correlation between how smart or kind someone is and their ability to access wisdom. For emphasis, it does not matter if you are a Nobel Prize-winning physicist, the President of the United States, or a religious leader, your worldview can be informed from an ego-dominated perspective.

There are certain hallmarks of an ego-dominated perspective. For example, an outlook centered on the mind imagines life as a threatening zero-sum game. It perceives a finite quantity of resources, fame, wealth, and ideas. For some people, this creates an impulse for accumulating or hording as many resources as they can—often at the expense of others. This "scarcity mentality" is responsible for the competitive, dog-eat-dog cultures in business, politics, and society generally. Other people respond by closing their minds to any idea that does not align with their preconceived notions of reality. For them, the defense of their fragile concept of self takes priority over striving for the truth.

Of course, we see these destructive behavior patterns playing out in all facets of life. From the greed of the power elite to violent acts of tribalism, to the indiscriminate ravaging of our planet—everywhere you look, you see the effects of our ignorant, ego-dominated mentality.

An ego-dominated existence also creates a host of weaknesses that are exploited by our power structures and institutions. A diverse cast of players—including politicians, religions, advertisers, and even social justice reformers—all prey upon our fears and insecurities. They are masters at tapping into the ego-dominated psyche and exploiting our unenlightened inclinations for their own gain. All of this creates a perpetual feedback loop that reinforces these ignorant perceptions. Is it any wonder so many well-meaning, intelligent people harbor such destructive ideals?

Thankfully, ignorance is not a terminal condition (for anyone). However, it is critical to realize that moving away from an ego-oriented viewpoint is an individual endeavor. Wisdom cannot be imposed upon anyone. You cannot bully someone into deviating away from their ego-based perspective. This only leads to the ramping-up of more ego-based energy. Each of us must find our own way out of the darkness and into the light.

Instead, the key to moving yourself, or anyone else, from ignorance to wisdom is unconditional love and acceptance. We can see this dynamic at play when we interact with someone who has a different worldview from our own. We always have two choices. Either we condemn the individual (which is an assault on their ego/sense of self), or we accept the individual for who they are at that moment. Notice that their opinion is irrelevant. Either we choose to operate from a place of unconditional love and acceptance, or we don't.

It is far better to approach the ego, either yours or someone else's, with nonthreatening openness, acceptance, and love. This takes the mind out of its defensive mode and creates an environment that fosters communication. As the mind relaxes, there is a much better chance that it will be open to new concepts and ideas. Let's face it; an honest, caring dialogue resonates with almost anyone. Who knows—you might also gain new insights in the process.

CHAPTER 60

YOUR SPIRITUAL-MIND CAN ONLY BE ACCESSED IN THE PRESENT MOMENT

OPERATING IN THE PRESENT MOMENT is difficult. Most of us have trouble focusing on the here and now. I find people fall into one of two categories. Either their mind dwells on the past, or it dwells in the dreamworld of the future. My mind loves to inhabit the future. In the future, I am fulfilling my dreams and ambitions. I am living my highest and best life. I am a rock star! Of course, we cannot be in two places at once. If I focus only on the future, I am neglecting the present moment. I am not living my highest and best life *right now*.

Today, the phrase "living in the moment" is easy to discount because it is such a popular platitude. However, for millennia, ancient wisdom has been pointing to this concept as the key to happiness and fulfillment. The reason? Conscious awareness of the present moment requires bypassing the brain and accessing our higher Spiritual-Mind. Let's look at how the brain can impede our desire to live in the moment.

First, our biology is genetically hardwired with a host of subconscious, instinctual responses that bypass our conscious awareness. These include everything from "fight-or-flight" reactions and sexual arousal to reflexive responses for dangerous things in the environment (e.g., pulling your hand away from a flame). While these instinctual reactions are of vital importance, they can also distract us from tuning into our Spiritual-Mind. As an example, many people become so affected by the sensory overload of modern society, they cannot shut down their acute sensory responses. When you live in a constant state of heightened stress, it is difficult to reach beyond your primitive reactions and connect with Source in the present moment.

Next, your mind processes present reality from the perspective of the past. On its own, the brain's comprehension of the world around it relies on prior experiences and learned behaviors. The brain takes sensory input from our five senses and filters this data through its bank of stored memories. As a result, any moment has the potential to mutate into a symbolic representation of the past, transporting with it all the emotional triggers associated with that memory. Once this happens, the present moment ceases to exist; it transmutes into a re-broadcast of past events.

The mind favors projecting into the future. The future is unknown and scary, so we compensate by using our experience, hopes, and dreams to visualize a future that looks familiar. These expectations can have either positive or negative ramifications, but the net effect is to remove us from experiencing what is taking place in the moment.

All these machinations of the brain make it difficult to live in the "now." In contrast, through our Spiritual-Mind we are rooted in the vastness of the current moment. In this state, we have none of the pathologies or projections of the past or the future. We are one with pure reality, and our only concern is using the present moment to develop the connection to Spirit. When you are connected to Spirit, the past and the future cease to exist. Instead, you become a conduit for moving energy into the "now."

Where do you spend most of your time? Are you dwelling on the past, projecting into the future, or living in the present moment? If you are like most people, you spend most of your waking moments in the imaginary world of the mind, not focused on living in the present. When this happens, you are short-changing your human experience in several ways. For starters, you are turning your life over to the mercurial world of the ego, which makes you vulnerable to its associated pathologies. You miss countless sensual details that make this material existence special. You stifle the flow of energy from your Spiritual-Core—all of which impedes your ability to reach your evolutionary potential for this lifetime.

To be clear, there is a time for remembering the past. However, you must have dominion over the memory instead of letting the memory control you. Likewise, there is a significant benefit to dreaming, planning, and projecting your intention into the world. But you must learn to dwell in the reality of *now* instead of in the fictional future. This involves feeling the pain, the joy, the thrill, the love, the sorrow, and the beauty that life offers in the moment in which it manifests.

Your spiritual growth is predicated on you being brave enough to occupy every moment. Revelations arise here. This is where you transform karmic energy. This is where miracles are made manifest. This is where lessons are learned. This is where we connect with this material realm. This is reality!

CHAPTER 61:

YOUR EGO NEEDS ENEMIES

WE ALL ENCOUNTER PEOPLE WHO lash out at their environments. Are you one of them? Within this group, there is a subcategory of individuals who are engaged in a constant search for someone to blame for their anger, fear, hurt, frustration, sadness, or dissatisfaction. These are the *enemy hunters*. If you find yourself in the crosshairs of one of these people, recognize that *you* are not the problem. They are simply projecting their negative impulses onto you. You have the power to choose what you do with this negative energy. If you absorb their dysfunctional behavior, you take on their low-frequency energy. However, you can protect yourself from the damaging effects by recognizing the pain behind their behavior, thus raising the frequency of the energy by generating compassion and understanding.

This is difficult. But the enemy-hunters in our lives can become valuable teachers for us as we learn to control negative energy in our environment.

∞

Life is hard and contentious enough without manufacturing enemies. However, it is a curious feature of the ego-dominated mind that imagines enemies around every corner. The psychology behind this phenomenon is rooted in the fragile nature of the ego, which hampers our ability to take responsibility for the negative features of our reality.

When your self-worth is tied to your physical presence—to your mind's concept of who you are—the world can seem like a very hostile place. Your instinctive response is to defend yourself against anything from the environment that might challenge your notions of self, including any negative energy that comes your way. To your ego, any admission of fault or error undermines who you think you are (or whom you aspire to be). This cannot be allowed! Over time, this defensive strategy establishes the ego as sole arbiter for defending right and wrong and deputizes the mind to exact vengeance upon anyone who does not conform to its concept of truth.

All of this adds up to an unpleasant cycle of self-reinforcing paranoia, whereby the individual is searching the environment for someone to blame for their misery. And guess what? We can find an endless stream of idiots... er... candidates... who will support our supposition.

For many enemy hunters, enemy hunting is a distinguishing personality trait. Not only does it provide their ego with purpose, but it supplies a self-indulgent "rush" of ego gratification when life conforms to their negative expectations. This has the same effect as any habit-forming drug, with the individual craving the next high—or, in this case, the next person to validate their fear, hate, jealousy, or insecurity. If left unchecked, this habit leads to a wholesale manufacturing of events to feed their compulsion. The individual sees conspiracy around every corner and destroys their closest, most trusted relationships. All this chaos is created in order to feed the insatiable appetite of the ego.

The problem of manufacturing enemies is rooted in the inability to take responsibility for life. The mind and ego want to focus blame anywhere but on the self. If you have this issue, the only solution is to take 100 percent responsibility for everything in your existence. Until you recognize you are liable for every moment—every encounter—every situation, you will continue searching for someone to blame.

If you know someone with this issue, the most you can do is extend love to them. Unfortunately, all efforts to illuminate this behavior will confirm you as enemy number one. For this reason, relationships with an enemy-hunter can be difficult. No one wants to provoke the enemy-hunter, lest they be branded an adversary. As a result, dysfunctional behaviors emerge that destroy everyone involved.

Each of us is responsible for every aspect of our personal reality. This includes our ability or inability to change. Breaking destructive habits is an individual journey. No one can do it for us, and we can't do it for anyone else. If someone is preoccupied with blaming external forces (including real or imagined enemies), they are robbing themselves of the power to change. You can love and encourage them, but they must awaken to the driving force behind their internal fear and take responsibility for it.

CHAPTER 62:

YOUR CONNECTION TO SOURCE-ENERGY MAY DETERMINE YOUR MENTAL HEALTH

My TUMULTUOUS CHILDHOOD LEFT ME with a catalog of serious mental health issues, all of which wreaked havoc in my life and took decades to resolve. Acute anxiety, debilitating depression, an uncontrollable dissociative condition, self-destructive behaviors. It was no picnic. But I am grateful that I experienced these challenges because they gave me a unique opportunity to explore the inner workings of my mind and develop an approach to heal myself. During this journey, I have come to understand that traditional treatments for mental conditions provide little more help than to bandage the symptoms. They do little to address the root cause.

As an alternative approach, I took the position that my issues emanated from the stuck energy in my mind and body. My mental problems were symptomatic of my inability to clear out negative energy and channel high-frequency energy into my life. I saw my maladies as arrows pointing to the energy that needed transforming. Sure enough, once I began applying this strategy, the mental illnesses that had plagued me for decades dissipated. They began fading into the background, and then vanished altogether.

I now have a clear path for handling pathological behaviors and connecting my subconscious mind to my conscious expression of Spirit!

Today, the term "mental illness" is broad beyond the point of being useful. It includes such a diverse array of afflictions that it is hard to separate them. There seems to be no medical consensus on the causes of these maladies. Is it nature or nurture? Do mental problems originate from our genetic makeup, or are they a byproduct of the way we are socialized? Or both?

An increased potential for exhibiting certain mental illness seems to be genetically encoded, or "hardwired," from birth. As an example, certain OCD behaviors, schizophrenia, and psychopathologies can manifest from early childhood. As genetic research continues to advance, science is discovering more and more genes that seem to be responsible for different afflictions. However, as the science makes clear, this genetic coding only represents the potential for a problem—not a certainty. A host of conditions (many of which are environmental—socialization, trauma, physical health, etc.) determine whether or not these genes are expressed.

The resulting complexity of causation leaves medical science at a loss as to how best to treat mental conditions. As a result, many treatments focus on regulating emotional and behavioral symptoms and make little progress toward addressing the sources of these manifestations. In short, treatments that mask unpleasant or negative feelings have limited value in treating the root cause of mental health problems. In fact, they often amplify the conditions.

Perhaps the problems we have with understanding, evaluating, and treating mental health problems are because we focus in the wrong areas. Instead, what if a person's connection to Source-Energy was the primary determinate for mental health? As an extreme example, assume for a moment that you were cut off from Source-Energy. What effect would this have on your mental well-being? Your isolated mind would have no choice but to become self-referential. Every moment would manifest through the lens of egotism. Imagine if your entire sense of worth and purpose was determined by the feedback you received from your environment. What if your definition of self were contingent on how you viewed yourself at any moment, on how you compared to everyone else in the world, or on how you stacked up cosmetically? This would put you into a desperate, dog-eat-dog competition for resources, recognition, and superficial validation. Everyone would become your rival. You would feel inferior to anyone who had more than you, and superior to anyone who had less. What effect would all this have on your mental health? In short, your mind would experience an onslaught of compulsive fear, anxiety, paranoia, and aggression. You would go insane!

In contrast, let's look at the effect of Source-Energy on the mind. A mind connected to Source is the opposite of self-oriented. It recognizes we are all connected and that each of us plays an important role in the evolution of this material realm. Therefore, the more we open up the channel to Source, the more we can manifest the joy, peace, and creativity that originate from this energy.

I theorize that mental health is correlated with our connection to Source-Energy and that mental health issues arise anytime we restrict our access to Source Energy. Many mental health treatments focus on using the mind as the tool for healing the mind. This approach is doomed to failure because the mind is the source of the problem. It is a bit like letting the inmates run the asylum. These techniques serve only to reinforce the brain's dominance, which inflames the problem.

A common example of this treatment attempts to heal the mind by assigning blame to external factors, such as life events or personal relationships. This method deflects responsibility for psychological scarring away from the individual and into an external circumstance. Unfortunately, this kind of ego-oriented treatment is also problematic. By removing responsibility from the individual, you remove their power to fix the problem—to heal themselves. You cannot change the past, no matter the amount of blame you heap upon it. If you want to heal, you must use the present moment, and only you can control the present moment!

Another example of faulty treatment is the use of drug compounds to change the "feeling-state" of an individual. While these drugs can stimulate the production of the various chemical compounds associated with *feeling good*, it is important to be clear on what is taking place. The chemicals are not causing the transformation. Instead, they are changing the brain's chemistry so that it no longer interferes with the flow of Core-Energy. This is an important distinction. The source of joy, happiness, and mental health is always present. It is the brain's conditioning that interferes with our ability to access this state of being. By bypassing the brain and allowing Source-Energy to flow in, these drugs can provide a positive, short-term effect. However, they often come with a host of side effects and do a poor job of contributing to a sustainable connection to this Energy.

So many people struggle throughout their lifetimes with mental illness. The primary culprit is an egocentric culture that feeds our brain with the lie that clarity and happiness is sourced outside of our beings. The solution cannot be found outside of ourselves, but is omnipresent within us, waiting to be uncovered. The "fix" is within us—it is our ever-present connection to Source!

Restoring Mental Health

Restoring mental health involves the slow, often painful process of reconditioning the mind to surrender its dominance to the higher intelligence of Source-Energy.

Step One: This step involves developing an intellectual framework for healing:
- The recognition that your compulsions, depression, anxiety, pathologies, mania, or fear are self-inflicted states, caused by a mind that is not in sync with your innate energetic power.
- The acceptance that you, and you alone, have the responsibility to deal with your illness.
- The understanding that the power of your Spiritual-Self is ready to guide and assist your mind throughout the healing process.

This framework serves two important functions. First, it garners the mind's participation in the healing process. It provides assurance that there is a much greater power outside of the brain that stands ready to help you through healing.

Step Two: In this step, you do the hard work necessary to identify and heal the wounds that are contributing to your associated pathologies. This process involves:
- Opening to the unknown and asking your Spiritual-Self for guidance and illumination.
- Identifying and acknowledging the pain in your life.
- Drilling down, step by step, until you uncover the roots of the pain.
- Experiencing the pain in each step along the way.
- Releasing the pain back to the universe.
- Forgiving the perpetrators.

Contrary to the avoidance techniques associated with many mental health initiatives, true healing requires facing the pain, consequences, and reality of your mental illness. Since it is caused by a blockage of Source-Energy, you must take the steps necessary to identify and release these obstructions, clearing the path to your Spiritual-Source. As you go through this painful process, the joy and peace of your renewed connection to Source-Energy will grow and your mind will clear. Once your mind becomes conditioned to accept a new reality centered on your connection to Source, true healing will take place!

CHAPTER 63:

THE ACT OF GIVING ATTRACTS HIGH-FREQUENCY CREATIVE ENERGY

Over the years, I have learned the art of consciously modifying my environment. Like furnishing and decorating a house, at any moment we can change our surroundings by channeling a particular type of Creative-Energy. The action of *giving* is a perfect example of doing something that has an immediate impact on your environment. The high-frequency energy that accompanies a selfless act of giving is miraculous. I find it provides an immediate lift to my spirit, and I have seen it have transformative effects on those around me. When in doubt, give. Give your time. Give a positive thought. Give your resources. Give a simple smile. Life will always reward the spirit of giving by giving back to you!

The act of giving feels good. It draws people to us; it brings resources; and it provides clarity to mind and body. But why? What is the spiritual science behind these amazing manifestations? To begin, let's define giving as "the focused offering of energy for the benefit of another." Giving can include anything, from a charitable donation to providing roadside help to a stranded motorist, or something as simple as offering a compliment. Anytime you spend energy to help the people, places, and things in your environment, whether this is smiling at a stranger or picking up trash on the street, you are triggering the beneficial *power of giving* in your life. The secret to the power of giving comes from your alignment with the complex nature of Creative-Energy itself. When we project energy, we align with the giving nature of life. The impact of this calibration on our minds and bodies is instantaneous—it feels good! It creates an open, cleansing, positive feeling that stems from the flow of energy through you and out into the environment.

We all know people who hoard energy for their own benefit. They are always bitter, angry, or unhappy. Those who give can be identified by their light, happy, positive nature. Whether or not they know it, they are tapped into the wellspring of Creative-Energy.

The act of giving also leverages the "attraction" characteristic of energy. Energies of the same frequency are always attractive to one another. Giving energy projects abundance to the universe, which attracts abundance back to the individual. This is the science behind the adage, "Give, and it will be given to you."[52] This aphorism is expressing a fundamental law of nature. Whatever you give will attract more of the same. If you give joy, caring, help, money— whatever—these things will come back to you. The universe recognizes these acts as confirmations of your intentions and will work to fulfill your desires.

Do you give your energy freely, or do you hoard it? A quick look at your reality will give you the answer. If there are areas of your

---

[52] Luke 6:38 (NIV).

life that seem stuck or that are going in the wrong direction, you need to assess the energy you project into the world. Unfortunately, the mind's impulsive response to scarcity is the opposite of how reality works. Its reaction is to conserve, to control, and to withhold resources. These actions signal a desire for poverty to the universe, and sure enough, Creative-Energy will go to work to give you what you are asking for. To change your circumstances, you must first change your perspective and learn to override your brain's impulse to pull back from giving. Once you project abundance, whether it is abundant joy, love, or material wealth, life will reward you in kind.

To explore the transformative power of giving in your life, you may need to start small. Give a smile, a good thought, or a few dollars to someone in need. Then take notice of how your energy grows. Notice how *good* it feels to be a conduit for Creative-Energy! As you move down this path, note the greater shifts in your reality. You will see this energy coming back to you. Opportunities will materialize, healthy relationships will enter your life, positive energy will be projected back into your existence. It will seem miraculous, but remember, you are getting back what you are giving!

CHAPTER 64

PAIN IS YOUR TEACHER

I HAVE HAD A LOT OF pain in my life. Like many people, as noted earlier, I spent a great deal of time and energy trying to avoid dealing with it. Despite my greatest efforts, it was futile. In fact, the harder I worked to bury my pain, the more it grew in strength. I concluded that pain must be treated like a living entity. It has its own will, its own sense of purpose, and its own objectives for entering my life. Also, pain cannot be ignored. It will not go away until it has achieved its mission. And this task always centers around enhancing my personal evolution.

In this way, I learned to develop a relationship with pain: to partner with it, to help it achieve its highest purpose, to honor pain as my greatest teacher!

It does not matter who you are or what you do. Pain is an unavoidable component of our daily experience. Given that pain is a permanent fixture in life, it is a wonder most people never develop a healthy relationship with it. In fact, most people's lives are defined by strategies to avoid the unavoidable—they change their reality to forestall all encounters with pain.

However, if we take a dispassionate step back and examine the role that pain serves in life, it is a gift to be understood and cultivated.

Why Do Emotional and Physical Pain Feel the Same?

There are two types of pain: physical pain and psychological (emotional) pain. As different as these seem, it is amazing how similarly we experience them. As everyone can attest, the pain of emotional hurt feels a lot like physical pain. But why? The explanation lies in our evolutionary history. Our central nervous system developed to provide the obvious benefits of experiencing physical pain. Of course, this primitive pain response not only lets us know that something is wrong with our body, but it teaches us how to avoid damaging situations in the future. Over time, as the brain's capacity for sentience emerged, we developed the capacity to absorb various frequencies of emotional energy. However, this novel energy is being processed through the same primitive brain and central nervous system that processes physical pain. Our brain is simply ill-equipped to distinguish between these two distinct types of energy inputs. As a result, the brain registers emotional pain in much the same way as being physically hurt does. They are, of course, different, but both play a similar, beneficial role in life.

The Importance of Pain

Let's look at a couple of extreme examples of a life without pain. There are rare individuals who, because of a defect in their central nervous system, cannot feel physical pain. Life for these people is like running a gauntlet of hidden dangers. Even mundane, ordinary activities such as cooking dinner have potential life-threatening ramifications because there is no feedback that tells them when they have injured themselves. In addition, they struggle to develop the quick-response subconscious memory necessary to avoid destructive behavior in the future. What might seem like a blessing is, in fact, an affliction that leads to bodily harm and even a shorter lifespan.

Likewise, there are those who do not have the normal capacity to feel emotional pain. In extreme cases, we label these individuals as psychopathic or sociopathic. Because their ability to interpret low-frequency energy is inhibited, there is no feedback to help them regulate damaging behavior. Of course, this has potentially dire consequences for an individual and all those within their sphere of influence.

So, we may think we want a life without pain, but as we can see, this would be devastating. Pain is our greatest teacher and should be honored. Pain lets us know when we are damaging ourselves and it guides us into nurturing behaviors. It alerts us to areas of life that require attention and offers feedback to keep us on a healthy track. Our natural reaction is to mask or ignore pain energy. No one enjoys feeling uncomfortable, and dealing with pain is certainly not pleasant. However, the healthier option is to face the sensation of pain and strive to interpret the messaging behind it. For physical pain, this messaging might be straightforward. You have an injury, it hurts, and your body signals the brain to tend to the injury.

Psychological pain is a bit more complex. It always results from the blockage of Core-Energy in your being. These blockages can originate from anywhere and/or in any timeframe: your current behavior, events throughout your lifetime, even activities from prior lifetimes. To complicate matters further, an energetic blockage can take many forms: it can live in your biological body; it can live in your subconscious mind; it can dwell within the energetic body that surrounds you; and it can even inhabit multiple areas. Therefore, the only way to fix these blockages is to spend the time and effort needed to identify not only where they live but also their root causes.

This healing cannot take place if you are avoiding the pain. The cure requires facing the pain, developing a relationship with it, and allowing it to guide you to the source of the problem. Pain is just the symptom illuminating a greater core issue. Each of us must make a conscious decision not to mask a pain-symptom, but to follow the pain into the obstacle that is obstructing the flow of Core-Energy.

Pain is not the problem. Its job is to serve as a guidepost pointing to the problem. If you treat only the pain and ignore the core issue, it increases until you deal with the core problem. Any sort of chronic pain, whether physical or psychological, will continue to persist until you address its root cause. Of course, our impulse is to avoid pain altogether, but to reiterate, painful energy *will not* dissipate or go away unless you act upon it.

If someone "hurts your feelings" or causes you psychological pain, it highlights an emotional wound buried within your psyche that you have avoided. It may seem ludicrous, but the pain is doing you a favor. It is serving as your teacher—your guide, directing you to the area that needs attention.

CHAPTER 65:

THE KEY TO SPIRITUAL GROWTH IS TO MAINTAIN A FLUID IDENTITY

OUR DEFINITIONS OF SELF DEFINE what we do with this lifetime. My mother, to her ever-loving credit, instilled in me the notion that I could rise above my circumstances—that I had greatness within me—and that I could actualize my dreams and ambitions. Even at our lowest moments, she never stopped believing I could escape our cycle of poverty and abuse and make my dreams come true. She didn't believe this for herself, but she believed it for me. As I reflect on my improbable life and how far I have traveled, I am so grateful she never placed a label on me. She never defined her expectations. For her, my life was wide open. I could achieve anything.

This wisdom—this seed of belief, was planted deep within me. What continues to drive me and inspire me to this day is the notion that I am limitless!

The Danger of a Static Identity

"I am... " These are the two most dangerous words in any language. Anytime you anchor your concept of self to *anything*—to an emotion, a belief, a physical characteristic, a social construct, an aptitude, a perceived strength or weakness—you create problems for yourself, as well as the people within your sphere of influence.

The psychological construct of "I am" denotes that somehow, within a dynamic and ever-changing universe, you can be a static participant. You cannot! It is impossible! This kind of thinking causes immediate tension between you and the Creative-Energy within and around you. Your true nature is one of evolution. Change. Growth.

Once you define yourself as *something*, once you fix your identity, you are tethering yourself to an imagined stationary object while the universe continues to move, grow, and change around you. You are setting yourself up for a great deal of pain. As a metaphor, imagine holding an elastic band in a fixed position with one hand and stretching it with the other. The farther you stretch it, the more tension you create, the more effort is required. It gets harder and harder... and then... *snap!* It hurts like hell. This happens when you (attempt to) remain static. You are creating hardship and pain. You are placing yourself in an impossible situation.

Besides causing tension, adopting a static identity robs you of the ability to evolve. The energy that could apply to growth and improvement is focused instead on maintaining your fixed illusions of self. This is not what your Creative-Energy wants to be doing. It wants to create cool *new* stuff. Instead of fighting against the tide of change, it wants you to play a positive role in moving yourself and humanity forward.

Let's test this concept by considering a few ways we consciously and unconsciously shackle our growth:

- Identifying with a tribe: "I am American. I am a New Yorker. I am an Irish Catholic American New York Mets fan." You can define your tribe as broadly or finitely as you like, but the net result is always the same. It is a trick your ego uses to set you apart from others. It is an attempt to bring a feeling of superiority or "specialness" to your existence. It not only fixes you into a stereotype of belief and behavior, but it also creates a psychological separation between you and those outside of your group. In its most extreme form, this separation devolves into dehumanization and creates the justification for all manner of heinous actions against those outside of your tribe. Of course, tribalism is the basis for every group war and conflict that ever was and ever will be. This is because tribalism is an illusion—it is a false concept. In reality, we are not separate from one another. We share everything from our genetic code to the air we breathe. The idea that we are separate creates a tension with reality that leads to harmful, low-energy behaviors.
- Identifying with ideologies: "I am a capitalist. A communist. A Christian. A Muslim. A conservative. A liberal." (Or fill in the blank.) No matter what label you put on your belief system, anytime you hitch your wagon to an ideology, you are creating misery for yourself and those around you. Because this entire material realm changes and evolves, the experience of watching reality march away from you invariably causes fear, anxiety, and internal conflict.
- Identifying with fixed definitions of self: "I am smart/dumb, aggressive/passive, beautiful/ugly, creative/uncreative, social/antisocial." Any label you put on yourself, positive or negative, is a harmful illusion. Anytime we define who we are, we restrict the emergence of our true self. We are handcuffing our ability to change, grow, and express the desires of our Spirit.

Instead of defining our limitations, we need to free our Creative-Energy to maximize our evolutionary potential. Instead of creating fixed definitions of Self, we need to direct our attention away from the ego and toward the desires of our Spiritual-Mind. If we accept that anything is possible, we cut the anchor, stifling our existence, and empower the winds of change to carry us to our intended destination.

The key to evolutionary growth is to maintain a fluid identity. Sure, we all possess certain distinguishing characteristics, as well as strengths and weaknesses. But we can never let them define who we are, how we respond to the world, or where we are heading. Instead of thinking in terms of "I am _____," think in terms of "My physical form is now _____."

Acknowledge where you are without restricting your ability to change. It is healthy to be realistic about where you are within the context of achieving a seamless link between yourself and Source-Energy. We all fall short of achieving this aim. However, we need to ensure that our Creative-Energy is free to continue its evolutionary work in our life.

Instead of relying on your faulty ego or external pressures to define who you are and what you should manifest in life, listen to your Spiritual-Self for guidance. This guidance can best be observed by paying attention to your innate passions and interests. What brings you joy and excitement? What increases your overall vibrational frequency and gives you energy? The answers to these questions illuminate your true path and point to what you are meant to create in this moment. Of course, this could change in the next moment—but such is the nature of life!

CHAPTER 66:

DEATH IS NECESSARY FOR EVOLVING YOUR LINK TO SOURCE-ENERGY

THE MOTIVATION FOR MY LONG journey to discover the nature of reality can be distilled down to one phrase: *Fear of death!* The entire process began with the cold-sweat-inducing realization that I had no satisfactory vision of what lies beyond life. This uncertainty produced an emotional collapse, plunging me into a pit of all-consuming fear and a dark depression. I felt like a wild animal backed into a corner; the only strategy for survival was to fight my way out—to conquer my fear of death, or (*ironically*) die trying.

This fight has defined my path of discovery. You can't bluff your way out of a life-or-death struggle, and I could not (and cannot) satisfy myself with a half-hearted explanation of reality and the afterlife.

Thankfully, I now have a vision of existence that brings me peace—the kind of peace only achieved through understanding. I am not claiming that I am correct—only that I am *correct* for me. Isn't that what we are all seeking? We all want (need) a vision of reality that brings peace and comfort to our chaotic existence, that infuses our life with meaning, and that gives us hope for the future.

Death, "the final frontier." But is it? As a practical matter, death is necessary because matter is finite, and biologically oriented matter is even more finite. Eventually, all matter breaks down into its parts and dissolves back into pure energy. This is just the nature of matter. Of course, this rationale for death leaves out a very important component (at least for sentient life): what about consciousness? Does our consciousness die along with the body? This is the question that drives all spiritual exploration.

Consciousness Lives On

Death is part of a continuum—a component of the ongoing process of evolving the link between energy and matter. Death of our physical bodies is necessary because our bodies are made of matter, and matter "does what it does." However, an evolutionary *link* is not possible without something that carries on the evolutionary process. After the death of your physical body, there needs to be a part of you that continues to serve as a platform for future evolution. Otherwise, evolution is a non-starter—it is not possible.

In this case, the "something" that continues to evolve is our consciousness as our Spirit; our Soul; our Spiritual-Mind. This is the "link" that is building the connection between Source-Energy and our material universe. From lifetime to lifetime, in a continual parade of death and rebirth, we are marching steadily toward perfection.

So, what happens when we die—when we transition out of our material form and into a realm of pure energetic consciousness? What do we experience? What becomes of existence? Of course, no one knows for sure, but perhaps we can gain some insight into death by exploring our experience with our Spiritual-Self while we are alive.

Experiencing the Afterlife

If, as I contend, the Spirit is your repository for consciousness after death, it should offer a fair representation of what to expect in the "afterlife." As we have explored in this book, your Spirit is far from a detached abstract concept. Instead, it collaborates with your physical presence at every moment of life. When you align with your Spirit, you become a channel for high-frequency energy, and you experience the benefits of this energy:

- intense feelings of joy, peace, and love;
- boundless physical and mental energy;
- clarity of thought and a sensation of lightness; and
- an overwhelming sense of oneness with all of existence.

It stands to reason that these same experiences await you upon death. However, because you are no longer encumbered by your physical mind, these attributes should magnify beyond comprehension!

Incidentally (and not surprisingly), these positive, high-frequency experiences also match up with research conducted on near-death experiences (NDE's). They also correspond with many people's experiences in deep meditation, and even with psychedelic drugs.[53]

---

[53] Aristos Georgiou, "Most people who have near-death experiences report the same thing after," *Newsweek* (Aug. 24, 2022), https://www.newsweek.com/most-people-near-death-experiences-report-same-thing-psychedelic-1736504; Mayo Clinic Staff, "Meditation: A simple, fast way to reduce stress," *Mayo Clinic*, https://www.mayoclinic.org/tests-procedures/meditation/in-depth/meditation/art-20045858.

Returning to Spirit and Planning for the Future

Death represents a return to our complete Spiritual form. It (temporarily) removes the dichotomy that is present while we are alive. While we may not have access to the tactile perceptions of the material realm, we are blessed with an unobstructed pipeline of Source-Energy.

As Spirit, you house all of your experiences from every past incarnation. This includes all the karmic energy from every lifetime. Because karmic energy can only be expressed in the material realm, it has no negative impact on your Spiritual-Self. However, all of this energy and all of your prior experiences have a direct impact on how you plan for your next incarnation. The afterlife gives your Soul a chance to assess where you are in the evolutionary process and come up with a strategy for moving the ball forward. This includes collaborations with other Spiritual entities.

When Spirit and Matter Merge

Envision a seamless merger between your physical lifetime and your Spiritual-Self. Ponder having all the blessings of Source-Energy while experiencing all the tactile wonderment of our material world. Imagine a time when death and rebirth are but the transition between moments. This, my friend, is heaven. Heaven is not the afterlife but an evolved life!

The End

GLOSSARY OF TERMS

Term	Explanation (with synonyms)
Amygdala	A roughly almond-shaped mass of gray matter inside each cerebral hemisphere of the human brain involved with the experiencing of emotions. Some spiritual practices identify this primitive area of the brain as important for channeling Creative-Energy.
Attraction Characteristic of Energy	Energies of the same frequency are always attractive to one another.
Avatar	The embodiment or physical manifestation of an individual's Spiritual identity; the physical body as a projection of someone's Spiritual form; the evolving human being. Synonyms: physical body; material body; material self; human body; human form; human being.
Awareness, The Practice of	The practice of being consciously aware of thoughts as they enter the mind.
Blockchain Program	A blockchain is "a distributed database that maintains a continuously growing list of ordered records, called blocks." These blocks are linked using codes to protect the identity of the sender and receiver. Each block contains an equation used to verify the validity of the previous block, a timestamp, and transaction data.
Brain	The biological thought machine capable of storing massive amounts of data, as information, feelings, memories, etc. The brain uses this data to create programming that produces an unlimited array of material objects, items, concepts, actions, and ideas.

Burning Off Karma	Taking harmful negative karmic energy and turning it into high-frequency energy that is helpful and beneficial to evolving one's connection to Source.
Chakra	See: Energy center.
Consciousness	See: Sentience.
Conservation of Energy	A fundamental law of physics and chemistry stating that the total energy of an isolated system is constant despite internal changes. It is most commonly expressed as "energy can neither be created nor destroyed" and is the basis of the first law of thermodynamics.
Core	See: Creative Energetic Force.
Core-Energy	See: Creative Energetic Force.
Creative Energetic Force	The creative force emanating out of the Realm of Energy that is responsible for creating all of material reality. This energy is infinite, creative, and evolutionary.
	Synonyms: God; Core; Core-Energy; Source; Source-Energy; God-Force; the Divine.
Creative-Energy	Energy channeled into the material realm that creates everything in our known reality.
	Synonyms: Creative-Force; Creative Impulse.
Creative-Field	See: Field of Energy.
Creative-Force	See: Creative-Energy.
Creative-Impulse	See: Creative-Energy.
Cross-Dimensional	Energy transfer between different dimensions, such as between the material dimension and a dimension of the Spiritual Realm.
Distributed Evolution	Distributing the evolutionary load over as many unique entities as possible.

Divine Wisdom	The process of first analyzing, accepting, and then using information in a way that supports the initiatives of your Core-Self.
Divine, The	See: Creative Energetic Force.
Dreamworld	A version of reality created in the mind through imagination. Pertaining to a dream-state during sleep.
Drug-Induced Ego Dissolution	The experience of a compromised sense of "self," termed ego dissolution, is a key feature of the psychedelic experience.
Economies of Scale	Efficiency gained by an increased level of production.
Ego	The impact of a person's history (socialization, childhood, experiences, beliefs, etc.) on the human thought process.
Energetic Body	The existence of a nonphysical and massless extension of matter that interacts with the environment, composed of energy. In human beings, this comprises psychological, emotional, and intellectual states and spiritual states of consciousness.
	Synonym: subtle body.
Energetic Communication	Communication between energy fields or energetic bodies.
Energy Center	Areas within the body that facilitate the flow of energy between the physical body and the environment.
	Synonym: chakra.
Energy Profile	All the energy accumulated from our past, residing within our material being in the present moment.
	Synonym: karmic profile.

Equanimity	The ability to process life events in a calm, positive manner by focusing on a sense of self that is located beyond the physical body and material existence.
Field	See: Field of Energy.
Field of Energy	The invisible pool of energy that permeates and surrounds all of existence. Creative-Energy emerges from this field to create everything in our known reality.
	Synonyms: Field; Creative-Energy; Creative-Field.
Freak Flag	A characteristic, mannerism, or appearance of a person, either subtle or overt, which implies unique, eccentric, creative, adventurous, or unconventional thinking or behavior.
Frequency of Energy	The amount of energy transferred by the wave frequency of a subatomic particle.
Freudian Model	Freudian theory postulates that the adult personality is made up of three aspects: (1) the id, operating on the pleasure principle, generally within the unconscious; (2) the ego, operating on the reality principle within the conscious realm; and (3) the superego, operating on the morality principle at all levels of consciousness.[54]
God	See: Creative Energetic Force.
God-Force	See: Creative Energetic Force.
God-Realm	See: Realm of Energy.

---

[54] Julie Blaskewicz Boron, K. Warner Schaie, and Sherry L. Willis, "The Aging Personality and Self: Diversity and Health Issues," *Brocklehurst's Textbook of Geriatric Medicine and Gerontology* (Philadelphia: Elsvier, 2017), https://sls.psychiatry.uw.edu/wp-content/uploads/2020/03/Aging-Personality-and-Self2010.pdf.

High-Frequency Energy | Energy associated with formless manifestations in the material realm, such as thoughts and feelings, and communication between energy states. Also associated with energy flowing directly from Source-Energy, which creates positive and beneficial manifestations of reality.

Hyper-Evolved Beings | Individuals whose evolutionary link to Source-Energy far exceeds that of the general population.

Instant Karma | Negative karma that is burned off immediately or shortly after the causal action.

Karma | In Hinduism and Buddhism, the sum of a person's actions in this and previous states of existence, viewed as deciding their fate in future existences.[55]

Karmic-Force | A general term for both the positive and negative type of karmic aftermath that is either a constructive or destructive phenomenon and which will ripen into a result. It is the inseparable energetic link between our actions and the reality we create.[56]

Karmic Profile | See: Energy Profile.

Law of Creative Expansion, The | The universal principle that Creative-Energy will always respond to our expectations, beliefs, feelings, and actions to create our reality.

Low-Frequency Energy | Energy associated with the formation of matter. Also associated with energy states channeled through the mind in the absence of an influence from Source-Energy that often create negative or harmful manifestations of reality.

---

[55] *Oxford Languages,* "Karma," Oxford University Press, 1989, https://www.google.com/search?q=karma&rlz=1C1CHBF_enUS802US802&oq=karma&aqs=chrome..69i57j0i67j0i67i433j0i67j46i131i199i433i465i512j0i131i433i512j0i433i512j46i433i512j0i131i433i512j46i433i512.1004j0j15&sourceid=chrome&ie=UTF-8.
[56] Dr. Alexander Berzin, "Study Buddhism" (Berzin Archives e. V., 2003-2022), https://studybuddhism.com/en/glossary/karmic-force.

Manifesting	Bringing about in the material realm. Converting energy into material reality.
Mind	Cognitive response resulting from a person's interaction with material life, experiences, and biological coding, without the influence of the Spiritual-Mind. Egocentric thoughts emanating from the brain.
	Synonyms: brain, material self, ego-mind, ego.
Mind of God	See: Spiritual-Self.
Mistakes	Decisions or actions that led to behavior harmful to you or others.
Newtonian Physics	In Newtonian physics (also called Newtonian or classical mechanics), scientists use the laws of motion and gravitation to describe the mechanical forces acting upon matter as formulated in the late seventeenth century by English physicist Sir Isaac Newton.
	Synonym: classical mechanics.
Nirvana	
Overt Communicating	Communication registered through our body's five senses.
Power of Giving	The flow of Creative-Energy resulting from a focused offering of energy for the benefit of another (the act of giving).
Pre-Matter Energy	Energy in a wave state before it "becomes" a particle of matter.
Quantum Communication	A field of applied quantum physics closely related to quantum information processing and quantum teleportation.
Quantum Energy	*Quantum* refers to a particular packet of substance or energy in chemistry and physics. The energy is not transferred continuously but as discrete packets of energy.

Quantum Entanglement — Quantum entanglement states that two particles are connected and affect one another even if those particles are light-years apart.

Quantum Superposition — A fundamental principle of quantum mechanics. It states that, much like waves in classical physics, any two (or more) quantum states can be added together ("superposed"), and the result will be another valid quantum state; and conversely, that every quantum state can be represented as a sum of two or more other distinct states.

Quantum Theory — The theoretical basis of modern physics that explains the nature and behavior of matter and energy on the atomic and subatomic levels. The nature and behavior of matter and energy at these levels are sometimes referred to as quantum physics and quantum mechanics.

Quantum-Field — A theory in physics which describes the interaction of two separate physical systems (such as particles) within a field that extends from one to the other and is manifested in a particle exchange between the two systems.

Quasi-Material — The nature of a past event that continues to have material repercussions in the present moment. A ghost reality supported by karmic consequences and mental projections, at once material and non-material.

Synonyms: trapped energy; past karma.

Realm of Energy — The realm beyond physical existence made up of pure energy. The realm beyond time, space, and matter. The invisible energy field from which our universe emerged.

Synonym: God-realm.

Real-Self — See: Spiritual-Self.

Reincarnation — The transfer of your Spiritual-Self from one lifetime to another lifetime.

Scientism	The belief that science alone can render truth about the world and reality.
Sentience	The mind's capacity for rational thought, self-reflection, and deep awareness.
	Synonym: Consciousness.
Soul	See: Spiritual-Self.
Source	See: Creative Energetic Force.
Source-Energy	See: Creative Energetic Force.
Spirit	See: Spiritual-Self.
Spiritual-Center	See: Spiritual-Self.
Spiritual-Link	See: Spiritual-Self.
Spiritual-Mind	See: Spiritual-Mind.
Spiritual-Personality	See: Spiritual-Self.
Spiritual Science	Filtering new spiritual concepts through a process of examination and experimentation to determine their effectiveness in a "real-world" setting.
Spiritual-Self	The energetic expression of our individual consciousness which resides within the Realm of Energy. It is responsible for perpetuating one's spiritual evolution from lifetime to lifetime. It is the link between the Creative Energetic Force and human material existence.
	Synonyms: Spirit; Spiritual-Personality; Spiritual-Center; Spiritual-Voice; Soul; Real-Self; Mind of God; Spiritual-Link; Spiritual-Mind; True-Self
Spiritual-Voice	See: Spiritual-Self.
Subconscious	Hidden or repressed energy residing outside our field of awareness. An action driven by forces outside of our field of awareness.
	Synonym: Unconscious.
Subtle Body	See: Energetic body.

Subtle Communication	Communication that takes place through the transfer of energy between energetic bodies.
Subtle Energy	Energy flowing from energetic bodies. Subtle energy is registered through our feelings.
True-Self	See: Spiritual-Self
Unconscious	See: Subconscious.

BIBLIOGRAPHY

Except where noted, all URLs were accessed December 16, 2022.

Alexander, Stephon and Salvador Almagro-Moreno. "Is life the result of the laws of entropy?" *NewScientist*, June 11, 2022. https://www. newscientist.com/article/2323820-is-life-the-result-of-the-laws-of-entropy/.

Kasas, Sandor, et al. "Detecting nanoscale vibrations as signature of life." *Proceedings of the National Academy of Sciences of the United States of America*, Dec. 29, 2014. https://www.pnas.org/doi/abs/10.1073/pnas.1415348112.

Barlow, Roger. "If atoms are mostly empty space, why do objects look and feel solid?" *Phys.org,* Feb. 16, 2017. https://phys.org/news/2017-02-atoms-space-solid.html.

Beck, Don Edward. *Spiral Dynamics in Action: Humanity's Master Code.* United Kingdom: John Wiley & Sons Ltd, 2018.

Bergner, Raymond M. "Intelligent Design: Maybe True, Maybe False, But Not Absurd." *Research Gate.* 10.13140/RG.2.2.15653.91367, 2017. https://www.researchgate.net/publication/317332700_Intelligent_Design_Maybe_True_Maybe_False_But_Not_Absurd.

Berzin, Alexander. "Study Buddhism." Berzin Archives e. V., 2003-2022. https://studybuddhism.com/en/glossary/karmic-force.

Blaskewicz Boron, Julie, K. Warner Schaie, and Sherry L. Willis. "The Aging Personality and Self: Diversity and Health Issues," in Fillet, Howard M. *Brocklehurst's Textbook of Geriatric Medicine and Gerontology.* Philadelphia: Elsvier, 2017. ScienceDirect.com. https://sls.psychiatry.uw.edu/wp-content/uploads/2020/03/Aging-Personality-and-Self2010.pdf.

Blifernez-Klassen, Olga, V. Klassen, A. Doebbe, K. Kersting, P. Grimm, L. Wobbe, and O. Kruse. "Cellulose degradation and assimilation by the unicellular phototrophic eukaryote *Chlamydomonas reinhardtii.*" *Nature Communications* 3, no. 1214, 2012. https://doi.org/10.1038/ncomms2210.

Boston University. "Entropy and the second law," December 12, 1999. http://physics.bu.edu/~duffy/py105/Secondlaw.html.

Caltech Science Exchange. "What Is Superposition and Why Is It Important?" *Caltech Science Exchange*, 2022. https://scienceexchange.caltech.edu/topics/quantum-science-explained/quantum-superposition.

Campbell, Joseph. *The Hero with a Thousand Faces*. 3rd ed. Novato, CA: New World Library, 2012.

Carnegie Science. "Plants' Threat-Detection Mechanisms Raise the Alarm." *Phys.org,* June 14, 2022. https://carnegiescience.edu/plants-threat-detection-mechanisms-raise-alarm-0

Carrey, Jim. *What Oprah Learned from Jim Carrey*. Oprah's Life Class, 1997. Oprah Winfrey Network, 3:50. https://www.oprah.com/oprahs-lifeclass/what-oprah-learned-from-jim-carrey-video.

Chu, Jennifer. MIT News Office. "Light from ancient quasars helps confirm quantum entanglement," August 19, 2018. https://news.mit.edu/2018/light-ancient-quasars-helps-confirm-quantum-entanglement-0820.

Cornell University. "Plants alert neighbors to threats using common 'language.'" *ScienceDaily*, 3 October 3, 2019. www.sciencedaily.com/releases/2019/10/191003135713.htm.

Emoto, Masaru. *The Hidden Messages in Water*. New York: Beyond Words Publishing, 2004.

Folger, Tim. "The war over reality." *Discover Magazine*, May 2017.

Gamow, George. *Thirty Years That Shook Physics: The Story of Quantum Theory*. Dover ed. New York: Dover Publications Inc., 1985.

Georgiou Aristos. "Most people who have near-death experiences report the same thing after." *Newsweek*, Aug. 24, 2022.

Gibbins, John. "Quantum Physics in 10 Minutes." *BBC Science Focus*. Issue 284, Aug. 2015.

Groundhog Day. Directed by Harry Ramis, Producer Trevor Albert (1993, United States: Columbia Pictures).

Hicks, Esther and Jerry. *Ask and It Is Given: Learning to Manifest Your Desires*. Carlsbad, California: Hay House Inc., 2004.

Hunt, Tam. "The Hippies Were Right: It's All about Vibrations, Man!: A new theory of consciousness." *Scientific American*, Dec. 5, 2018. https://blogs.scientificamerican.com/observations/the-hippies-were-right-its-all-about-vibrations-man/.

Judith, Anodea. *Wheels of Life: A User's Guide to the Chakra System.* 2nd ed. Woodbury, MN: Llewellyn Publications, 2018.

Kelley, David. "What is Objectivism?" *The Atlas Society*, June 14, 2010. https://www.atlassociety.org/post/what-is-objectivism.

Konyukhov, A. "Wave cancellation conditions for the double impact of finite duration in an arbitrary structure." *Acta mech* 231, 2773–2798, 2020. https://doi.org/10.1007/s00707-020-02672-0.

Letzter, Rafi. "There's a Giant Mystery Hiding Inside Every Atom in the Universe." *Live Science*, Jan. 3, 2020. https://www.livescience.com/mystery-of-proton-neutron-behavior-in-nucleus.html.

Lincoln, Don. "Quantum Foam." *Fermilab Today* (Feb. 1, 2013), https://news.fnal.gov/2013/02/quantum-foam/.

Liu, Tianjun. "The scientific hypothesis of an 'energy system' in the human body." *Journal of Traditional Chinese Medical Sciences.* Volume 5, No. 1, 2018: 29-34. ISSN 2095-7548, https://doi.org/10.1016/j.jtcms.2018.02.003.

Luskin, Casey. "An Introduction to Intelligent Design." *Intelligent Design and Evolution Awareness Center.* https://www.discovery.org/m/2015/08/Introduction_to_ID_Luskin_2015.pdf.

Mason, N.L., K.P.C. Kuypers, F. Müller, J. Reckweg, D.H.Y. Tse, S.W. Toennes, N.R.P.W. Hutten, J.F.A. Jansen, et al. "Me, myself, bye: regional alterations in glutamate and the experience of ego dissolution with psilocybin." *Neuropsychopharmacol.* 45 (2003–2011), 2020. https://doi.org/10.1038/s41386-020-0718-8.

McTaggart, Lynne. *The Field: The Quest for the Secret Force of the Field.* 1st ed. United States: Harper Collins, 2002.

Mohandas E. "Neurobiology of spirituality." National Library of Medicine. *Mens Sana Monogr.* 2008 Jan;6(1):63-80. doi: 10.4103/0973-1229.33001. PMID: 22013351; PMCID: PMC3190564. https://www.ncbi.nlm.nih.gov/pmc/articles/PMC3190564/.

Morris, Henry M. "The Scientific Case Against Evolution." Institute for Creation Research. https://www.icr.org/home/resources/resources_tracts_scientificcaseagainstevolution/.

Moskowitz, Clara. "Tangled Up in Spacetime." *Scientific American*, January, 2017: 33-37.

Musser, George. "Quantum Weirdness Now a Matter of Time." *Quanta Magazine*, January 19, 2016. https://www.quantamagazine.org/time-entanglement-raises-quantum-mysteries-20160119/.

Nagasawa, Yujin. "Where does consciousness come from?" *BBC Focus*, August 2017: 64-69.

New International Version, 2011. BibleGateway.com. http://www.biblegateway.com/versions/

New-International-Version-NIV-Bible/#booklist.

Nichols, D.E. "Psychedelics." *Pharmacological Reviews* (2016 Apr;68(2):264-355. doi: 10.1124/pr.115.011478.) Erratum in: Pharmacol Rev. 2016 Apr;68(2):356. PMID: 26841800; PMCID: PMC4813425.

Oxford Languages. "Karma." Oxford University Press, 1989. https://www.google.com/search?q=karma&rlz=1C1CHBF_enUS802US802&oq=karma&aqs=chrome..69i57j0i67j0i67i433j0i67j46i131i199i433i465i512j0i131i433i512j0i433i512j46i433i512j0i131i433i512j46i433i512.1004j0j15&sourceid=chrome&ie=UTF-8.

Pappas, Stephanie. "Faster-Than-Light Discovery Raises Prospect of Time Travel." *Live Science,* January 31, 2022. https://www.livescience.com/16207-faster-light-discovery-time-travel.html.

Perkowitz, Sidney. "E = mc2." *Encyclopedia Britannica*, August 16, 2022. https://www.britannica.com/science/E-mc2-equation. Accessed 18 November 2022.

"Radioactive Decay." United States Nuclear Regulatory Commission, March 09, 2021. https://www.nrc.gov/reading-rm/basic-ref/glossary/radioactive-decay.html.

Radin, Dean, Leena Michel, Karla Galdamez, Paul Wendland, Robert Rickenbach, and Arnaud Delorme. "Consciousness and the double-slit interference pattern: Six experiments." *Physics Essays* 25 (2), 2012: 157-171. 10.4006/0836-1398-25.2.157. https://hal.archives-ouvertes.fr/hal-00719707.

Ridgway, Andy. "Your quantum brain: A new theory suggests that the bizarre world of quantum physics could be at play between our ears." Magzter.com. *BBC Focus*, March 2017. https://www.

magzter.com/stories/Science/BBC-Focus-Science-Technology/Your-QuantumBrain.

Schonefeld, Lisa-Maria and Lars Wojtecki. "Beyond Emotions: Oscillations of the amygdala and their implications for electrical neuromodulation." *Frontiers in Neuroscience*, April 18, 2019. https://www.frontiersin.org/articles/10.3389/fnins.2019.00366/full.

Shapiro, Ilyak and Guilherme de Berredo-Peixoto. *Lecture Notes on Newtonian Mechanics: Lessons from Modern Concepts.* New York: Springer, 2013.

Siegel, Ethan. "Observing the Universe Really Does Change the Outcome, and This Experiment Shows How." *Forbes.com,* May 26, 2020. https://www.forbes.com/sites/startswithabang/2020/05/26/observing-the-universe-really-does-change-the-outcome-and-this-experiment-shows-how/?sh=69f5cc4467af.

"Starts with a Bang: 70-year-old quantum prediction comes true, as something is created from nothing." *Big Think*, Sept. 13, 2022. https://bigthink.com/starts-with-a-bang/something-from-nothing/.

Singer, Michael A. *The untethered soul: the journey beyond yourself.* Oakland, CA: New Harbinger Publications, 2007.

Smith, George. "Newton's Philosophiae Naturalis Principia Mathematica," 2007. https://plato.stanford.edu/entries/newton-principia/#toc.

Stapp, Henry P. "Attention, intention, and will in quantum physics." Ernest Orlando Lawrence Berkley National Laboratory. LBNL-42650 reprint, May 1999. https://escholarship.org/content/qt5xr366vq/qt5xr366vq_noSplash_a451774ff5e46f7a5bdc665ed65c09f8.pdf?t=p21mxm.

Thomas, William, Baron Kelvin, Hans Bethe, Lev Davidovich Landau, Lyman Spitzer, and James Prescott Joule, eds. The Editors of Encyclopaedia Britannica. "Energy." *Encyclopedia Britannica*, Oct. 18, 2022. https://www.britannica.com/science/energy. Accessed 18 November 2022.

Tretkoff, Ernie, et al. APS News. "This month in physics history: December 1706: Birth of É'milie du Châtelet." *American Physical Society Sites.* Vol. 17, No. 11, Dec. 2008. https://www.aps.org/publications/apsnews/200812/physicshistory.cfm.

University of Haifa. "Groundbreaking study uncovers first evidence of long-term directionality in the origination of human mutation, fundamentally challenging Neo-Darwinism." *American Association for the Advancement of Science*, Jan. 31, 2022. https://www.eurekalert.org/news-releases/941828.

van Leeuwen, Paul J. "Experimenter effect in parapsychological experiments?" *Quantum Physics & Consciousness*, Nov. 09, 2019. https://quantumphysics-consciousness.eu/index.php/en/2019/11/09/experimenter-effect-in-parapsychological-experiments/.

Volk, Steve. "Down the quantum rabbit hole." *Discover Magazine*, March 2018.

Walchover, Natalie. "A New Physics Theory of Life." *Quanta Magazine*, January 22, 2014. https://www.quantamagazine.org/a-new-thermodynamics-theory-of-the-origin-of-life-20140122/#comments.

"Chakra." Wikipedia. www.en.wikipedia.org/wiki/chakra.

Zyga, Lisa. "Physicists investigate lower dimensions of the universe." *Physics.org*, March 18, 2011. https://phys.org/news/2011-03-physicists-dimensions-universe.html.

TABLE OF DIAGRAMS

ACKNOWLEDGEMENTS

On the PUBLISHING SIDE, THANK you to my wonderful team. Special thanks to my lead editor, the incomparable Michael Ireland, for your insight, expertise, and patient guidance. Also, thanks to Rachel de Leon and Zora Alexandra Knauf. Thank you to my publishing group, PRESStinely, LLC—to Kristen Wise, Maira Pedierra, and their amazing staff. I could not have done this without you. A special shoutout to Ross Hostetter for your encouragement, mentorship, insight, and friendship.

I owe a debt of gratitude to the many Souls who have partnered with me on this mortal journey. To my parents, my brother, my extended family, my friends and antagonists—I appreciate each one of you. I am especially grateful for my amazing wife. Brooke, thank you for all the love and support you have given me during our long and crazy journey. You are my rock and my inspiration—God only knows where I would be without you. To my children: Austin, Sean, Savannah, and Chase, you are my greatest joy and the impetus for all my efforts.

And to you, the reader: Thank you for joining me on this journey of discovery. May your curiosity always lead the way.

ABOUT THE AUTHOR

Marc Max Pollock's life story is an extraordinary example of over-coming adversity. Having grown up experiencing poverty, abuse and homelessness, Marc made it his mission to harness the power of the universe to change his reality from a life of hopelessness to a life of abundance. Marc's calling is to share his transformational secrets to help you heal and live your best, abundant life. Marc is an entrepreneur, author, visionary, spiritual adventurer, energy practitioner, and Reiki Master. Marc and his wife Brooke, an accomplished businesswoman, have built an amazing life of true partnership and enjoy traveling the world with their children. Marc loves playing music, painting, and communing with nature.